COPING
WITH
TRAUMA

THE VICTIM AND THE HELPER

EDITED BY
Rod Watts *&*
David J de L Horne

First published in 1994 by
Australian Academic Press
32 Jeays Street, Bowen Hills, Brisbane QLD 4006, Australia

National Library of Australia
Cataloguing-in-Publication data:

Coping with trauma: The victim and the helper
Bibliography.
Includes index.

ISBN 1 875378 08 1
1. Post-traumatic stress disorder — Australia — Case Studies.
I. Watts, Rod. II. Horne, David J. de L.
616.8521

Designed and typeset in Garamond 10/11 by Australian Academic Press, Brisbane
Cover design by Elke Ploetz
Printed by Shortrun Books, Melbourne

Foreword

I N the last 25 years the field of traumatic stress studies has seen an unparalleled growth of knowledge such that today there are over 5000 articles in scholarly journals on different aspects of psychological trauma (e.g., childhood abuse, warfare, torture, disasters, industrial and technological accidents, etc.) as well as scores of books and a new *Journal of Traumatic Stress*. More recently, the first *International Handbook on Traumatic Stress Syndromes* was published (Wilson & Raphael, 1993) which reflects the interests of researchers, clinicians, trauma specialists, and others throughout the world in building a common source of reference as well as international cooperation to aid victims of trauma. Further, in the United States there are now five National Centers for the study and treatment of Posttraumatic Stress Disorders (PTSDs). This type of national commitment strongly suggests the importance of addressing the adverse effects of traumatisation. Further, the International Society for Traumatic Stress Studies (ISTSS) and the more recent establishment of an Australian counterpart (ASTSS) within the auspices of the parent organisation, indicate that the scientific study of trauma and victimisation is now mainstream in many disciplines such as psychiatry, psychology, social work, neuroscience, childhood development, and gerontology as well as the medical sciences.

The present volume is another important contribution to the field of traumatic stress studies. The nine chapters and appendix that comprise the volume cover both sides of the coin: the victim and the helper.

In Chapter one, Beverley Raphael and Lenore Meldrum present a conceptual overview of trauma, bereavement through traumatic loss, and the Posttraumatic Stress Disorder (PTSD). Additionally, models of care are reviewed with specific recommendations for preventive assessment and management of 'at risk' persons and groups (which includes, of course, trauma specialists).

In Chapter two, Rod Watts presents a discussion of a multi-fatality road accident which killed 11 people when a motor coach rolled off a cliff. Twenty-nine passengers survived and were immersed in a scene of chaos, death, and injury. Many, if not all, of the survivors displayed symptoms of PTSD. The psychological care and follow-up of the survivors are described in this chapter. Especially noteworthy is the proactive nature of the aftercare in which counsellors sought out survivors who were highly likely to have been traumatised to make available supportive care by specialists knowledgeable in PTSD.

In Chapter three, Mark Creamer discusses some of the central issues which mental health professionals face when organising a program of intervention following a disaster. In this chapter, the disaster described is the Queen Street shooting in the Australia Post building during which a deranged gunman terrorised employees working in the building in a brutal and sadistic manner, killing eight people and wounding may others. Later, the gunman committed suicide by jumping from a window of the building and falling to his death on the street below. Throughout the ordeal, the gunman moved to different floors of the building and generated terror and horror in nearly all of the workers there. As would be expected, many of the threatened workers developed symptoms of PTSD and sought out supportive counselling.

The program developed to aid the distressed workers was unique because it was purposely designed to occur in the workplace with the endorsement of management and staff. Through the cooperation of several mental health agencies, the intervention strategy ranged from the immediate intervention to longer-term services. However, the mutual cooperation between the mental health specialists and the management staff afforded opportunities for the traumatised workers to come to grips with the post-traumatic psychological consequences of the shooting disaster. Perhaps what is most fascinating about the intervention program was that it was creatively adapted to assist workers in the location where the trauma occurred. This nontraditional approach to treatment is interesting and underscores how the treatment of PTSD may require innovative outreach efforts.

Chapters four and five both contain discussions about the impact of trauma on professionals who work with victims of disaster and trauma. In Chapter four, Michael Stewart and Peter Hodgkinson detail common psychological reactions among rescue workers to such catastrophes as the Hyatt Regency Hotel skywalk collapse, the Mount Erebus DC 10 airplane crash, and the football stadium fire in Bradford in the United Kingdom. The authors discuss a number of common difficulties for rescue workers, including performance guilt, acute anxiety states, increased states of irritability, forms of re-enactment, decreased occupational interest, and symptoms of PTSD. These common and expectable post-disaster reactions are further discussed by Robyn Robinson in Chapter five who reviews the different types of programs that have been developed for emergency service providers. They include: critical incident stress debriefing, group counselling, family support, de-fusings, demobilisations, and one-to-one counselling services. The rationale for these different approaches is explained and points to the reality that despite professional training, emergency responders continue to be at risk for powerful impacts to their sense of well-being and therefore need the implementation of specialised programs to care for those exposed to trauma in the line of duty.

In Chapter six, the psychology of working with victims of traumatic accidents is discussed. David Horne outlines a number of very practical clinical guidelines in this chapter. These guidelines begin by describing the nature and extent of problems confronting the professional working in a medical setting when a patient enters the system for treatment. Clearly, the team responsible for care must assess both the nature of physical injury and psychological impact, especially PTSD and co-morbid conditions. Differential diagnosis is especially important since the absence of hard medical findings on head injury, for example, should not preclude careful follow-up on symptoms of PTSD which may be similar to those of 'soft' neurological signs. For this reason, Horne recommends that extensive psychological assessment be performed prior to psychotherapy.

To illustrate the complex interplay of factors that confront mental health professionals in case management, Horne presents a discussion of a case which involved PTSD, anger, and phobia following a motorcycle accident. The patient not only had disrupted psychosocial functioning but was violent and abusive to his spouse and children. The report of this successful treatment illustrates the need to understand how the cyclical tendencies of hyperaroused affective states and psychic numbing get expressed in behavioural forms of coping and ego-defence.

Chapters seven and eight concern traumatic impacts on children. In her chapter, Ruth Wraith discusses a broad range of topics associated with childhood trauma, including some common myths that have existed for many years in the mental health community (for example, 'children are resilient and will naturally recover from any effects by forgetting the experience, getting over it, or growing out of it'). The author explores the various ways that trauma impacts on children in terms of the damaged inner-self, developmental stages, cognitive capacities, interpersonal functioning, and family dynamics. Further, the management and treatment of children's responses is discussed, including practical clinical recommendations on how to protect the child's vulnerability throughout the recovery process.

In Chapter eight, Denise Brunt focuses on the long-term consequences of sex abuse in childhood. To begin, the author lists a number of basic questions prior to a discussion of how sexual abuse causes damage to the self. And since the primary blow of childhood sexual abuse is a loss of trust and feelings of boundary violation, there are typically many thematic issues which carry forth throughout psychosocial development such as feelings of low self-esteem, the need for power and control, conflicted gender identity, and the capacity for intimacy. The chapter presents models of intervention and notes that mental health specialists might be especially prone to countertransference reactions when working with children who relive the pain of their violation by those whose role it was to nurture them.

In Chapter nine, the role of culture in the treatment of PTSD is explored. Harry Minas and Steven Klimidis note that because of its history, Australia has a rich and diverse cultural heritage. In recent years the influx of refugees to Australia from Asian countries has resulted in a significant sub-culture of people who have endured the ravages of war trauma, civil violence, mass genocide, and political oppression. Predictably, immigrants who have survived traumatic events will have PTSD and other psychiatric disorders. Of particular interest in this chapter is the special concerns with the cross-cultural assessment and treatment of PTSD. The clinician needs to be aware of their own circumscribed belief system and how it might vary from that of clients from different cultural and religious backgrounds. The need for interpreters skilled in bridging gaps between cultures to facilitate disclosure of trauma is particularly important in the treatment process.

The appendix to this volume concerns the understanding and management of the deceased. Priscilla Nelson-Feaver and Ian Warren begin by discussing cultural needs and how different religions view death and the conception of the afterworld. This conceptual overview is useful and creates a foundation for the discussion that follows in regards to: (i) viewing the body of the deceased, (ii) the funeral and its alternatives, (iii) procedures for exhibiting the deceased, and (iv) legal considerations.

In conclusion, this book by some of the leading researchers in Australia, offers the reader a concise and practical text on traumatic stress reactions that is readable, well-referenced, and a valuable source for students and professionals alike.

PROFESSOR JOHN P. WILSON
Department of Psychology
Cleveland State University
Cleveland, OH, USA
Past President, International Society for Traumatic Stress Studies

Contents

Preface

T HIS book arose out of a perceived need, by both editors, to provide something authoritative and compact about the nature of trauma and its consequential reactions in both victim and helper, for busy practitioners or rescue workers. Since the early 1980s there has been an enormous growth in awareness of, and research into, the possible impact of traumatic experiences on people's lives. Articles on this theme quite regularly appear in professional journals, with several important major texts now available. Two recent examples are Charles Figley's *Trauma and Its Wake* (1985), and John Wilson and Beverly Raphael's recent *International Handbook of Traumatic Stress Syndromes* (1993). What was not readily available was a concise, readable, practically oriented text on this theme.

The lack of availability of this type of information is addressed by this unique book, which also systematically looks at the impact of traumatic experiences on both the victim and the helper. Since the interaction between these two groups of people is crucial to the successful resolution of traumatic experiences, it seemed sensible to unite both perspectives in the same book. Thus, the aim of *Coping with Trauma: The Victim and Helper* is to provide information on trauma that is directly applicable to clinical practice, whether it be for an individual victim, or following a large-scale incident or disaster. There is, therefore, an emphasis both on outlining major principles of assessment and intervention, which are based on contemporary research and experience, and providing vivid case histories and vignettes to illustrate what actually happens.

Contributors for each chapter were selected because of their demonstrated clinical expertise and prominence in their respective fields associated with the effects of trauma. The book is organised into nine chapters and an appendix, some of which have two authors. Titles of the chapters are self explanatory and the chapters are loosely grouped together in the following way.

The first chapter provides an overview of the most important principles to be adhered to as a clinician assisting traumatised victims. Chapters two to five primarily focus on the impact, on both victims and helpers, of moderate to large-scale disasters. Referring to recent research, the plight of survivors of large-scale road accidents is described in Chapter two, as are some principles to be used in psychological follow-up. The third chapter addresses the important area of community recovery following trauma. The consequential horror often faced by personnel when attending disasters is aptly described in Chapter four, with suggestions as to how best to promote effective coping skills. The fifth chapter elucidates one particular facet of enhancing helpers' coping, through organising peer support: the chapter also briefly describes how to do this.

Generally, victims of trauma are unlikely to initiate a search for assistance, at least in the short term, following their ordeal. In terms of treatment, early detection is the most effective response. Chapter six addresses this issue within the context of providing appropriate counselling and psychological help to accident and disaster victims who attend an acute medical setting, such as a emergency department of a general hospital.

Children do not escape the effects of trauma when exposed to it. This critical issue is addressed in Chapter seven, including some discussion of the specific needs of children at different developmental stages. The suffering of children has a particularly poignant traumatic impact on workers involved in their treatment. Chapter eight is about the long-term impact of child sexual abuse and discusses a specific type of trauma and its effects on the victim and on workers. This book does not try to present a range of traumata and their effects, its focus is primarily on large-scale incidents and/or disasters. However, this chapter was included because the field of child trauma is so important, and the increasing number of reports each year of its occurrence must be of grave concern. While a disaster, as a single incident, is likely to capture the greatest attention from the media, and therefore the community at large, child sexual abuse, perhaps more than any other type of trauma that occurs to an individual, has widespread impact at all levels of society. As the chapter describes, reactions to this type of trauma entail both similar and different sequelae to those typically found following disasters. They question the definition of trauma itself, and pose a threat to the psychological health of the workers and associated professionals who work in the field.

An important area of trauma, not adequately covered as yet in the literature, is that of cultural influences in reactions and treatment response. Chapter nine looks at these cultural differences in response to trauma, particularly fully developed Posttraumatic Stress Disorder (PTSD), and alerts practitioners to the importance of this factor in their approach to clients. The book concludes with an unusual, but crucial appendix that describes, in some detail, the procedures associated with the preparation of bodies following death, and rites of passage, and includes discussion of important cultural aspects to these processes.

Reactions to trauma range in severity, extent, and over time. Psychological strategies, accordingly, must be based on current knowledge of trauma and development in psychological treatments, but used according to the specific needs of each individual affected. This applies whether the event has only affected one person, or is so large that it has virtually decimated an entire community. People affected by trauma are referred to as victims, clients, patients, or some other term, which does have an influence upon how they are perceived and reacted to by others. What we, the editors and authors hope, is that this book helps reduce ignorance about traumatic stress reactions, as well as elucidating ways in which the victims of traumatic experiences can receive optimum care. All of the writers have attempted to show that although there are many innovative assessment and intervention techniques available today, to forget the underlying healing quality of human compassion means that many people will suffer far more than they need to.

ROD WATTS & DAVID J DE L HORNE
1994

About the Authors

ROD WATTS is Manager of Social Work Services at Bethesda Hospital, Richmond, Victoria working in the clinical area of the head-injury unit. He has researched extensively into the effects of large-scale road trauma and has conducted workshops on bereavement, loss, and trauma, including training mental health professionals in critical incident stress debriefing.

DAVID J de L HORNE is Associate Professor/Reader in Medical Psychology and Head of the Behavioural Science and Medical Psychology Unit at the University of Melbourne. He also conducts a private clinical practice as well as consulting at the Royal Melbourne Hospital, and has been working since the 1980s to promote the need for improved psychological research, assessment and treatment for victims of road trauma.

BEVERLEY RAPHAEL is Professor and Chairperson of the Department of Psychiatry at The University of Queensland and Director of Psychiatric Services, Royal Brisbane Hospital. She is an advisor to a number of international bodies in the field of bereavement, traumatic stress and disasters including the World Health Organisation and the European Disaster Action Group and founding president of the Australasian Society for Traumatic Loss and Grief Studies.

LENORE MELDRUM is a research assistant in the Department of Psychiatry at The University of Queensland in the field of posttraumatic stress disorder and crisis intervention. She has designed, conducted and evaluated a number of surveys of critical incident stress management in trauma service organisations and professionals, and is the Australian representative on the Ethics Committee of the International Society for Traumatic Stress Studies.

MARK CREAMER is a clinical psychologist based at the University of Melbourne. He has worked extensively on both the research and treatment perspectives of a broad range of traumatic incidents involving individuals, groups and communities. He is a member of the editorial board of the *Journal of Traumatic Stress*.

MICHAEL STEWART and **PETER HODGKINSON** are the founders of the Centre for Crisis Psychology in the UK, a consultancy working with the aftermath of trauma. The centre was established following their work in the aftermath of the Bradford City football stadium fire in 1985 and the Zeebrugge ferry disaster of 1987. They are the authors of the highly successful book *Coping with Catastrophe*.

ROBYN ROBINSON is Clinical Director of the Victorian Ambulance Crisis Counselling Unit and Director of Trauma Support Consultants. She trained the first combined emergency services debriefing team in Australia and has since trained further debriefing and peer support teams in Australia and overseas. She is the founding president of the Australasian Critical Incident Stress Association and coauthor of *Developing Peer Support Programs in Emergency Services*.

RUTH WRAITH is Senior Psychotherapist at the Royal Children's Hospital in Melbourne and consultant to the Victorian Disaster Plan. She also conducts a private practice specialising in trauma, and has worked with children, families and communities in the aftermath of such events as the Ash Wednesday bushfires, the Queen Street Massacre and the Manresa Kindergarten siege. She is founding convenor of the Australasian Society for Traumatic Stress Studies.

DENISE BRUNT is Lecturer in Clinical Psychology at the Victorian University of Technology and currently researches in the area of clinical and health psychology. Her interest in trauma developed from her earlier work as a senior clinical psychologist in hospitals, schools and a community health centre, and she has since been instrumental in establishing a parallel group program for sexually abused children and their mothers.

HARRY MINAS is Director of the Victorian Transcultural Psychiatry Unit and Associate Professor of Transcultural Psychiatry at the University of Melbourne. His research interests include the relationships between culture, migration and mental illness, as well as the development and evaluation of mental health services for immigrant communities.

STEVEN KLIMIDIS is a clinical psychologist at the Victorian Transcultural Psychiatry Unit. His clinical and research interests lie in how cross-cultural psychology may be of benefit to the conceptualisation and management of clinical problems, and how the individual and family processes surrounding migration and resettlement relate to mental health.

PRISCILLA NELSON-FEAVER is director of her family company Nelson Bros. Funeral Services in Melbourne and established the firm's Bereavement Resource Centre in 1987. She is actively involved in bereavement education and support and is past president of the National Association for Loss and Grief, Victoria.

IAN WARREN is Funeral Director for Nelson Bros. Funeral Services in Melbourne. He has more than 16 years experience in the area of embalming and funeral services, and has worked extensively on funerals of families of differing ethnic and cultural backgrounds.

Helping People Cope With Trauma

CHAPTER ONE

Beverley Raphael and Lenore Meldrum

O NE of the most vital elements of the healing process following trauma is the quality of human compassion for another person's suffering, regardless of the nature of the trauma. There are, however, a number of aspects which are important in understanding traumatic events. There is the *sudden, unexpected, untimely,* facet of the trauma. The trauma is often violent and shocking. Other elements can contribute to trauma, but these are universal.

Traumatic loss and traumatic encounter with death

Two of the most prevalent subcategories of stress or traumatic experiences that can occur are traumatic encounter with *death* and *traumatic loss.* Traumatic loss refers to those losses of close attachment figures which occur in association with sudden, unexpected, untimely or otherwise traumatic circumstances of death, for which we suffer grief and in which we need the help, support and comfort of our family and other people (Raphael, 1983).

Traumatic encounter with death refers to the stresses experienced in confronting death which may lead to Posttraumatic Stress Disorder (PTSD). This is the type of reaction people have after severe exposure to combat or violence — whether they are direct victims or incidentally exposed, as bank customers often are in a hold-up. The exposure emergency workers experience when dealing with the consequences of someone else's death in a traumatic or violent manner may also evoke these reactions.

Disasters that occur within our community, such as motor vehicle accidents (Horne, 1993) or large-scale disasters like the Ash Wednesday bushfires (McFarlane & Raphael, 1984), the Granville rail disaster (Singh & Raphael, 1981), the mass shootings at Hoddle Street and Queen Street in Melbourne[1] (Creamer, Burgess, Buckingham, & Pattison, 1990) have all caused stress reactions in people involved.

One of the critical elements in coping with trauma and traumatic encounter with death is how the experience is appraised. How a person perceives the stressfulness of their experience is one of the variables that is likely to lead to a more severe stress effect and the greater likelihood of the need for care.

Perhaps the most tragic impetus for the understanding of trauma has come from war, particularly studies of Vietnam veterans (Figley, 1978, Laufer, Frey-Wouters & Gallops, 1985; Wilson, 1980). Studies in the USA, where systematic data is available, suggest that at least 500,000 Vietnam veterans are suffering from PTSD related to the severity of the stressful experience they had during combat in Vietnam. (Kulka, et al., 1991).

Traumatic loss

Bereavements which are sudden and unexpected, involve children, or are violent and shocking lead to greater stress for the survivors and greater diffi-culty in resolving and coming to terms with the loss. Many studies describe the impact of deaths of children and how families bereaved in this manner may suffer for many years afterwards. (Gordon & Wraith, 1993; Pynoos & Eth, 1985; Pynoos & Nader, 1989). While death from cancer may not be sudden or unexpected, the prolonged suffering of the victim may be traumatic for family and friends.

Some of the specific reactions that may occur when a person is exposed to a any loss are listed below:

• intense yearning for the lost person
• preoccupation with images of the dead person which come to the mind all the time

---

[1] Bushfires which broke out in country areas of Victoria and South Australia on Ash Wednesday, 16 February 1983, were intensified by air temperatures of 43 degrees Centigrade and gale-force winds. As many as 30 fires raged at the peak of the disaster with 4000 firefighters and 1000 soldiers battling the inferno. Flames 240 m high and travelling at speeds of 100 kilometres per hour killed 72 people and 345,000 livestock. Seven towns were destroyed, 200 homes burnt out, and 4200 square kilometres of land were devastated.

The Granville rail crash on 19 January 1977 killed 83 passengers and injured another 80 when a commuter train from the Blue Mountains, west of Sydney, struck a bridge which collapsed onto the overturned train and crushed several carriages.

On 9 August 1987, a 20-year-old man started shooting at people and vehicles in Hoddle Street, Melbourne, killing 19 and wounding seven.

For information on the Queen Street shooting, see Chapter 3.

- pangs of grief triggered by any reminder
- disorganisation
- numbness
- anxiety
- anger
- dreams of the dead person
- angry protests, 'Why did this have to happen to my loved one?'
- searching, looking for perceptual cues that the person might return
- sadness, crying, pain at being separated from the person who has gone

In the case of traumatic loss, these reactions of grief may be much more intense and have superimposed traumatic stress symptoms and reactions as described below. These reactions to traumatic loss are normal, yet many people may not understand this and become frightened by their own response. They may fear they are going insane, particularly if they hear the voice or feel the presence of the lost person. This may be just part of the perceptual set of longing for them to return.

There are nonspecific reactions which are not relevant to loss, exclusively, but occur with any acute stressful situation. These are anxiety, agitation, restlessness, depression, withdrawal, disorganisation, and general symptomatic disturbance including sleep and appetite disturbance.

Having a reaction to a traumatic loss or a traumatic encounter with death is normal. This is not an illness, but a natural reaction to an abnormal situation. When providing support and counselling after a trauma, it is important to understand what the role of the helper is. To facilitate the normal resolution of the experience, the therapist treating a person exposed to trauma must reinforce the idea that theirs is a normal reaction to an abnormal situation.

The *normalisation*, and *educational* aspect is a critical part of early intervention and therapy provision for those who have been acutely exposed to such traumatic experiences.

Catastrophic loss with its associated bereavement can affect people in many different situations. It is particularly likely to lead to difficulties in the following circumstances:

- when there are multiple bereavements
- when there are multiple losses; multiple deaths (even if they are not at the same time but over an extended period of time)
- where there has been previous extreme deprivation
- where the person has been very deprived of support and security
- where the individual has trouble in basis trust

People in these circumstances are more likely to have a catastrophic response even in what may appear to be a lesser loss situation. For those who are already suffering chronic extreme stress and marginally coping, the loss may become catastrophic.

Incidents such as domestic fires may cause death and total loss of a household, exposing people to multiple levels of stress. The belief that death only comes to the elderly in a quiet, peaceful manner is challenged when a person is confronted with an inexplicable, violent death. Stress reactions are particularly likely to be exacerbated if the traumatic loss involves violence perpetrated by one person upon another.

A number of elements contribute to the levels of stress experienced after traumatic loss. Personal vulnerability, the levels of support available, and often the personal involvement with victims puts an additional burden on those affected, placing them more at risk. A double burden is carried by emergency workers in country areas of Australia who are often personally associated with road accident victims injured or killed in their locality. The workers may already be significantly stressed by their repetitive exposure to mutilation and death, by the retrieval of burnt bodies from automobiles, or trying to extract people before they die, and by the continual frustration encountered in their role. The additional personal sense of loss experienced by these workers often impedes their ability to cope with the situation.

Traumatic encounter with death

The second major type of trauma is a traumatic encounter with death. This term is used when death itself, rather than loss, seems to be the stressor experience. Generally, people develop a sense of personal invulnerability, 'That's the sort of thing that happens to other people, not me'. This belief is challenged by a traumatic encounter with death. An encounter with death makes us aware of our own mortality. A stressful encounter with death — particularly multiple and gruesome deaths of others, the helplessness experienced while someone close to us dies, or a close encounter with our own death — can have an effect which imprints the experience on our mind.

This may lead to post-traumatic stress reactions or, in some instances, ongoing psychological problems such as PTSD and other psychiatric disabilities.

Personal life threats, mutilating deaths, and entrapment can be referred to as 'inescapable horror' (Burges Watson, 1987). When this type of traumatic stressor is experienced in either a personal or community disaster, such as the Granville rail disaster, it can lead to great difficulties in subsequent adjustment and mastery (Raphael, 1977; Raphael, 1979; Raphael, Singh, & Bradbury, 1980). The massive encounter with death that occurs when there are multiple deaths leads not only to grief for those who are involved and massive grief for the community, but also to a sense of the overwhelming amount of death that is present. Emergency workers and the wider community are quite often traumatised by this. Years after the

Granville rail disaster, many of the emergency workers involved still had images imprinted in their minds of when the slab was lifted, exposing the dead bodies crushed beneath. As one worker said, 'Like sardines in a can' (Raphael, 1977).

Research has found that there is a common pattern of reactions that occurs in acute stressors such as accidents — an alternation of *shutting out, denying, numbing* and *reexperiencing, intrusive thoughts*, and *hyperalertness* (Malt, Blikra, & Hoivik, 1989).

Reactions after a traumatic encounter with death may also involve overwhelming fear, rage, or sadness. This pathological response is not frequent and research into disasters has shown that no more than 25 per cent of the totally affected population are likely to be overwhelmed in that way and rendered incapable of further action. (Green, Grace, Lindy, Titchener, & Lindy, 1983). Studies of disasters have shown that panic behaviour is extremely rare and only likely to occur when we have an escape channel that is closing (Gleser, Green, & Winget, 1981). A person may attempt to deny what is happening; a shutting-out process comes into play and that may lead to an inappropriate response (Horowitz, 1976). Police officers, for example, who have attempted to shut out of their minds some of the trauma to which they have been exposed, have later encountered problems because they are required to keep the memories of incidents alive to give evidence. They often will be challenged in court to present facts, and attacked if they are inaccurate. There can therefore be factors at work which interfere with the ability to integrate the traumatic experience, by facing it and letting go.

Past the denial phase is *intrusion*, when the memories of the event emerge along with subsequent reactions to them. At the same time, a mastery and acceptance of the traumatic experience may begin to occur (Green, Wilson, & Lindy, 1985).

Components of PTSD

There are a number of components to the diagnostic criteria of PTSD. The first of these is the occurrence of a severe traumatic event, one which would be defined as such by most people in the society.

The second is a set of symptoms or experiences which are the reexperiencing and intrusive phenomena: the memories, distress caused by triggers that remind the person of the event, and nightmares which frequently disturb the person's sleep. Flashbacks may also occur which are like a reliving of the experience. Often these are associated with panic and sweating.

The third group is the numbing, denying phenomena, which attempt to shut out feelings.

Finally there are the arousal symptoms: irritability, sleep disturbances, hyperalertness. Having experienced something so threatening, staying aroused seems a protection against it occurring again (American Psychiatric

Association, 1987; Horowitz, 1976; Horowitz, Wilner, Kaltreider, & Alvarez, 1980).

The reactive process is a similar group of processes but not prolonged. It may involve the intrusive experience of the return of the event, the attempts to shut out and shut down feeling, and the alertness that makes people prepared to deal with any trauma that may confront them again. These patterns of response occur in the acute time, and for the first few weeks. They may continue, or reemerge after a period of latency, developing as major patterns of symptoms in PTSD, perhaps of such severity as to warrant treatment.

Studies of people who have been first victims of a disaster, as well as helpers, show rates in the initial weeks of post-traumatic stress reactions reaching sometimes as high as 70–90 per cent of those exposed (Patrick & Patrick, 1981; Taylor & Frazer, 1982; Weisaeth, 1989a). This may or may not go on to disorder.

Two years after the Ash Wednesday bushfires, nearly 20 per cent of the firefighters studied were suffering from PTSD as a result of their experience (McFarlane, 1988). They had not previously been psychiatrically ill but were people exposed to severe stress. PTSD is not an indication of 'weakness' in the people who have been exposed; it is a manifestation of the severe effects of trauma.

Traumatic stress may involve the reactions of the individual, coping processes, and avoidance of things that are reminders. It may also involve the wish to shut out feelings, and the wish to withdraw and not to talk about what has happened, as well as increasing irritability. These factors often impact on marital relations and family life, so that the healing process of talking through cannot occur (McFarlane, 1987a, 1987b).

When traumatic loss has occurred, patterns of morbidity post-bereavement may reflect pathological grief or depression. Alcohol and drug abuse may be common because people attempt to repress their symptoms. This is a form of self-medication and may be an attempt to shut out memories of the experiences. For many, the shutting-out process develops because the event is so frightening that there is an unwillingness to face it. When this occurs, that portion of life experience is closed off and part of the personality becomes deactivated.

It is very important to understand that, therapeutically, it is totally inappropriate to tear down a person's defences and force the trauma story out at all costs. One of the main components of care is assisting victims to feel safe enough to talk about the trauma, but they cannot be forced to do so. Procedures which attempt to force people may repeat the trauma for the victim. While helping the person bring out and come to terms with the traumatic experience is often a very important aim of support and counselling, defensive barriers should never be torn down.

To understand the effects of a stressful experience, it is necessary to examine the nature of the experience itself, characteristics of the individual, their pre-trauma personality, the coping behaviours they use, their pattern of defences, and how they gauge the event. If someone appraises the event and feels they can master it, then they may be less traumatised than if it was assessed as more threatening (Raphael, 1986). This particular point is important because when pre-trauma training and education is provided to those in emergency services who are likely to be at risk, it provides a support mechanism which helps them deal with a trauma when they are exposed to it (Dunning, 1988).

Post-traumatic cognitive processing is the way in which the mind tries to come to terms with the experience. The processing of the event and the resultant emotions are normal reactive responses to exposure to trauma, just as grief is normal in exposure to traumatic loss. Horowitz (1976) suggests that phases of remembering and reexperiencing alternate with denial, shutting out, or avoidance until the experience attenuates and is integrated.

Gradually, all being well, there is a working-through process which involves facing the reality of what has happened, leading to mastery and acceptance of what has occurred. This process may continue for many years until it is dealt with or, if never dealt with, can become the pattern of the person's existence. They become physically numb and incapable of emotional response or, alternatively, stuck in time and totally preoccupied with the trauma (Raphael, 1975, 1986).

The *recovery environment* is particularly important in helping the person assimilate the traumatic experience: the social support network is vitally important. Support of those who have experienced the same traumatic event can occur in the acute period or later. It is part of what might be done in debriefing. It is also part of a natural process of mastering what was experienced and each person's actions (Hodgkinson & Stewart, 1991). At a later stage, it might occur in mutual support or self-help organisations.

The perception that a person did not handle the event as they felt they should have is a possible complication. There is a particular burden of stress associated with personal perceptions of failure in a traumatic situation. Coming to terms with actions during the trauma is one difficulty experienced during the reaction afterwards. An example would be someone having to leave others to die in order to escape. The person may not have been able to do anything else to survive, but the ultimate cost may be a burden of guilt, a psychological issue in terms of the capacity to resolve the trauma.

Social supports are therefore vital and mobilising them in the recovery environment is critical (Green, Grace, & Gleser, 1985). If the community and normal social networks are disrupted, as in the extensive destruction by Cyclone Tracy of the city of Darwin in Australia in 1974, there is a further burden to be dealt with. Deprivation and financial problems cause additional stress after disasters. Often, the practical assistance rendered after a disaster may make people feel that they should not complain about the distress they may still feel inside.

Cultural characteristics and *societal attitudes* may interfere with the expression of feelings. Some cultures believe that, 'if something happens to you it is your fault', in others, 'it is karma', 'it is how it is'. Understanding the cultural background of the person is vital. It is particularly important to recognise that for recent immigrants there may be stresses in relation to their migration and the lack of social support may add to their trauma.

Models of care

The model of care in *When Disaster Strikes* (Raphael, 1986, p. 248) was designed for use in a major disaster, but the principles are the same for a smaller disaster and in traumatic loss. The range of levels and processes are relevant. There are two key themes within this umbrella of care: recognition of the suffering; and recognition of the strengths of those who have been rendered victims. Secondary problems occur for victims when they are visualised as helpless, passive, and unable to participate actively in the recovery process. This may add to their trauma and may reinforce the helpless traumatised role that was suffered at the time of stress.

Therefore inherent in any healing after trauma is a recognition of suffering that has occurred. 'I am sorry you have suffered,' acknowledges a person's experience. It is important also to recognise personal strengths. A key concept is that people will usually go on from being a victim to becoming a survivor (Ochberg, 1988). It must be recognised that the person has been hurt and has been a victim, but the process of mastery and strength involves moving on beyond that stage. Part of the message given when helping is, 'Yes I'm sorry, I know that you suffered. I know it was awful, I'm glad that you didn't die, we will go on'

Three of the best writers in the field of traumatic stress in the world are men who survived the Holocaust: Victor Frankl (1963), who evolved logotherapy; Henry Krystal (1971), who has written of trauma and healing; and Leo Eitinger (Eitinger & Askevold, 1986), who was the first person to bring to the attention of the world the impact that the concentration camps had on health and well-being. We have learned from the immediate post-war period that although people expected to return to 'normal' once the business of daily living was resumed, the ability of many to do so was compromised by the 'scars on the mind' of their war-time experiences. The essential principles are that education and consultation processes are very important. The more understanding we gain about the processing of traumatic reactions, the more assistance will be available for future victims of traumatic loss and traumatic encounter with death.

Psychological first aid is part of the first stage of triage, the organising of care for the injured, including those psychologically injured. When trauma occurs it is necessary to do kind, reasonable things with people as part of the psychological first aid. This may include holding them, touching them, or bringing them a warm drink. Touching is a very individual matter and it is necessary to understand what touch involves for that particular person. Touch in an acute situation is different to that in a long-standing relationship where it may have more personal or sexual connotations.

Another way of helping may be to let the victim talk, assisting them to express their feelings, especially if they are acutely distressed. Often just spending time with them as a comforting presence is enough.

The next stage beyond just triage and first aid is psychological support and assessment alongside other aid and care. That is, when the physical and material needs are being attended to, such as a splint for a broken leg or a roof overhead, it is also the time to provide the psychological arm to aid. This may be the time people are ready to talk about their experience. In follow-up studies after the Granville rail disaster, it was found that counselling was often best accepted when it came alongside the other areas of support provision (Singh & Raphael, 1981).

Preventive assessment and management of 'at risk' groups

Most people do recover from trauma. However, the more severe the trauma, the lower the rate of recovery. Therefore the degree of severity of the traumatic event is a primary indicator which may assist in the presentation for professional care. Establishment of 'at risk' criteria is important in achieving preventative early intervention.

Ten questions evolved from research in Norway about the post-traumatic affect that occurs after exposure to a traumatic event (Weisaeth, 1989b). There could be other questions that are relevant, but the checklist of these 10 provides an indication of who may be at risk:

1. Difficulty with sleep.
2. Nightmares about the accident or disaster.
3. Depressed feelings.
4. Tendency to jump or startle at sudden noises or unexpected movements, indicating the arousal.
5. Tendencies to withdraw from others.
6. Irritable feelings, getting easily irritable or infuriated.
7. Frequent swings of mood.
8. Bad conscience, self-accusations or guilt.
9. Fears when approaching the place of the accident or situations which act as reminders.
10. Tension in the body. (Raphael, Lundin, & Weisaeth, 1989, p. 58)

This is a useful checklist. It does not cut across the understanding of the individual, and it covers what is most relevant. If a number (six or more) of these reactions are present after the first week and increasing, then this person may need further support and counselling to help them adapt to the loss or trauma.

After traumatic events, recognition of at-risk groups is critical so that they can be targeted for counselling and support. McFarlane's (1984) studies after the Ash Wednesday bushfires found that even though the communities responded well by providing support and education through the bush-fire relief workers, many were hesitant to refer people on with PTSD. Relief workers had been given programs to outline what it was, yet were reluctant to refer because they thought doing so would make people worse. As a result, it appears that many people's suffering may have been prolonged. It is far worse for people not to be referred and to go on suffering, often at significant cost to their personal relationships, their capacity to function at work, their sexual lives, and to their self-esteem, and ultimately sometimes even with risk to their lives. For some people, it will prevent longer-term disability. Referral should hold no shame, it should be an appropriate part of the spectrum of care, the umbrella of care provided.

WHAT MAKES PEOPLE MORE AT RISK FOR THE DEVELOPMENT OF CHRONIC PTSD?
Usually, 90 per cent of people have some reaction to trauma in the first day or so which begins to lessen by the end of the first week. However, a number of things make people more vulnerable. Instead of resolving the stress over the first four to six weeks and settling down to occasional memories or nightmares, reactions can disrupt the person's life and functioning and become PTSD. Certain factors which influence the development of PTSD are summarised below.

1. Nature and intensity of the stressor
It has been found that levels of exposure and stressfulness of the experience were contributing factors to morbidity but they seemed to have a threshold level before any disability from post-traumatic stress reactions became evident (McFarlane, 1987a). Other factors that influence the outcome may be personal, property, and financial losses or physical injury.

2. Characteristics of the individual victim or helper
Individuals may be more at risk if general health is impaired. Studies have shown that some people are more sensitively aroused by stress, and this may make them more prone to ongoing long-term problems (Green, Grace, et al.,1985). People with coping styles involving more active mastery or problem-solving may also go on to more positive outcomes (Gleser et al., 1981).

3. History of past stressful life experiences
A history of many stressful life events and prior unresolved loss experiences, or past psychological and/or psychiatric treatment may indicate vulnerability — but does not automatically do so. It is important to understand the context of these and the meaning to the individual. Why has this stress affected this person in this way? The more severe stress that someone has

been exposed to previously, the more likely they are to be vulnerable again. Previous stress can be reawakened. So past loss, past severe stress, mean that there are more likely to be ongoing difficulties (Raphael, 1986). Some people may be strengthened by trauma and there is a need to know more about how such resilience develops (Kobasa, 1979).

4. Characteristics of the recovery environment
The availability of family and social support, professional counselling, and financial support may make a difference. Survivors of the Zeebrugge disaster (see p. 60) who reported family conflict exhibited worse stress reactions (Hodgkinson & Stewart, 1991). Even in a supportive family atmosphere, where people can talk about their traumatic experience, family members may feel that they cannot respond because they were not there. Working in a small group with people who have been through the same experience can be enormously helpful. That is why the provision of psychological debriefing as part of the role and work situation of those exposed to stress may be helpful.

We must also recognise that there are issues where both the professional and family networks may be unhelpful (Hodgkinson & Stewart, 1991). People who have been through traumatic experiences often tell sad stories of what is called the 'second trauma' when health professionals were unable to listen to them, when they did not want to know about what had happened (Symonds, 1980). This has happened to rape victims, victims of incest, and victims of torture and trauma. Trauma also distresses the helpers (Raphael, Meldrum, & O'Toole, 1991). Countertransference reactions within ourselves as professional carers are very natural if we work with trauma victims. We need to understand and deal with these reactions, and use our professional systems to support us in that role (Wilson, 1989).

Adaptation and mastery

Adaptation and *mastery* are critical concepts in the process of recovery. Human resilience plays an enormous role in the intensity of post-trauma reactions. An example of this adaptation was shown by the helpers at the Granville rail disaster: a great many of them related that it was an awful, terrible, and frustrating experience and that they had been acutely stressed, but it made them reevaluate their lives more positively and do things differently afterwards (Raphael et al., 1980).

Human attachments to other people are very important and are often what help people to survive. Survivors of the *Bell Star* shipwreck off Tasmania, Australia, which occurred in October, 1973, spent time in an open boat and then in the bush before they were rescued. Images of those they loved helped their survival (Henderson & Bostock, 1977). Human attachments are motivating factors: they assisted the survival of people in the concentration camps; they can help to keep people alive through trauma when they think they are going to die.

Images of those we love motivate us to endure and survive dreadful diseases — to live on, to do battle, and to stay alive. They are also the factors which empower people to get better.

It is important not to treat the victim or those who have been hurt or traumatised, as passive and unable to respond. It is important to engage them in making decisions about the processes of recovery so they may achieve a greater sense of empowerment.

Active mastery is another vital concept. Workers should help victims to identify past strengths, how they mastered stress previously, what future strengths they will display. That very act in itself will be most important in their active mastery of what has occurred. One of the values of talking through the traumatic event is enabling the person to master, in retrospect, what has happened. Children's traumatic play stems from the wish to master what has happened. This may be an active mastery process in some instances, (Lacey, 1972) but in others it is a sign of ongoing traumatisation (Terr, 1991). It has been suggested that, after disaster, those who are involved in active rescue and recovery operations are less likely to suffer PTSD than those who are not, because the active rescuers have had an opportunity for active mastery (Raphael, 1986).

Pre-trauma training

Training of those who are likely to be in a vulnerable situation is one step towards preventing PTSD. People need to be encouraged to think ahead, to prepare a plan of action in their minds. International reports suggest that if there has been training in dealing with a trauma and planning to implement response, people seem less vulnerable and the mastery process is assisted. The training program should include education in identifying normal reactions to trauma, advice on what actions can be taken, how behaviour may be affected, and a possible plan of action. This is part of an active mastery spectrum that can be activated.

Implications for prevention arise during the trauma also. It is known that those who can continue to engage with what is happening in the trauma rather than dissociating from it, may be helped in the issues that follow. Not all are able to do that and, for some, dissociation may be necessary for survival.

It may be useful when working with people to help them go back over the trauma and ask them what they would have done differently, what advice they would give someone else if the same thing occurred in the future. However, this must be done carefully, for perceived mistakes or negligence may be a source of guilt and distress, and need to be dealt with.

Assisting workers

During the reactive time, (that is, the early days and weeks post-trauma) there are achievable programs that will assist rescue and other workers to process post-traumatic reactions. Shortly after exposure to the trauma, a debriefing process can allow people to express their thoughts of the experience, the feelings aroused by it and may provide support for them. Emergency services are now recognising that the issue of stress debriefing is important and may be helpful as part of the balancing process for those who work in this area.

It is very important that hospital systems also have opportunities for debriefing. When stress is a repetitive part of work these should ideally be once a week, or at least once a fortnight. They should be at the end of the working week, covering case review and allowing a chance to disengage. The carrying home of that stress can burden relationships. Workers' families, while they may want to share some of that burden, also want to share the positive parts of the relationship as well.

Forward treatment is a model similar to debriefing, and refers to procedures such as those used in the army to deal with acutely stressed combat troops. This is treatment of proximity, immediacy and expectancy, and back in the front line again (Solomon & Benbenishty, 1986). This approach has some value, but also some risk. Treating people with the intention that they will be able to return to work, to return to normal functioning, is an important ethos, but recognising that they can come to a situation where the overload is too much is also of great consequence. The traumatised person may need protection from any reminders of the stressor, at least until some healing has taken place. They can then confront the trauma at their own pace, with opportunity to integrate it.

Beyond the immediate reaction

During the reactive period it may be best to employ strategies specifically for high-risk groups: looking at those who may be at particular risk, facilitating their active mastery, assisting their coping, and helping them diminish and control the intrusive phenomena and to manage the arousal better.

The approach used during the intermediate period may be an extension of these techniques, but should concentrate on techniques that help people talk in small groups or to review what has happened to them. People need to review the experience, with positive goals of unloading feelings, sharing distress, and moving on, having commenced some process of mastery.

Finally, in the longer-term, more intensive therapies and their effects should be considered. There is only one systemic study demonstrating the effectiveness of any specific therapy in the treatment of PTSD and there is an urgent need for more (Brom, Kleber, & Defares, 1989). A few studies exist of small groups of veterans and other people in the USA but after all these years of gradually growing understanding of this disorder, there is yet no adequate delineation of the most effective treatments. For some people, a counselling, behavioural, or psychotherapeutic approach will be adequate to treat their PTSD, for example, cognitive-behaviour therapy after rape (Foa, Rothbaum, Riggs, & Murdock 1991). For others it will be necessary to prescribe from a range of medications depending on arousal, depressive, and other phenomena of the disorder as it presents. It is critically important that the most effective treatments for particular groups of patients are better understood (Davidson, 1992).

Critical incident stress debriefing

In Australia, debriefing is now being offered to emergency and other organisations. It is extremely important that this be done from the background of expertise, by or involving a mental health professional; this is not as simple a measure as is sometimes presented. There is no magic — people conducting critical incident stress debriefings need to recognise that while there are some good general principles, they need to have access to expertise in the mental health area, to help them define when people need additional specialised help.

There are several parameters relevant to critical incident stress debriefing. The first of these is commonly called *defusing*, often in the emergency time immediately after an acute episode. The terms don't specifically matter, but peers or others (not necessarily professionals) help those involved let down, talk about what has happened, express some feelings *if they want to*, and just release tensions generally. A common response to an emergency situation is to want to stay working longer than the tour of duty, often beyond tolerable levels of stress. The 'high' that occurs from working as emergency workers in an emergency situation generates the feeling, at the time, that it can be done. Defusing allows a worker to let go of what happened on their shift. It should be part of the process of going from on duty in an acute stressful situation to off duty. People need a certain amount of relief from being on duty and it is critical that any emergency organisation build this in.

Debriefing can follow the immediacy of the defusing within a few days, perhaps up to a week afterwards. This is a formal situation where the debriefer works with those who have been exposed to the stressful situation, providing educational input about the normal reactions to abnormal events and the stressor effects previously described. People are given the opportunity to talk about what happened, preferably in a small group, although it can be done one-to-one if that is the most appropriate. There is value in those who have been through the event talking about it together, talking about what happened. This is an opportunity to facilitate emotional release, as is appropriate for people if they wish to at that time. There should be no pressure for expressing feelings but a recognition that many complex human emotions are normal at this time, including those which are sometimes seen as weak, like fear, anxiety, tears, or helplessness.

Participants often find it helpful to review actions during the traumatic incident and then draw together the experience in an active way — what might have been done differently, what would be recommended to others in the future. It is helpful to end with a positive, constructive review, a sense of care, and of active achievement. The concluding review should tie the session together, even with the opportunity of further review soon after or several weeks later if needed.

Treatment of specific disorders

The *treatment of specific disorders by mental health professionals* is a critical issue. It has been found again and again that people who are suffering from significant psychiatric disorders, including PTSD, are often not referred on for proper psychiatric assessment even when this disorder is severe and entrenched. (McFarlane, 1988; Clark, Minas, & McKenzie, 1991). This often arises from a fear that to call a person disordered will mean that they are being made sick. There should, instead, be recognition of the value of early and appropriate specialist care when this is needed.

Critical elements of therapy

1. TRUST
It is important to establish a relationship in which some level of trust exists between the counsellor and the person who has been affected by the trauma. The counsellor cannot expect people to unload their feelings to a stranger.

2. EDUCATION
Within that relationship of trust, an important educational process should occur: advising people of the normality of their reactions and that anyone exposed to such an abnormal situation might experience them. From there, the therapist can allow the person to talk further. Education can be broadly based and may need to involve family members as well.

3. OVERALL HEALTH
General health is an important aspect and requires a holistic approach. Physical health and emotional well-being may contribute to the general health of the person. The active processes involved in those aspects of health may assist with the process of recovery and general well-being, as may nutrition, exercise, and rest.

4. SOCIAL SUPPORT
The provision of support within the family is important and the therapist may need to help build this for the family, or in a broader way, for a group of people who have all been exposed to stress. The type of support that

needs to be available must include education, to assist recognition of what traumatic experience is and how it is dealt with. It needs to provide an opportunity for people to talk through their experience as they wish, without being judged. There needs to be provision of an opportunity for the release of feelings if and when these are appropriate. It particularly needs to be non-judgmental, to recognise there is a wide range of human response, and that an extensive variety of coping mechanisms may be implemented to assist people in coming to terms with such trauma. Support may involve practical as well as emotional assistance.

5. DEALING WITH THE TRAUMA ITSELF

The more specific aspects of therapy involve dealing with the trauma itself, and this is the clinical work that needs to be done. It involves building the sense of trust so that the person can come to the stage of releasing their story of trauma. This cannot be demanded, nor can the tears or the release of feelings.

Two vital principles are: (a) looking at when it is right for this person; and (b) taking the time necessary. Firstly, it is quite often only when the person feels trust enough in the relationship that they may be ready to talk about a little of what has happened. The second important concept is what is called dosing of affect, dosing of emotions. People who have intense painful emotions about traumatic experiences can often only let them out in small doses. The counsellor has to go along with this process, providing support as these releases occur. Sometimes there will be an enormous outpouring, a catharsis and a release. However, for many people it can only be done a bit at a time, much the same as grieving can, and may go on for a long period.

The catharsis that may occur for some people either in a good group support system or in the support and trust of one-to-one therapy may be very helpful. This may result from the person being ready to tell their story when they trust enough, when they know the listener can bear it. For counsellors, this is part of having to deal with personal experiences of trauma. If the counsellor has personally experienced substantial trauma, its reawakening may be a painful part of working with trauma victims even though it may bring a special empathy to the relationship. Counsellors may need to know themselves well enough to say when they cannot handle this sort of trauma.

Also important, in dealing with the trauma, is pace: taking it at the pace that is appropriate for the particular person. The concept of recovery should always be remembered, the goal of helping this person move from being a victim to becoming a survivor who has integrated and mastered this experience. This requires progress, not just enduring the painful, helpless, humiliating, terrifying horror aspects of the experience, but also the positive growth: the, 'I've mastered it', 'I survived' aspects.

Survival has many meanings for people. It is often bought at the cost of someone else. The person may need help to integrate their sense of responsibility for whatever they contributed, what they feel they might have done that would have helped others, and what they feel they did that hurt others. Those are parts of the trauma story that are gradually integrated in a therapeutic way over time, again without judgment, facilitating the gentle dosing of emotional release as is suitable for the person. Many professional techniques may be brought into play, such as some behavioural techniques, or some techniques with hypnosis, but none of these is a short cut. They need to be tailored to individual needs and have to be understood in the background of knowing the particular person as a human being, the nature of their own past experience, their social support, and what strengths they bring.

For counsellors, the ultimate aspect of their work is the depth of trusting relationship established with victims. It is important for the person to feel that the counsellor is caring and empathic enough to help them face this burden of the trauma gradually, in their own time, and that this person believes in their strength and capacity to go on from it. They must know that the counsellor gets no vicarious satisfaction out of knowing about it, that they don't have to 'get it out' for that person. Knowing that the counsellor will be there with them to deal with it over time is most meaningful for trauma sufferers. When the trauma has been severe, or the problems surrounding it have become chronic, the process is going to take time and is not going to be easy.

For loss, and the trauma encountered with it, the *processes of bereavement counselling reflect similar themes*. In traumatic loss it may, however, be necessary to provide counselling for trauma before counselling for grief, as both elements need care. Trust, letting the person review and talk about the lost relationship, letting the person come to terms with the pain of the death, and how it occurred, expressing their own mixed feelings are all important elements. The bereaved need to let out their feelings bit by bit — their anger, resentment, and rage at being 'deserted' by the person who has died. Many complex feelings are involved and there will be unique aspects relevant to particular individuals, certain relationships, and specific circumstances of death. There is no magic package available at the end which determines that the person has grieved, that they are alright, or that they have resolved the trauma. The counsellor and the bereaved reach agreement about a level of acceptance for now and an acknowledgment that the person will go on. If there has been a good relationship, the bereaved may come back again later on to do more work, or they may, as most people do, progressively over the years deal with it themselves. They will remember almost invariably what the trauma was, it will always be something significant in their lives, but it will not be an emotional burden disrupting and altering their lives and marking them as a victim forever. They will have survived it, they will have become a survivor.

Ultimately, what is done, is to comfort one another. All of this work is about the human response, of wishing to comfort others who have been hurt in some bad way. This is most basically represented when we put our arms around each other. That is not automatically part of therapy, and sometimes it is not at all appropriate, but it symbolises that comforting we offer to one another at a time of trauma.

References

American Psychiatric Association. (1987). *Diagnostic and statistical manual of mental disorders.* (3rd ed. rev.) (DSM-III-R). Washington, DC: Author.

Brom, D., Kleber, R.J. & Defares, P. B. (1989). Brief psychotherapy for posttraumatic stress disorders. *Journal of Consulting and Clinical Psychology, 57*, 607–612.

Burges Watson, I.P. (1987) Post-traumatic stress disorder in Australia and New Zealand. A clinical review of the consequences of inescapable horror. *The Medical Journal of Australia, 147*, 443–447.

Clark, D.M., Minas, I.H., & McKenzie, D.P. (1991) Illness behavior as a determinant of referral to a psychiatric consultation/liaison service. *Australian and New Zealand Journal of Psychiatry, 25*, 330–337.

Creamer, M., Burgess, P., Buckingham, W., & Pattison, P. (1990). Psychological response to trauma: The Queen Street shootings. *The Bulletin of the Australian Psychological Society,* November.

Davidson, J. (1992, November). Developments in the diagnosis of post-traumatic stress disorder. In *The spectrum of traumatic stress: A symposium on post-traumatic stress disorder.* Inaugural Lingard Symposium, Pokolbin NSW.

Dunning, C. (1988). Intervention strategies for emergency workers. In M. Lystad (Ed.), *Mental health response to mass emergencies: Theory and practice* (pp. 284–307). New York: Brunner/Mazel.

Eitinger, L., & Askevold, F. (1968). Psychiatric aspects. In A. Strom (Ed.), *Concentration camp survivors* (pp. 73–95). New York: Humanities Press.

Figley, C.R. (Ed.). (1978). *Stress disorders among Vietnam veterans.* New York: Brunner/Mazel.

Foa, E.B., Rothbaum, B.O., Riggs, D.S., & Murdock, T.B. (1991). Treatment of posttraumatic stress disorder in rape victims: A comparison between cognitive-behavioral procedures and counselling. *Journal of Consulting and Clinical Psychology, 59*, 715–723.

Frankl, V. (1963). *Man's search for meaning.* New York: Washington Square Press.

Gleser, G.C., Green. B.L., & Winget, C.N. (1981). *Prolonged psychosocial effects of disaster.* New York: Academic Press.

Gordon, R. & Wraith, R. (1993). Responses of children and adolescents to disasters. In J. Wilson, & B. Raphael (Eds.), *International handbook of traumatic stress syndromes* (pp. 561–575). New York: Plenum Press.

Green, B.L., Grace, M.C., & Gleser, G.C. (1985). Identifying survivors at risk: Long-term impairment following the Beverly Hills Supper Club Fire. *Journal of Consulting and Clinical Psychology, 53*, 672–678.

Green, B.L., Grace, M.C., Lindy, J.D., Titchener, J.L., & Lindy, J.G. (1983). Levels of functional impairment following a civilian disaster: The Beverley Hills Supper Club fire. *Journal of Consulting and Clinical Psychology, 50*, 573–580.

Green, B.L., Wilson, J.P., & Lindy, J.D. (1985). Conceptualizing post-traumatic stress disorder: A psychosocial framework. In C.R. Figley (Ed.), *Trauma and its wake: The study of post-traumatic stress disorder* (pp. 53–69). New York: Brunner/Mazel.

Henderson, S. & Bostock, T. (1977). Coping behaviour after shipwreck. *British Journal of Psychiatry, 131*,15–20.

Hodgkinson, P.E., & Stewart, M. (1991). *Coping with catastrophe: A handbook of disaster management.* London: Routledge.

Horne, D.J. de L. (1993) Traumatic stress reactions to motor vehicle accidents. In J. Wilson & B. Raphael (Eds.), *International handbook of traumatic stress syndromes* (pp. 499–506). New York: Plenum Press.

Horowitz, M.J. (1976). *Stress response syndromes.* New York: Jason Aronson.

Horowitz, M.J., Wilner, N., Kaltreider, N., & Alvarez, W. (1980). Signs and symptoms of post-traumatic disorder. *Archives of General Psychiatry, 37*, 85–92.

Kobasa, S.C. (1979). Stressful life events, personality and health: An inquiry into hardiness. *Journal of Personality and Social Psychology, 37*, 1–11.

Krystal, H. (1971). Trauma: Considerations of its intensity and chronicity. *International Psychiatric Clinics, 8*, 11–28.

Kulka, R.A., Schlenger, W.E., Fairbank, J.A., Jordan, K., Hough, R.L., Marmar, C.R., & Weiss, D.S. (1991). Assessment of posttraumatic stress disorder in the community: Prospects and pitfalls from recent studies of Vietnam veterans. *Psychological Assessment: A Journal of Consulting and Clinical Psychology, 3*, 547–560.

Lacey, G.N. (1972). Observations of Aberfan. *Journal of Psychosomatic Research, 16*, 257–260.

Laufer, R.S., Frey-Wouters, E., & Gallops, M.S. (1985) Traumatic stressors in the Vietnam war and post-traumatic stress disorder. In C.R. Figley (Ed.), *Trauma and its wake: The study and treatment of post-traumatic stress disorder* (pp. 73–89). New York: Brunner/Mazel.

Malt, U.F., Blikra, G., & Hoivik, B. (1989). The late effects of accidental injury questionnaire. *Acta Psychiatrica Scandinavica Supplementum, 353* , 59–64.

McFarlane, A.C. (1984). The Ash Wednesday bushfires in South Australia. Implications for planning for post-disaster services. *Medical Journal of Australia, 141*, 286–291.

McFarlane, A.C. (1987a). Family functioning and overprotection following a natural disaster: The longitudinal effects of post-traumatic morbidity. *Australian and New Zealand Journal of Psychiatry, 21*, 210–218.

McFarlane, A.C. (1987b). Posttraumatic phenomena in a longitudinal study of children following a natural disaster. *Journal of the American Academy of Child and Adolescent Psychiatry, 26*, 746–769.

McFarlane, A.C. (1988). The longitudinal course of posttraumatic morbidity. The range of outcomes and their predictors. *The Journal of Nervous and Mental Disease, 176*, 30–39.

McFarlane, A.C., & Raphael, B. (1984). Ash Wednesday: The effects of a fire. *Australian and New Zealand Journal of Psychiatry, 18*, 341–353.

Ochberg, F. (1988). *Post traumatic therapy of victims of violence.* New York: Brunner/Mazel.

Patrick, V., & Patrick, W.K. (1981). Cyclone 78 in Sri Lanka: The mental health trail. *British Journal of Psychiatry, 138*, 210–216.

Pynoos, R.S., & Eth, S. (1985). *Post-traumatic stress disorder in children.* Washington, DC: American Psychiatric Press.

Pynoos, R. S., & Nader, K. (1989). Children's memory and proximity to violence. *Journal of the American Academy of Child and Adolescent Psychiatry, 28*, 236–241.

Raphael, B. (1975). Crisis and loss counselling following a disaster. *Mental Health of Australia, 14*, 118–122.

Raphael, B. (1977). The Granville train disaster: Psychological needs and their management. *Medical Journal of Australia, 1*, 303–305.

Raphael, B. (1979). A primary prevention action programme: Psychiatric involvement following a major rail disaster. *Omega, 10*, 211–226.

Raphael, B. (1983). *The anatomy of bereavement.* New York: Basic Books.

Raphael, B. (1986). *When disaster strikes.* New York: Basic Books.

Raphael, B., Lundin, T., & Weisaeth, L. (1989). Appendix J Post-traumatic symptom scale: PTSS-10: Reactions following an accident or a disaster. *Acta Psychiatrica Scandinavica Supplementum, 353*, 58.

Raphael, B., Meldrum, L., & O'Toole, B. (1991). Rescuers' psychological responses to disasters. *British Medical Journal, 303*, 1346–1347.

Raphael, B., Singh, B., & Bradbury, L. (1980). Disaster: The helpers perspective. *Medical Journal of Australia, 2*, 445–447.

Singh, B., & Raphael, B. (1981). Postdisaster morbidity of the bereaved: A possible role for preventive psychiatry? *The Journal of Nervous and Mental Disease, 169*, 203–212.

Solomon, Z., & Benbenishty, R. (1986). The role of proximity, immediacy and expectancy in frontline treatment of combat stress reaction among Israelis in the Lebanon War. *The American Journal of Psychiatry, 143*, 613–617.

Symonds, M. (1980). The 'second injury' to victims. *Evaluation and Change*, Special Issue, 36–38.

Taylor, A.J.W., & Frazer, A.G. (1982). The stress of post-disaster body handling and victim identification work. *Journal of Human Stress, 8*, 4–12.

Terr, L.C. (1991). Childhood traumas: An outline and overview. *American Journal of Psychiatry, 148*, 10–20.

Weisaeth, L. (1989a). The stressors and the post-traumatic stress syndrome after an industrial disaster. Traumatic stress: Empirical studies from Norway. *Acta Psychiatrica Scandinavica Supplementum, 335*, 25–37.

Weisaeth, L. (1989b). Torture of a Norwegian ship's crew. *Acta Psychiatrica Scandinavica Supplementum, 355*, 63–72.

Wilson, J.P. (1980). Conflict, stress and growth: The effects of war on psychosocial development among Vietnam veterans. In C.G. Figley & S. Leventman (Eds.), *Strangers at home: Vietnam veterans since the war* (pp. 123–165). New York: Praeger.

Wilson, J.P. (1989). *Trauma, transformation and healing.* New York: Brunner/Mazel.

Follow-up to Survivors of Large-Scale Road Accidents

CHAPTER TWO

Rod Watts

'I WAS talking to the person next to me (who died), I looked up, and the bus was tipping, then everyone was on top of everyone else.'

'Looking out of the window over the edge, I saw the bus tilt, then heard all these screams, then a terrible crash, and then I blacked out.'

'After the bus left the road I remember sighing, I came to in the bus and noticed dead people around me, one woman was screaming and I noticed there was something through me.'

In the context of this chapter a survivor is defined as someone who escaped death when involved in a fatal accident. This is similar to, but not as broad as, the definition provided by Lifton (1988), 'A survivor is someone who had come into contact with death in some bodily or other psychic fashion and has remained alive.' (p. 18).

Understanding traumatic stress reactions and Posttraumatic Stress Disorder

Before describing the plight of survivors of modern-day large-scale road accidents, looking back in time shows us that, while knowledge about reactions following trauma has increased over the past decade, reports of their occurrence are not new. One of the earliest descriptions was provided by Charles Dickens after he was involved in a railway accident at Staplehurst, Kent, in 1865. Apparently, part of the train was derailed in the accident and the carriage in which Dickens was a passenger became suspended over the ruined parapet of a bridge. Writing of his reactions to a friend, some time later, he stated:

> I am getting right, though still low in pulse and very nervous. Driving in Rochester yesterday I felt more shaken than I have since the accident. I cannot bear railway travelling yet. A perfect conviction, against the senses, that the carriage is down on one side comes upon me with anything like speed, and is inexpressibly distressing. (Trimble, 1981, p. 28)

The set of typical psychological reactions observed following accidents was initially referred to as railway spine, or nervous shock, but from the 1960s began to be classified as accident or traumatic neurosis. This cluster of reactions consisted of anxiety, muscular tension, irritability, reduction in cognitive functioning, repetitive nightmares, withdrawal, and sexual difficulties. It was argued that these reactions were caused by the accident being frightening and potentially life-threatening. In such instances a 'psychic wound' occurred (Modlin, 1967), which is a key factor that differentiates trauma from stress, including cumulative stress. The perception of life threat is the crucial factor. For example, being threatened with a gun, but not necessarily shot, could have sufficient impact to comprise a traumatic event. The responsibility of the death of someone in a fatal accident is another cause of reactions to that of a narrow escape from death (Foeckler, Garrard, Williams, Thomas, & Jones, 1978).

It is also possible for accidents, such as those involving motor vehicles, to cause stress reactions, even when there are only slight injuries or none at all (Goldberg & Gara, 1990; Pilowsky, 1985). These reactions can be severe and persistent because the psychological impact of the experience is too large to assimilate. When this occurs, they become traumatic stress reactions. The ripples caused when a rock is thrown into a pond is an analogy to these reactions, which quite normally cause a disturbance for a period of time. Traumatic stress reactions can be categorised into the following three primary types:

- *Intrusion* consists of distressing recollections of the trauma, or some aspects of it, that occur involuntarily. The recurring sensation of being in the railway carriage was the example provided by Dickens. Symptoms include dreams about the event, nightmares, and flashbacks.
- *Avoidance* or numbing, reflect the need of the survivor not to be so severely distressed. Avoidance includes attempts to avoid thoughts and feelings about the accident or injury, avoiding reminders whenever possible, having diminished interest in significant events, and feeling detached. Returning to the accident site, or where the trauma occurred, can be distressing — as it was for Dickens when contemplating travelling again by train.

- *Persistent symptoms of increased arousal* such as difficulty falling or staying asleep, irritability, outbursts of anger, difficulty in concentrating, and exaggerated startle response.

The increase in understanding of the interplay between the intrusiveness of reminders of the trauma and the need to avoid them was an important component of the establishment of the diagnostic criteria for Posttraumatic Stress Disorder (PTSD) in 1980. This disorder was proposed as the most commonly diagnosed syndrome following trauma (Modlin, 1983), and led to an increase in recognition that the most severe types of trauma, ranging from individual traumas, such as rape or violent death of a family member, to large-scale catastrophes, such as war and natural disasters, commonly caused reactions. These typical reactions remained similar to those previously prescribed as anxiety or traumatic neurosis, but with a clearer differentiation between what was normal and what indicated long-term difficulties (Horowitz, Wilner, Kaltreider, & Alvarez, 1980).

The revised diagnostic criteria for PTSD, in 1987 (American Psychiatric Association, 1987), reflected further changes in the understanding, assessment, and treatment of people affected by trauma. It provided some examples that elucidated what constitutes trauma. These listed examples included serious threat to life; sustaining a severe injury; serious threat to one's children, spouse, or close other; sudden destruction of one's home or community; or witnessing the death of another. The more severe the trauma, the greater the likelihood of consequential reactions, including the development of a psychiatric disorder such as PTSD. As an example, one study of prisoner of war survivors, who would have experienced extreme stress, found high incidence rates of PTSD up to 40 years after their ordeal (Allodi, 1991). The occurrence of PTSD among this victim group was associated with the severity of their experience, such as the proportion of body weight lost and degree of torture they were subjected to.

Traumatic factors in motor vehicle accidents

The initial impact of an accident on each person who survives a multi-fatality on the road is a key factor associated with how they will be affected by it. This was the case among survivors of a coach accident on Mount Tamborine, Queensland, in 1990. Eleven people were killed as the touring coach skidded off the road, rolled down a steep embankment and crashed into a tree.

Part of the initial impact caused by trauma is the suddenness with which it occurs. In the case of the Mount Tamborine coach accident, this is encapsulated by the survivors' first memories quoted at the start of this chapter.

The accident mutilated the bodies of some of the deceased. All the survivors required admission to hospital after the accident. Hence, the trauma associated with surviving such an encounter leaves a disturbing impression on the psyche — what Lifton (1988) describes as a death imprint. This imprint is due to the inability of survivors to accept a large number of people killed in such circumstances, also referred to by Burges Watson (1987) as 'inescapable horror'.

In the context of what constitutes a traumatic event, it is not surprising that the majority of survivors of the Mount Tamborine coach accident remained severely affected in the long term: in addition to the 11 people killed, 38 more were injured. Twenty-nine of the survivors participated in a research project I conducted which examined the prevalence of reactions evident 13 months after the accident, plus the follow-up they received and their assessment of it.

Surviving such an accident necessarily meant a narrow escape from death, as approximately one-quarter of the passengers in the coach died. Survivors were also likely to have witnessed the death of fellow passengers and been exposed to the horror of mutilated bodies. All sustained injuries of sufficient severity to require admission to hospital, and many would have heard the pleas of other people who lay injured around them at the accident site. The majority of the passengers were members of, or associated with, a senior citizens club from Newcastle, New South Wales. Consequently, many had a close friend or family member die in the accident. Witnessing the death of a person, a narrow escape from death, being exposed to the anguish of the injured, sustaining a severe injury, and having a loved one suddenly and unexpectedly die, are all factors cited as examples of trauma. The likelihood of severe traumatic stress reactions would be expected to increase correspondingly to the number of these factors incorporated in the one experience; the magnitude of a trauma is an important determinant in the occurrence of PTSD among survivors. For example, a comparative analysis of PTSD among various survivor groups indicated that the degree of life threat, or loss, were predictors of the occurrence of the disorder (Wilson, Smith, & Johnson, 1985).

Assessment of survivors

Assessments of the survivors of the Mount Tamborine coach accident unequivocally identified them as being a high-risk victim group. Fifty-two per cent of the 29 survivors surveyed had, according to the Impact of Event Scale (IES), severe levels of intrusion or avoidance. The IES (Horowitz, Wilner, & Alvarez, 1979) is a 15-question self-report instrument that assesses the degree of intrusion and avoidance phenomena. The IES is a comparative scale, but some studies have categorised subscale scores into the following: low 0–8, medium 9–19, and severe 20+ (Hytten & Hasle, 1989; Malt, 1988). Furthermore, at the time of assessment, 79 per cent of the survivors were likely to have had a psychiatric disorder, according to their scores on the 12-item General Health Questionnaire (GHQ 12).

The GHQ 12 (Goldberg & Hillier, 1979) is a self-administered screening instrument designed to detect psychiatric disorders, which are indicated by a score of 2 or more.

Also, 31 per cent of survivors assessed, or just less than half of those who had a disorder, were assessed as having PTSD. Assessments of other types of psychiatric morbidity were not completed, but based on several studies following disasters, those who did not have PTSD, but a 'case' score on the GHQ 12, would predominantly have had a depressive or generalised anxiety disorder (Shore, Tatum, & Vollmer, 1986; Smith, North, McCool, & Shea, 1990). Surviving, for this group meant the likelihood of a legacy of psychological difficulties, with the statement 'I'll never be the same again' made by several survivors when describing the consequences of the accident on their lives.

Such a situation of extensive personal consequences is well illustrated by a case study, referred to as 'Mrs A'. Mrs A was 79 at the time of the accident, she regularly attended a social club, and played lawn bowls at least once a week. Due to lacerations on both legs, which required skin grafts, she remained in hospital for 35 days after the accident. When assessed after 13 months, Mrs A had a GHQ 12 score of 9, intrusion subscale score of 27, 23 for avoidance, and was assessed as having PTSD. Her symptoms included intermittent nightmares, which mostly involved images of people from the accident lying on the ground beside the coach; difficulty going to sleep; withdrawal from others; and the development of generalised anxiety. The image of a deceased woman lying at her feet was the most distressing recurring memory.

Mrs A also had difficulty using the local bus services, which had posed no problem before the accident. Whenever the bus travelled fast, or sharply turned a corner, the motion triggered memories of the accident, including feelings of anxiety and flashbacks. This limited ability to use the only available public transport led to social isolation. Although she described her two sons as being extremely helpful, Mrs A reported being unable to talk to them about the accident. Whenever she tried they became upset, which added to her distress. She also recounted that during her five weeks in hospital she rarely sought opportunities to discuss her reactions with hospital staff, in spite of believing they were willing to listen.

The extent of the plight of these survivors is exemplified by comparing the prevalence of reactions among them with other population groups. Firstly, the incidence of disorder was approximately four times that found in Australian general population studies (Henderson, Byrne, & Duncan-Jones, 1981). Secondly, at similar measurement periods, the prevalence of likely disorder was twice that of the victims of some other Australian events, such as the Queen Street shootings (Creamer, Burgess, Buckingham, & Pattison, 1989) or the Ash Wednesday bushfires (Clayer, Bookless-Pratz, & McFarlane, 1985). They were also far in excess of the estimated 30–40 per cent generally found among victims of disasters (Raphael, 1986).

Finally, they were significantly more affected than both the ambulance officers or State Emergency Service personnel involved in the response even though rescue workers who become involved in large-scale incidents, or disasters, can be affected, at least in the short-term (Dunning & Silva, 1980; Hytten & Hasle, 1989; Raphael, Singh, Bradbury, & Lambert, 1983–84). In fact, some claim that until this last decade, rescuers have been the 'hidden victims' of such events (Hodgkinson & Stewart, 1991; Kliman, 1976). Studies have also been able to document a small, but nonetheless important, percentage of personnel who remain severely affected for some time (Green, Grace, & Gleser, 1985; McFarlane, 1986). The significant differences in the prevalence of reactions between survivors and rescue workers involved in the Mount Tamborine coach accident do not deny that such events affect emergency workers, but do clearly identify those who narrowly escape death as being particularly vulnerable.

Factors associated with ordeals

Examining the factors associated with the bus crash survivors' ordeal leads to the realisation that severe and persistent reactions following such large-scale road accidents are normal. This could well apply to other multi-fatality accidents. For the survivors, seeing the deaths and/or bodies of fellow passengers was the most common cause of severe distress both at the time of the crash and for months afterwards. Not enough research has been done to show if the survivor of a single-fatality accident, particularly when a loved on is killed, is equally at risk. Mrs A's recurring nightmare of a dead woman lying at her feet is an example of the distressing and disturbing impact witnessing death can have. The exposure to death, the witnessing of fellow passengers dying and, in particular, the mutilation that occurred in the Mount Tamborine accident had a large psychological impact on survivors.

The impact of traumatic loss cannot be underestimated, nor can a quick recovery be expected. Sudden and unexpected death has a long-lasting affect on the bereaved (Lundin, 1984; Parkes & Weiss, 1983; Sanders, 1988). One study of sets of parents (Shanfield & Swain, 1984) of adult children who were killed in a motor vehicle accident found widespread psychological reactions persisted, particularly depression, after two years. Another study (Lehman & Wortman, 1987) found persistent and severe psychological reactions common among the bereaved relatives following motor vehicle accidents.We can expect that the bereaved of people killed in large-scale accidents would be more affected than those following single fatalities due to the intensification of the features of sudden and violent death (Hodgkinson & Stewart, 1991).

Certainly, bereavement was a salient factor in the traumatic experience that affected the survivors of the Mount Tamborine coach accident. Forty-one per cent of those surveyed had a close friend or family member killed in the accident. The following case outlines the added impact when a traumatic exposure to death is also associated with traumatic loss. 'Mrs B' remembered little of the accident and, after 13 months, reported that the death of her three close friends in the accident caused her by far the greatest amount of distress. For months after the accident she was distressed by the preoccupying thought that she had survived and they had not. This 'survivor's guilt' is not uncommon (Raphael, 1986). When the accident occurred, one of Mrs B's friends was sitting next to her in the coach, the two other close friends were in adjacent seats. She had an undeniably narrow escape from death.

When assessed, Mrs B had a GHQ 12 score of 5, intrusion levels of 14, avoidance levels of 24, and she had PTSD. During the year after the accident, there were often nights that she was unable to sleep, and for the first few months she remained mostly indoors. She reported having continual lapses in concentration and memory throughout that year; persistent ringing in her head, which at times caused her to feel nauseous; plus difficulty realising her friends had died. Because she was repeatedly being woken by fits of screaming, or by strong urges to shout, Mrs B was referred to a psychiatrist, whom she described as very helpful, Although still severely affected by the accident, particularly by the grief of having three of her close friends die, Mrs B was, after 13 months, beginning to believe that she would most likely recover sufficiently to regain something of a normal life. It is my experience that rarely, if ever, is life post-trauma the same as it was before the event occurred. Recovery can mean the regaining of control over reactions, or reactions not being as predominant when they occur, rather than not having them at all.

The occurrence of other severely distressing events in the lives of survivors is also an important factor to consider when examining the impact of trauma. The persistence of distress they cause is the key factor, not necessarily the length of time that has elapsed since they occurred. Of the survivors surveyed following the Mount Tamborine coach accident, 52 per cent reported having had at least one other severely distressing event in their lives at some time prior to the accident. These events predominantly involved the death of a family member, with some occurring during the year before the accident: for one survivor it was the death of a brother; for another it was the death of her husband after a protracted illness. Most of the distressing events occurred a number of years before the coach accident. Importantly, seven, or 47 per cent, of those who had experienced a previous traumatic event, reported being distressed by it during the year after the coach accident. This subgroup of seven had significantly higher levels of psychiatric disorder, intrusion, and avoidance than the other survivors.

The distress associated with other traumatic events was thus identified as a compounding factor to recovery for survivors. An example of this was 'Mrs C', aged 76, single with a sister and two brothers. During the year prior to the coach accident, her two brothers had died. In the coach accident she sustained five fractured ribs, facial bruising, and a bruised lung. She remembered little of what had occurred, and was distressed in the long-term by memories of seeing the deceased among the debris of the coach. Apparently, some time after the accident she awoke to find herself in an intensive care ward where she felt totally alone, and the memory of this caused her the most distress initially. She described thinking often of her brothers during the year following the coach accident. These thoughts always led to her becoming very upset. After 13 months, Mrs C's symptoms of distress included an inability to sleep, constant tiredness, restlessness, inability to relax, and a propensity to believe the accident had not taken place. These symptoms were reflected in a GHQ score of 10, intrusion levels of 19, and avoidance levels of 20, but she did not have PTSD.

Soon after being discharged from hospital, Mrs C had three counselling sessions, which she reported as being somewhat helpful. She rejected further assistance, however, because she no longer wanted to talk about what had happened, as doing so always made her upset. Becoming upset was something she was attempting to avoid at that time. Her situation was also an example of the interplay between reactions to traumatic loss and reactions associated with a traumatic encounter with death. In my experience, the horror of the imprint caused by the traumatic encounter with death, such as witnessing the death of a loved one, or seeing bodies lying on the ground, becomes a barrier to the grieving that is necessary if recovery is to be achieved following loss. The barrier occurs because the psychological disturbance associated with the imprint is avoided if possible. When this occurs the chance of poor recovery increases, as does the need for professional help.

Factors such as scope of impact, speed of onset, degree of life threat to individuals, degree of bereavement, prolongation of suffering, proportion of community affected (e.g., central or peripheral), and the cause of the disaster (natural or man-made) have been listed as key components that determine reactions caused by large-scale incidents and disasters (Gleser, Green, & Winget, 1981). Traumatic encounter with death and traumatic loss can both be components of the experience of surviving a large-scale road accident. The magnitude of psychological impact of being involved in such an accident (for further information on two other coach accidents, see Griffiths & Watts, 1992) means long-term reactions are common.

This is my central point. People who are directly involved in large-scale road accidents are highly vulnerable to having severe long-term reactions. Their well-being should be regarded as a priority by organisations with a responsibility to provide assistance, such as government health departments. Psychologically, the aim of this assistance would be to mitigate initial distress and facilitate recovery.

Psychological follow-up to survivors

Providing psychological follow-up to people affected by traumatic accidents is complex and difficult. An experienced mental health professional is needed to at least coordinate the response, as was the case after the Granville rail crash (Raphael, 1979). (For further details see chapter 1)

Using a framework which systematically organises those affected into identifiable groups is advisable. A useful model to do this was developed by Taylor and Frazer (1982) after their study of rescue workers involved in body retrieval and identification after the Mount Erebus DC10 plane crash in Antarctica. This accident, in 1979, killed all 257 passengers and crew on board (for further details, see Chapter four). The model, which seems to be the most frequently used (Raphael, 1986), consists of six hierarchical levels of victims based upon level of exposure as follows:

- Primary: People directly involved in the incident
- Secondary: Grieving relatives and friends of the primary victims
- Tertiary: Personnel involved in the response to help
- Fourth-level: The community involved in the incident, including those who converge on the scene
- Fifth-level: People with a degree of emotional fragility who become disturbed although not directly associated with what occurred
- Sixth-level: Others indirectly involved, such as those who could well have been primary victims but for a change of circumstance

How this differentiation of affected groups translates into the provision of psychologically oriented services following large-scale incidents or disasters is comprehensively discussed by Raphael (1986). I argue here that the primary victims are far more affected than the tertiary group and so must have at least equal access to assistance.

Evidence suggests that, like people injured in motor vehicle accidents, the high-risk victims of large-scale road accidents do not receive the follow-up they are likely to need. The lack of detection and treatment of people injured in road accidents was identified as a problem as early as the 1960s (Mann & Gold, 1966) and several authors claim this service gap still exists (Burnstein, 1989; Hodgkinson & Stewart, 1991; Horne, 1993). Limited information from the survivors of two other large-scale coach accidents at Grafton and Kempsey[1] indicated that the follow-up they received was disjointed and at times ineffectual (Griffiths & Watts, 1992).

The lack of adequate follow-up after these coach accidents, particularly the Grafton one, was anticipated by a consultant engaged by the New South Wales Roads and Traffic Authority following the Grafton coach accident

---

[1] The first accident occurred in October, 1989, just north of Grafton, NSW. A semitrailer crossed into the path of an interstate coach carrying 43 passengers. Twenty-one people were killed and 23 injured. The second accident occurred just two months later near Kempsey, NSW, when two interstate passenger coaches collided head-on. This disaster claimed the lives of 35 people, injured a further 39, and remains the worst road accident in the history of Australia.

(Humphries, 1989). Follow-up to the survivors was organised by the State Health Department, primarily personnel working in community health centres located closest to each of the accident sites. One major difficulty was that all of the survivors lived outside the community serviced by these centres. This meant that when the survivors were transferred to acute metropolitan hospitals or to hospitals closer to their homes, or discharged, the follow-up relied on referral. The referral process adopted consisted of writing letters to survivors that informed them of who to contact, if they so wished, to receive assistance. This reliance on letters to the survivors did not result in them receiving help.

PRO-ACTIVE FOLLOW-UP

Relying on survivors to initiate contact will not, normally, lead to many accessing available assistance. This general unwillingness to seek assistance is a key reason why the detection and treatment of people psychologically affected by accidents has remained a problem since the 1960s (Burnstein, 1989; Foeckler et al., 1978). Only a small proportion of people directly involved in a disaster will take advantage of psychological follow-up services, even when they are specifically established for them. This was the case in the USA following the Beverly Hills Supper Club fire in 1977, for example, where the building burnt to the ground killing 165 people (Lindy, Green, Grace, & Titchener, 1983). Two of the exits became blocked by some of the estimated 2,500 people inside the club at the time, as they tried to escape the fire. Few survivors contacted the Fire Aftermath Centre established following this tragedy (Lindy, Grace, & Green, 1981). How to provide psychological follow-up to survivors of large-scale road accidents, or following other disasters, remains an issue.

One method is by pro-actively providing the assistance on an individual basis. This was the method used by the Newcastle Community Counselling Service following the Mount Tamborine coach accident. This mental health service was established the year before the coach accident, as part of the follow-up to the Newcastle earthquake in New South Wales at the end of 1989 which killed 11 people. Counsellors from the service initiated contact with most of the 19 survivors who lived in the Newcastle area, as they were discharged from their respective hospitals in Queensland, or when transferred to the John Hunter Hospital in Newcastle. This approach is unlikely to make survivors, or victims in general, feel intruded upon if it is conducted in a professional manner, with sensitivity. Those affected (victims) must be encouraged to take charge of the situation, or at least to exercise their right to accept or reject the assistance offered. This was the case for the survivors following the Mount Tamborine coach accident, as none of those surveyed reported feeling intruded upon by the counselling staff of the Community Counselling Service. Conversely, they expressed an appreciation of the service's efforts and were supported by the care they felt the approach expressed to them as members of the community.

The pro-active approach by the counselling service led to 68 per cent of the 19 survivors who lived in the Newcastle area receiving counselling. This compares to 20 per cent of the remaining survivors, who mostly lived in Sydney, receiving counselling. Clearly, receiving psychological follow-up was greatly determined by geography, rather than a reflection of need. This finding shows that survivors of road accidents, even large-scale ones that attract widespread media publicity, are unlikely to gain psychological follow-up by traditional services. Without the pre-existing Community Counselling Service, and its outreach approach, a much lower percentage of survivors from Newcastle would have received psychological follow-up.

TIMING OF FOLLOW-UP

Another crucial factor that influences the use of psychological follow-up by survivors is when it is provided. Early detection of psychological reactions and subsequent treatment has been identified as the most effective strategy to assist victims of trauma (Burges Watson, 1987; Horowitz et al., 1980; Kuch, Swinson, & Kirby, 1985). Also, psychological aid is more readily accepted when provided alongside practical help following disasters (Raphael, 1986). The difficulty with expecting victims to engage in counselling in the acute phase is that they may not perceive the need for it, or feel too out of control to be confident that the personal risks associated with disclosure are warranted. Reluctance to disclose, or indicate the existence of difficulties, is common following trauma generally; victims feel a need to protect themselves against their own feelings of vulnerability and helplessness, as well as fearing further victimisation by well-meaning but unskilled and inexperienced professionals (Wilson, 1989).

Certainly this applied to the survivors of the Mount Tamborine coach accident. At 13 months post-accident, only one reported feeling the need for counselling during the first two weeks. In contrast, 17, or 59 per cent, felt the need for counselling at some point during the subsequent 12 months. Furthermore, 66 per cent of the survivors stated they did not, or rarely wanted, during this first two-week period, to talk to hospital personnel about their experience. The following comments document their general unwillingness to disclose the enormity of their distress to hospital personnel at this acute phase:

'I didn't talk to them often because I was in a lot of pain and couldn't hear, I just got through those days.'

'I even went a week before asking about two friends. I thought they had died because no-one mentioned them, I avoided talking about it.'

'I didn't talk to staff unless they asked, I talked to those in the accident, mostly to find out how the others were going.'

'I felt I just wanted to have a good cry, I thought once I get to my sister's I could let go and have a cry, but not before.'

This general unwillingness to discuss their distress was also evident in the case study of Mrs A previously described. Following such a large psychological impact, the victims were too vulnerable to be able to re-enter the experience, which is part of the counselling process. Significantly, several reported they were helped by talking to fellow survivors during this time.

The reported reactions over time by survivors of the Mount Tamborine coach accident were as would be expected following such a trauma. Generally, reactions were the most intense during the first three to four months, some felt there was no change throughout the first year, with a small number encountering delayed reactions. More specifically, when asked which had been the most distressing months, 34 per cent reported there had been no change, of which 60 per cent had PTSD at the time of interview. A small number of survivors, who perceived no fluctuations of distress over time, were relatively unaffected by the accident in the long term, but the majority of this 34 per cent experienced persistent and constant severe distress throughout the entire 13 months. In contrast, the remaining 66 per cent of those assessed encountered severe distress for the first three to four months, with a relatively rapid decline between four and six months. The first anniversary was associated with a resurgence of distress among approximately half of the survivors.

FLUCTUATIONS OF REACTIONS AND NEEDS

These patterns of reactions identify another issue in the provision of psychological follow-up after large-scale road accidents. Reactions can fluctuate over time, as can their cause, as can the perceived need for, and ability to engage in, follow-up such as counselling/treatment. The case of Mrs C illustrates this last point. She discontinued counselling after three sessions because each one caused her to become upset, which at the time she was endeavouring to avoid. Victims discontinuing treatment, prior to completing the recommended number of sessions, has been found to be the case after other disasters (Lindy et al., 1981). Delayed reaction is one factor influencing the fluctuation in reactions over time. This occurred for two survivors of the Mount Tamborine accident. They reported not being distressed at the time of the accident, but became so in the short to long term. One lost their partner in the accident, the other a close friend.

As the reactions to trauma and the factors that cause these reactions vary in influence, so must the focus of the follow-up change over time. For example, among the survivors surveyed after the Mount Tamborine accident, being trapped and the condition of other passengers lost impact over time. Conversely, the memories of the accident and those associated with the period of time in hospital became more predominant causes of distress in the short to long term. The counselling process needs to incorporate this change in reactions; the fluctuations in need for, and avoidance of, assistance; plus the variation in influence of factors associated with the experience. These are some of the reasons why psychological follow-up after disasters is complex and requires experienced and suitably trained clinicians.

In conclusion, and as a cautionary note, psychological follow-up (counselling/treatment) should not be presented as a guarantee for recovery. In some situations, nothing can possibly lessen the intensity of distress. One survivor of the Grafton accident, whose son, daughter, son-in-law, nephew, and son's fiancee were killed in the tragedy, asked this question: how could anyone possibly help?

Large-scale road accidents are similar to other major transport accidents in that they are man-made as opposed to natural (Hodgkinson & Stewart, 1991; Raphael, 1986): they also occur without warning; cause multiple deaths, including mutilation of bodies; and expose survivors to the sight of the dead while they lie trapped and await rescue. The survivors are likely to sustain injuries and possibly incur permanent disabilities. As a group they are highly at risk for severe and long-lasting traumatic stress reactions, including psychiatric morbidity, such as PTSD, and therefore need an effective and comprehensive safety net of psychological follow-up.

Many survivors of the Mount Tamborine accident reported that the counselling they received was helpful, but not all of them did. The psychological follow-up after major road trauma, as is the case for trauma generally, is most effectively implemented on a pro-active basis which uses a framework identifying those most in need. Such services must also be conducted by suitably trained and experienced professionals. Support from family and friends may not be sufficient to mitigate distress, or prevent long-term psychological difficulties. The 'inescapable horror' that survivors are exposed to in major road trauma becomes a component of the phenomena that are continually re-experienced, at least in the short term, in an involuntary and intrusive way. As it was for Mrs A, at times family can themselves be distressed by being indirect victims and therefore are unable to sensitively encourage their injured loved one to repeatedly describe the accident. This re-telling is necessary to facilitate integration of what occurred. Ventilation of reactions is also necessary. For families, this too can be quite distressing. Being able to hear the victim's story is an important function of the professional.

The development within Australia, particularly over the past five years, of services to help rescue workers recover from the effects of traumatic incidents, including disasters, is to be commended. Unfortunately, however, there is little, if any, evidence of a comparable development of similar services to these victims who are directly involved. This inequity needs to be addressed.

References

Allodi, F.A. (1991). Assessment and treatment of torture victims. *The Journal of Nervous and Mental Disease, 179*, 4–12.

American Psychiatric Association. (1987). *Diagnostic and statistical manual of mental disorders* (3rd. ed. rev.). Washington, DC: Author.

Burges Watson, P. (1987). Post-traumatic stress disorder in Australia and New Zealand: A clinical review of the consequences of inescapable horror. *The Medical Journal of Australia, 147*, 443–447.

Burnstein, A. (1989). Posttraumatic stress disorder in victims of motor vehicle accidents. *Hospital and Community Psychiatry, 40,* 295–297.

Clayer, J., Bookless-Pratz, C., & McFarlane, A.C. (1985). *The health and social impact of the Ash Wednesday bushfires.* Adelaide: Mental Health Research and Evaluation Centre, South Australian Health Commission.

Creamer, M., Burgess, P., Buckingham, W., & Pattison, P. (1989). *The psychological aftermath of the Queen Street shootings.* Unpublished manuscript, University of Melbourne, Department of Psychology, Melbourne.

Dunning, C., & Silva, M. (1980). Disaster-induced trauma in rescue workers. *Victimology: An International Journal, 5,* 287–297.

Foeckler, M., Garrard, F., Williams, C., Thomas, A., & Jones, T. (1978). Vehicle drivers and fatal accidents. *Suicide and Life Threatening Behavior, 8,* 174–182.

Gleser, G.C., Green, B., & Winget, C. (1981). *Prolonged psychosocial effects of disaster. A study of Buffalo Creek.* New York: Academic Press.

Goldberg, L., & Gara, M. (1990). A typology of psychiatric reactions to motor vehicle accidents. *Psychopathology, 23,* 15–20.

Goldberg, D.P., & Hillier, V.F. (1979). A scale version of the General Health Questionnaire. *Psychological Medicine, 9,* 21–29.

Green, B.L., Grace, M.C., & Gleser, G.C. (1985). Identifying survivors at risk: Long-term impairment following the Beverley Hills Supper Club fire. *Journal of Consulting and Clinical Psychology, 53,* 672–678.

Griffiths, J.A., & Watts, R. (1992). *The Kempsey and Grafton bus crashes: The aftermath.* Lismore, NSW: Instructional Design Solutions, University of New England.

Henderson, S., Byrne, D., & Duncan-Jones, P. (1981). *Neurosis and the social environment.* Sydney: Academic Press.

Hodgkinson, P., & Stewart, M. (1991). *Coping with catastrophe: A handbook of disaster management.* London: Routledge.

Horne, D. (1993), Traumatic stress reactions to motor vehicle accidents. In J.P. Wilson & B. Raphael (Eds.), *The international handbook of traumatic stress syndromes* (pp. 499–506). New York: Pitman.

Horowitz, M., Wilner, N., & Alvarez, W. (1979). Impact of event scale: A measure of subjective stress. *Psychosomatic Medicine, 41,* 209–18.

Horowitz, M., Wilner, N., Kaltreider, N., & Alvarez, W. (1980). Signs and symptoms of posttraumatic stress disorder. *Archives of General Psychiatry, 37,* 85–92.

Humphries, M. (1989). *Report of behavioural data, semi/bus crash, Cowper.* Sydney: Roads and Traffic Authority.

Hytten, K., & Hasle, A. (1989). Fire fighters: A study of stress and coping. *Acta Psychiatrica Scandinavica 80*(Suppl. 355), 50–55.

Kliman, A.S. (1976). The Corning flood project: Psychological first aid following a natural disaster. In H. Parad, H. Resnick & L. Bowie (Eds.), *Emergency and disaster management: A mental health sourcebook* (pp. 16–25). Baltimore, MD: Charles Press.

Kuch, K., Swinson, R.P., & Kirby, M. (1985). Post-traumatic stress disorder after car accidents. *Canadian Journal Psychiatry, 30,* 426–427.

Lehman, D.R., & Wortman, C.B. (1987). Long-term effects of losing a spouse or child in a motor vehicle crash. *Journal of Personality and Social Psychology, 52,* 218–231.

Lifton, R.L. (1988). Understanding the traumatized self: Imagery, symbolism and transformation. In J. Wilson, Z. Harel & B. Kahana (Eds.), *Human adapation to extreme stress* (pp. 7–31). New York: Plenum Press.

Lindy, J.D., Grace, M., & Green, B.L. (1981). Survivors: Outreach to a reluctant population. *American Journal Orthopsychiatry 51,* 468–478.

Lindy, J.D, Green, B., Grace. M., & Titchener, J. (1983). Psychotherapy with survivors of the Beverly Hills Supper Club fire. *American Journal of Psychotherapy, 37,* 593–609.

Lundin, T. (1984). Morbidity following sudden and unexpected bereavement. *British Journal of Psychiatry, 144,* 84–88.

Malt, U.F. (1988). The long-term psychiatric consequences of accidental injury — A longitudinal study of 107 adults. *British Journal of Psychiatry, 153,* 810–88.

Mann, A., & Gold, E. (1966). Psychological sequelae of accidental injury. *Canadian Medical Association Journal, 95,* 1359–1363.

McFarlane, A.C. (1986). Long-term psychiatric morbidity after a natural disaster. *The Medical Journal of Australia, 145,* 561–563.

Modlin, H.C. (1967). The postaccident anxiety syndrome: Psychosocial aspects. *American Journal of Psychiatry, 123,* 1008–1012.

Modlin, H.C. (1983). Traumatic neurosis and other injuries. *Psychiatric Clinics of North America, 5,* 661–669.

Parkes, C.M., & Weiss, R.S. (1983). *Recovery from bereavement.* New York: Basic Books.

Pilowsky, I. (1985). Cry to trauma and 'accident neurosis'. *British Journal of Psychiatry, 146,* 310–311.

Raphael, B. (1979). A primary prevention action programme: Psychiatric involvement following a major rail disaster. *Omega, 10,* 211–226.

Raphael, B. (1986). *When disaster strikes.* New York: Basic Books.

Raphael, B., Singh, B., Bradbury, L., & Lambert, F. (1983–84). Who helps the helpers? The effects of a disaster on the rescue workers. *Omega, 14,* 9–20.

Sanders, C.M. (1988). Risk factors in bereavement outcome. *Journal of Social Issues, 44*(3), 97–111.

Shanfield, S.B., & Swain, B. (1984). Death of adult children in traffic accidents. *The Journal of Nervous and Mental Disease, 172,* 533–538.

Shore, J.H., Tatum, L.E., & Vollmer, W.M. (1986). Psychiatric reactions to disaster: The Mount St. Helens experience. *American Journal of Psychiatry, 143,* 590–595.

Smith, E.M., North, C.S., McCool, R.E., & Shea, J.M. (1990). Acute postdisaster psychiatric disorders: Identification of persons at risk. *American Journal of Psychiatry, 147,* 202–206.

Taylor, A.J., & Frazer, A.G. (1982). The stress of post-disaster body handling and victim identification work. *Journal of Human Stress, 8,* 4–12.

Trimble, M. (1981). *Post-traumatic neurosis.* New York: John Wiley & Sons.

Wilson, J.P. (1989). *Trauma, transformation and healing*. New York: Brunner/Mazel.

Wilson, J.P., Smith, W.K., & Johnson, S.K. (1985). A comparative analysis of PTSD among various survivor groups. In C. Figley (Ed.), *Trauma and its wake* (pp. 142–172). New York: Brunner/Mazel.

Community Recovery From Trauma

CHAPTER THREE

Mark Creamer

I T has become common practice, both in Australia and overseas, to use community-based interventions following disasters of both human and natural origin (Lystad, 1988; Raphael, 1986). The purpose of this chapter is to discuss the fundamental issues to be considered in the implementation of a community-based mental health recovery program following disaster. These general principles apply not only to geographically defined neighbourhoods (villages, towns, and cities), but also to smaller units of the population such as workplaces. The major points of this chapter are illustrated by reference to a recovery program implemented following a multiple shooting in a city office block.

The unique nature of disasters demands that interventions are tailored to the specific needs of the affected community. While there are, of course, guiding principles, the challenge is frequently one of adapting interventions to the unique characteristics of the particular disaster. A central theme, however, is that recovery from trauma is an active process; mental health recovery programs should aim to involve people from all levels of the community.

Case example: The Queen Street shootings

The Queen Street shootings of 8 December 1987 occurred in the Australia Post building, an 18-storey office block located in the centre of Melbourne, Victoria. A gunman entered the building late on a Tuesday afternoon and proceeded to the fifth floor where he asked to see a particular staff member.

(It emerged during the coronial inquest that the gunman had known this person at school and had developed an intense and irrational hatred of him in the intervening years). When the staff member appeared, the gunman produced a sawn-off, semi-automatic rifle. As people ran for cover, he pursued them, firing a number of shots and killing a 19-year-old female staff member.

Unable to catch his intended victim, he proceeded to the 12th floor. He entered the work area and fired repeatedly at people hiding under desks and behind partitions. He killed three people on this floor and severely injured one other. He then left this work area and proceeded down the stairs to the 11th floor. In a similar fashion, he paced up and down between the desks, firing frequently at individuals where they were hiding. He killed four people on this floor and injured four others. He reportedly spoke often throughout the incident, saying such things as, 'You're all scum. Well, who's laughing now? I'm going to take you all with me'. Individual killings were prolonged and sadistic in nature, with the gunman tormenting and mocking his victims. Eventually he was tackled from behind and a brief struggle ensued, during which the gun was taken from him. He managed to break free and clambered through a broken window. Despite attempts by staff to hold on to him, he finally kicked loose and fell to his death on the pavement below.

It should be noted that the gun was not functioning properly throughout the incident. So although a total of 41 shots was fired, a further 184 unspent cartridges were ejected from the rifle during the incident as the gunman repeatedly tried to make it operate. Thus, a number of people had the gun pointed at them and the trigger pulled but the weapon failed to discharge. Clearly, this was an extremely traumatic experience for them despite the fact that they received no physical injuries.

At the time of the shootings, approximately 850 people were employed in the building, although many had left to go home by the time the incident occurred. Those still in the building experienced a range of exposure to trauma, with many fearing for their lives. Even those on the floors not directly affected knew that a shooting was taking place and barricaded themselves in their work areas; they did not know they were safe until the police came through the building some time later.

The shootings constituted a severe trauma for those involved. The incident was characterised by a number of features normally associated with severe post-trauma reactions, such as sudden onset, significant threat to life, bereavement, unpredictability, and exposure to grotesque sights. Details of the psychological reactions of those involved are provided elsewhere (Creamer, Burgess, Buckingham, & Pattison, 1989), but it was clear that many people were troubled by a range of symptoms typical of a post-trauma reaction. These included intrusive thoughts and dreams of the incident, tendencies to avoid reminders, and generalised symptoms of anxiety and depression.

Rationale for a recovery program

In broad terms, mental health programs should try to help communities and individuals recover from disaster. While it is not the purpose of this chapter to discuss the community effects of disaster in detail, a few points are worth noting. Experience suggests that disasters severely disrupt community functioning. The hierarchies, structures, rules and conventions within which the community operated before the disaster no longer apply in the aftermath of devastation. Although the community may unite strongly immediately after an impact, this phase is usually short-lived and the community quickly starts to rebond. The networks formed at this stage, however, rarely resemble those stable groupings that existed prior to impact; rather, the community re-forms according to disaster experience. Following a natural disaster, for example, individuals or groups who previously had little or nothing in common might unite because of their shared experience of material loss; feelings of resentment and anger may develop towards friends and neighbours who appeared to escape major material damage. Location may form another basis for bonding, with individuals in one part of the community or building becoming close and excluding people from other areas. Other splits may occur over issues such as bereavement, compensation, shared experiences during the disaster, and so on. These divisions may result in considerable anger being expressed towards others within the community, with major rifts occurring and relationships between friends, relatives and colleagues being irrevocably damaged. The long-term effect may be a shattered and destroyed community. The primary task of a mental health team following disaster is to prevent these potential splits from permanently dividing and fracturing the community.

The second goal of a community recovery program following disaster is to help individuals recover from trauma. Previous research (Foy, Resnick, Sipprelle, & Carroll, 1987; Green, Wilson, & Lindy, 1985) has suggested that the severity of post-trauma reactions depends upon potential etiological factors in three domains:

1. Pre-trauma variables (such as socio-demographic factors, personality characteristics, and exposure to previous traumas)
2. Experience of the traumatic event (such as degree of bereavement, life threat, and rate of onset)
3. Recovery environment (such as social support, additional stressors, and community attitudes)

The pre-trauma and trauma variables (1 and 2 above) clearly cannot be changed after the disaster, although they may provide information about individuals at high risk. The aim of a community-based program, however, is to address point 3 by maximising the recovery potential of the post-trauma environment. Such interventions should be preventive, designed to reduce the occurrence of severe reactions such as Posttraumatic Stress Disorder (PTSD; American Psychiatric Association, 1987). Naturally, what constitutes an effective recovery environment will vary and a number of factors need to be considered: the nature of the threat; the location of survivors; the extent of material damage; and the psychological needs of the affected communities, are some of these factors. In addition, the needs of the community will vary over time. What is appropriate immediately after the trauma may be seen as quite intrusive and inappropriate some months later. Finally, although the intervention may be community based, remember that it involves individuals. What is helpful for one person may be counter-therapeutic for another.

A recovery program should be flexible and reactive, constantly adapting to the changing needs of the affected community. However, within that flexibility, a number of specific elements are important in any recovery plan.

INFORMATION

The need for survivors to receive information about the incident and related issues has been highlighted by a number of authors (e.g. Maguire, 1985). Unless survivors know the facts about the trauma incident, extensive rumours and misunderstandings develop. These misconceptions fuel the splits within the community referred to above, and, on an individual level, are likely to increase feelings of vulnerability and distress. Accurate information helps people process the event, assisting survivors in answering the key questions of 'What happened?' and 'Why it happened?' (Figley, 1985). Thus, any forum that promotes the dissemination of accurate information should be encouraged. Public meetings (with appropriate 'experts' in attendance), newsletters, and effective use of the media are good ways of spreading information. Two-way communication should also be promoted, with survivors encouraged to ask for the information they require.

EDUCATION

The sudden onset of symptoms and intense emotional reactions in an individual with no previous psychological problems can itself be extremely distressing. A person's lack of understanding of their own reactions can significantly impede their recovery. Victims need to be educated about common responses to trauma, and to be reassured that these are normal responses to an abnormal situation.

EXPOSURE TO THE TRAUMATIC MEMORIES

A recent review by Fairbank and Nicholson (1987) concluded that all successful treatments of PTSD involved some element of controlled exposure to trauma-related stimuli. Thus, a recovery environment that facilitates and encourages exposure on cognitive, behavioural and affective levels is likely to be therapeutic. A general philosophy, or ethos, needs to be developed within the community that encourages open discussion of topics such as what happened, why it happened, how people reacted, and so on. This approach is in contrast to the commonly held belief that the way to recover is simply to 'forget about it and put it behind us'; such beliefs need to be openly acknowledged, but gently disputed.

SOCIAL SUPPORT

A common research finding in the area of recovery from trauma is the importance of social support networks (Soloman, 1986). The potential role that social support may play in attenuating or serving as a buffer against acute or chronic stress reactions is now widely accepted (Cohen & Willis, 1985). An effective recovery environment therefore needs to promote the development and use of social support networks by survivors. Wherever possible, such support needs to be generated through existing community structures such as neighbourhood houses, sports clubs, church groups, and workplaces.

REGAINING CONTROL

A central feature of post-trauma reactions is a feeling of loss of control (Janoff-Bulman, 1985; Taylor, 1983). This is often exacerbated by well-meaning helpers who attempt to take the difficult decisions out of the hands of those directly affected. A recovery environment that assists individuals to re-establish control by taking an active part in making decisions about their environment and their recovery from the trauma is probably beneficial.

AVAILABILITY OF PROFESSIONAL ASSISTANCE

A number of authors (Hodgkinson & Stewart, 1991; McFarlane, 1984) have emphasised the importance of having appropriately trained professionals available to work with any welfare service providing disaster relief. Formal treatment is then readily accessible when required. When appropriate (such as in the period immediately post-trauma and during subsequent inquiries), an assertive outreach approach may be adopted, in which those individuals and groups known to be severely affected can be actively sought out. At other times, of course, such assertive outreach may be seen as intrusive and inappropriate. How assertively such services should be delivered is always a difficult clinical decision. Nevertheless, it is probably true to say that, following a disaster, many people will be reluctant to ask for psychological assistance and may not even be aware that such assistance could help them.

It must again be emphasised that although recovery programs should be based on the above principles, they are likely to constantly evolve over the period following the disaster, adapting to the changing needs of the community.

Initial considerations

Implementing a community-based recovery program following trauma requires careful consideration of a number of issues. A disaster-affected community may resent services being imposed that imply it has widespread psychological problems. Many of those in need may be reluctant to make contact with the helping professions or may not perceive their needs as being related to mental health services (Raphael, 1984). Individuals with no history of psychological problems are unlikely to use assistance that is identified solely in terms of mental health (McFarlane, 1984). While this may be due, in part, to the avoidance and denial that is commonly associated with psychological response to trauma, it is probably as much a function of more widespread community attitudes towards mental health issues. This stigma of psychological problems may be intensified when a visible and foreign mental health service is set up independent of mainstream community life. In addition, a high-profile mental health presence may be perceived as exacerbating distress and impeding recovery by reminding the community of the trauma, or as invading what little privacy remains in the lives of those most severely affected. Mental health teams must be sensitive to these issues in a disaster-affected community. Wherever possible, mental health services need to be presented in a non-threatening manner by working through existing community structures and agencies.

An important feature of the Queen Street shootings recovery program was the way in which it was integrated into the organisational structure of the affected community. Since the operation was based in the workplace, the recovery strategies required endorsement from the 'owners' of the recovery environment (i.e., staff and management within the building). It was considered important that the program was not seen as imposed from outside (by health professionals) or from above (by management), but rather that it was owned and developed by the community, with the benefit of expert advice. To achieve this goal, there were constant negotiations with both staff and management as new issues arose and as the recovery program evolved over the first 12 months post-trauma.

To help integrate the recovery program into the affected community, a consultative group can be set up, comprising a range of volunteer representatives from all sections of the community. At Queen Street, a task group was established comprising myself, senior management, and staff representatives. This forum allowed change to occur rapidly, with appropriate consultation and with the minimum of bureaucratic delay. A staff consultative group was also formed, including representatives from each floor of the building. This group was responsible for canvassing staff views on a range of issues, identifying areas of need, and disseminating information.

This on-going dialogue with staff and management also helped to clarify and continually reassess the boundaries of the recovery team's responsibilities. Although advice was appropriately sought on a range of issues, occasional conflicts of interest were apparent and there was a danger of the recovery team being inappropriately used as an intermediary or arbitrator between staff and management. The continued involvement of the community in the evolution of recovery strategies also provided an opportunity to respond to fears that the program may be impeding recovery by providing frequent reminders of the trauma.

A key issue to be addressed in the early period post-disaster is that of inter-agency coordination. Typically, the disaster area will be inundated by well-intentioned representatives of a variety of government and non-government organisations. Health workers, counsellors, welfare workers, disaster agencies, the clergy, and many others will descend on a vulnerable and frightened community. It is vital that the valuable assistance available from these groups is provided in a coherent and organised manner. Thus, an inter-agency meeting should be scheduled as soon as practicable after the disaster to coordinate the recovery operation. Such a meeting needs to be handled with great sensitivity, since inter-agency conflict often occurs after the initial convergence on the disaster scene (Hefron, 1977). Naturally, further regular meetings will need to be held as recovery progresses.

At Queen Street, the coordination of several agencies was a delicate but important issue to be handled throughout the first year post-trauma. Although the community took responsibility for the recovery program, under my coordination, a number of groups perceived particular facets as being their domain. Inevitably, this occasionally resulted in some conflict which was resolved with varying degrees of success.

Program staffing

Recovery program staffing is an important issue that ideally should be considered before any disaster occurs. Regional response and recovery plans need to be developed that specifically include a mental health component. Disaster plans need to identify a 'lead agency' to coordinate recovery, with consideration given to both material and mental health needs; such an agency is likely to be in the health or community services area. Further, a specific position (or positions) needs to be identified as the 'disaster recovery coordinator'. This person will be responsible for coordinating responses to any large-scale disaster. Other staff can then be seconded or employed according to the needs of the affected community, although funding for such positions is always a contentious matter.

Further discussion on the content of a statewide disaster recovery plan is beyond the scope of this chapter. Nevertheless, the importance of including a mental health role cannot be underestimated; such a component provides the framework for implementing a program like the one discussed in this chapter.

With regard to the Queen Street shootings, I was seconded from Health Department Victoria to Australia Post immediately following the incident to oversee the recovery operation; that position was retained for 12 months post-trauma. Specific areas of my responsibility included individual, group, and community-based treatment; consultancy to other counsellors; and consultancy to the management of the organisation.

The recovery team also comprised staff from the Welfare and Employee Assistance section of Australia Post. These staff had varying levels of training and expertise in counselling and welfare. Involving staff from within the organisation was critical to the success of the operation and it reinforced community responsibility for the program. In addition, it probably helped to reduce the stigma and inferences of personal inadequacy that may have been associated with a purely mental health service. In the first two weeks post-trauma, a variety of government and non-government organisations contributed to the service, operating under the auspices of the State Disaster Recovery Plan (Health Department Victoria, 1987).

The recovery team at Queen Street was retained for most of the year and was responsible for all aspects of psychological recovery from the trauma. This team provided individual and group counselling as required, initiated community-based recovery strategies, provided advice on a range of issues, and generally ensured that community recovery continued to progress.

Immediate interventions

Establishing a 'recovery centre' as soon as possible after the disaster is useful because it acts as a focal point for the recovery operation. Such a centre rapidly becomes identified as a place where people can obtain information, meet with others to discuss the incident, and gain access to counsellors in an informal, non-threatening way. At Queen Street, such a centre was established within the building immediately following the trauma and remained in operation for approximately two weeks. As well as performing the above functions, it also acted as a convenient 'receiving point' for staff re-entering the building for the first time. After approximately two weeks, the recovery team was given a more permanent location, which became the recovery centre for the remainder of the year.

The degree of dislocation from the community has been identified as a major factor in the development of post-trauma pathology (Wilson, 1989). Community members should only be evacuated as a last resort and survivors should be encouraged to return to the community as soon as possible following the disaster. At Queen Street, every assistance was provided to staff returning to the building. This was considered important both from an 'exposure' perspective and also because the most effective support networks were thought to be colleagues who had also been through the incident. The majority of staff returned to the building within the first two days with little or no assistance. Those who did not return to work after two days, however, were contacted at home and, if required, a counsellor was sent out to assist their return to the building. The floors on which the shootings took place remained vacant for some time following the incident and support was provided for staff wishing to visit these areas.

The first two weeks post-trauma may be a time when assertive outreach of informal counselling services is required. Some of the most important mental health work following disasters may be this kind of 'kerbside counselling'. Brief, informal chats with mental health professionals (usually identified only as 'recovery workers') may not only facilitate recovery directly, but may also set the scene for further psychological assistance at a later date, should it be required. It is possible to be assertive in this process without being intrusive, but a delicate balance between the two is clearly required. Generally, such approaches will be met with appreciation as an opportunity to chat with someone who seems to understand. At Queen Street, a variety of counselling staff spent time going through the building over the first two weeks post-trauma, talking to individuals and groups informally at their workplaces and identifying those people most obviously distressed.

During the first two weeks, it is essential that information about the incident, available services, and the recovery process is widely disseminated. As noted above, this may take the form of public meetings, sensitive use of the media, or newsletters (discussed further below). Where appropriate, individuals should be encouraged and assisted to access more intensive treatment.

In some post-disaster situations, particularly those occurring in small and cohesive communities such as workplaces, group debriefings for survivors can be considered. Adapted from the work of Mitchell (1983), these groups have a number of aims:

- To educate people about the common responses to trauma and to emphasise the notion of 'normal reactions in normal people to an abnormal event'. To reinforce this education, handouts covering the important aspects of response to, and recovery from, trauma should be distributed and discussed.

- To encourage individuals to talk about their experience of the trauma, in order to learn of others' experiences and to gain more information about the incident. This process will also maximise group cohesion. Group leaders should take this opportunity to encourage people to talk about the trauma and their reactions whenever they feel the need.

- To assist people to identify and use their own resources and support networks, as well as informing them about the professional assistance available.

Contrary to popular images, the aim of these debriefing groups is not to provide an opportunity for emotional release. Remember that survivors at this stage are feeling vulnerable and out of control; the last thing they need is to feel that they have lost control of their emotions in front of friends and work colleagues. A debriefing group is not a therapy group. Rather, the aim of the group is to assist individuals to develop psychological frameworks by which they can understand their reactions to trauma and the personal recovery process. Following the Queen Street incident, debriefing groups were run for everybody in the building at 3 and 10 days post-trauma.

Short to medium-term interventions

At some point — usually about two weeks post-trauma — much of the external assistance and multi-agency involvement will need to be withdrawn. It is vital at this time that a reasonably high-profile and competent recovery team is left in place, since the community is likely to feel deserted after the initial flood of assistance. It needs to be made clear that the community, with the help of the recovery team, is now ready to take over responsibility for its own recovery.

To encourage active involvement in the recovery process, it may be useful to initiate a newsletter a few days following the disaster. The newsletter at Queen Street, symbolically titled *Together*, was distributed to everyone in the building and was maintained (at varying intervals according to perceived need) until the first anniversary. It provided an opportunity to keep people informed about a range of issues (such as the progress of the injured, relocation to the affected floors, the coroner's inquest, and so on), to continue the process of education regarding normal responses to trauma and simple coping strategies, and to give individuals an opportunity to express their own opinions and feelings arising from the incident.

The psychological impact of a major disaster may affect many other groups, in addition to the immediate survivors, and their needs should be considered at this point. These groups may include emergency services workers, journalists, and relatives of those involved. Following the Queen Street incident, it was clear that the families of those people working in the building were likely to be affected by the shootings. They often had to cope with quite dramatic post-trauma reactions in their spouse, parent or child (including withdrawal, anger and irritability, sleep disturbance, anxiety, and depressed mood). In an attempt to begin to address some of these issues, families were invited to attend an evening organised by the recovery team. Local clinicians with expertise in the area of disaster recovery provided input in a format similar to the group debriefings described above. Didactic presentations on the effects of trauma on individuals and their families were followed by small group discussions, led by counsellors. Participants were given an opportunity to share their experiences and provide mutual support. Finally, information about available resources was also provided.

Medium to long-term interventions

Any disaster recovery program needs to be sensitive to the fact that there will be several 'mini-traumas' after a major disaster. Survivors may have to cope with a range of economic, political, environmental, and social repercussions, each of which may constitute a highly stressful event. In addition, they may have to be involved in legal processes, such as criminal trials, inquiries, or inquests. The recovery team must be able to predict such events as far as possible, in order to prepare the community for the likely distress. Issues need to be dealt with in an active manner as they arise. Mental health recovery workers must recognise that there may be no clear 'right' way of doing things; rather, the team must make an assessment of the specific mood and needs of the community at the time. As a general rule, however, it is probably better to do something rather than nothing; crises should always be managed actively and there is no substitute for good preparation. A few examples from the Queen Street recovery operation may help to illustrate the point.

The coronial inquest into the deaths of nine people during the shootings was scheduled to occur 10 months after the incident. Because this inquiry was to be a major investigation, running for four weeks and addressing the wider issues of violence in the community, considerable effort was devoted to preparing for this period. The recovery team recognised that the inquest would be accompanied by extensive media coverage resulting in uncontrolled exposure to traumatic material. Those staff appearing as witnesses were extensively briefed on the process of the inquest and visits to the court were arranged. Practical arrangements were made for transport to and from the court and nearby facilities were secured for debriefing and personal support. Staff at all levels within the organisation were made aware of what to expect in terms of individual reactions and media interest. Representatives from each floor attended the hearing as observers and reported back daily to their colleagues on the proceedings. This strategy was adopted so that staff did not have to rely solely on media reports for information. Individual and group counselling was provided throughout as required. Following the inquest, debriefing groups were offered to everyone in the building and information regarding the proceedings and the findings was made available to all staff.

Considerable thought and community discussion was devoted to the first anniversary; eventually, the decision was made to handle it in a relatively low-key manner since it followed so quickly after the inquest. A memorial service was arranged; staff closely involved in the incident and the families of the bereaved took an active part in both planning and running the proceedings. Additional support was also made available during this period. The subject of an appropriate memorial was also an issue for some time. Again, the views of individuals within the affected community were sought through a variety of forums; it was eventually decided to commission a stained glass window to be placed in the Melbourne General Post Office.

At some point, it will be necessary to withdraw all external support from this community. Hopefully, by that time, the community will be in an advanced stage of recovery and will have developed structures to continue the process. Following the Queen Street shootings, I made individual treatment available throughout the first year post-trauma, and other initiatives such as *Together* and the consultative mechanisms also continued. In consultation with management and staff groups, however, the recovery process began to wind down following the inquest in October 1988. Long-term plans were formulated to continue the support after the disbanding of the recovery team, which occurred shortly after the first anniversary. Prime responsibility was handed over to the internal counselling services, and staff were made aware of appropriate outside agencies which could help them if required.

Support for recovery program staff

A detailed description of the support required by mental health recovery workers is beyond the scope of this chapter. Nevertheless, it is a vital issue that must be given serious consideration in the development of any program. The work is demanding and emotionally draining; workers will be exposed to continuous stories of devastation, loss, pain, and suffering. Frequently, recovery workers themselves will be the target of individual or community anger; this can be particularly hard to cope with but is almost inevitable at some stage. Strong support is essential if the team members are to continue functioning effectively. Regular, compulsory, debriefing and support meetings are recommended for all mental health recovery workers. In the aftermath of disaster, it is all too easy to see such support as an unnecessary luxury, but time and resources must be made available for the purpose. Group and/or individual support should be provided at least weekly, and daily during intense periods. This support should be provided by a mental health professional, with experience in disaster recovery, who is not directly involved in the provision of services to survivors.

In the absence of appropriate debriefing and support, mental health recovery workers are likely to experience a range of post-trauma symptoms themselves. The major dangers are probably avoidance, denial, and withdrawal on the one hand, and 'prosocial overcommitment' or loss of appropriate boundaries on the other (Wilson, 1989). Either way, the worker ceases to be an effective clinician. The wealth of literature on psychological support for emergency workers (see, for example, Dunning, 1988; Mitchell & Bray, 1990) can often be adapted to mental health recovery workers.

Evaluation of recovery programs

Formal evaluation of community-based interventions following disaster is rarely possible, since no control groups are available. Nevertheless, a number of areas may be examined. Below is a brief evaluation of the Queen Street recovery program.

COST-EFFECTIVENESS

An accurate assessment of the financial cost incurred as a result of the shootings is beyond the scope of this chapter. Initial projections by senior management in the compensation section of Australia Post, however, suggested a figure approaching A$4 million in compensation payments alone (Bishop, 1989). An estimate of the final total cost to the organisation was put at A$2.5 million, a figure considerably less than originally expected; this was thought to be largely a function of the better than anticipated return to work pattern. The majority of staff returned to work within one or two days of the shootings and most of the remainder within two weeks. The financial cost of the recovery operation itself, of course, constituted a relatively small fraction of the total cost.

STAFF EVALUATION

Feedback to the recovery team from staff in the building was generally very positive: the efforts of the team were widely appreciated and were also perceived as being beneficial. In addition, management was seen to be caring for staff during their recovery from the shootings. Inevitably, however, a small minority viewed the recovery team in a less positive light, seeing the program as occasionally intrusive and exacerbating symptoms.

ORGANISATION

The degree to which the organisation may have benefited from the recovery process in the long term remains to be seen and will be difficult to assess. Certainly, the incident and the guiding principles of the recovery process served to increase staff cohesion. The mechanisms for staff input (such as the Staff Consultative Group and *Together*), although they terminated at the end of the first year post-trauma, may have served to improve open communication within the organisation.

Summary

The case example used to illustrate this chapter, the Queen Street shootings, provided an unusual opportunity to mount a comprehensive mental health recovery program. Since the shootings occurred in the workplace, the recovery environment offered many opportunities for intervention and access to the affected population. It may be speculated how the needs and interventions would have differed had the incident occurred in the busy city streets outside the building. Nevertheless, the general principles apply across all types of community disasters. Similar programs have been implemented successfully in Victoria under the State Disaster Recovery Plan following a range of traumas including bushfires, floods, other shootings, and hostage-takings.

Effective recovery from community disasters frequently requires considerable innovation on the part of the recovery team to determine the most suitable strategies, as well as the courage to make the important decisions. At Queen Street, the physical location made information-dissemination and education relatively easy, and the opportunity to place appropriately qualified professional staff within the building ensured easy access for those requiring assistance. Support networks, composed of people with similar experiences of the trauma, were readily available; one of the prime tasks of the recovery team was to 'give permission' and encouragement regarding use of this natural resource. While lessons are continuously learnt about optimal mental health responses to disaster, each event will continue to challenge human services providers in their attempts to meet the needs of survivors more effectively.

References

American Psychiatric Association. (1987). *Diagnostic and statistical manual of mental disorders.* (3rd ed. rev.). Washington, DC: Author.

Bishop, E.W. (1989, September). *Workplace recovery: The Melbourne Queen Street tragedy.* Paper presented to the Industrial Safety Exposition of Victoria, Melbourne, Victoria.

Cohen, S., & Willis, T.A. (1985). Stress, social support and the buffering hypothesis. *Psychological Bulletin, 98,* 310–357.

Creamer, M., Burgess, P., Buckingham, W.J., & Pattison, P. (1989). *The psychological aftermath of the Queen Street shootings.* Unpublished manuscript, University of Melbourne, Victoria.

Dunning, C. (1988). Intervention strategies for emergency workers. In M. Lystad (Ed.), *Mental health response to mass emergencies* (pp. 284–310). New York: Brunner/Mazel.

Fairbank, J.A., & Nicholson, R.A. (1987). Theoretical and empirical issues in the treatment of posttraumatic stress disorder in Vietnam veterans. *Journal of Clinical Psychology, 43,* 44–55.

Figley, C.R. (1985) From victim to survivor: Social responsibility in the wake of catastrophe. In C. Figley (Ed.), *Trauma and its wake* (Vol.1., pp. 398–416). New York: Brunner/Mazel.

Foy, D.W., Resnick, H.S., Sipprelle, R.C., & Carroll, E.M. (1987). Premilitary, military and postmilitary factors in the development of combat related posttraumatic stress disorder. *Behavior Therapist, 10,* 3–9.

Green, B.L., Wilson, J.P., & Lindy, J.D. (1985). Conceptualizing post-traumatic stress disorder: A psychosocial framework. In C. Figley (Ed.), *Trauma and its wake* (Vol.1., pp. 53–72). New York: Brunner/Mazel.

Health Department Victoria. (1987). *State disaster recovery plan.* Melbourne: Government Printer.

Hefron, E.F. (1977). Inter-agency relationships and conflict in disaster: The Wilkes-Barre experience. *Mass Emergencies, 2,* 111–119.

Hodgkinson, P.E., & Stewart, M. (1991). *Coping with catastrophe.* London: Routledge.

Janoff-Bulman, R. (1985). The aftermath of victimization: Rebuilding shattered assumptions. In C. Figley (Ed.), *Trauma and its wake* (Vol.1, pp. 15–35). New York: Brunner/Mazel.

Lystad, M. (1988). *Mental health response to mass emergencies.* New York: Brunner/Mazel.

Maguire, M. (1985). Victim's needs and victim services: Indications from research. *Victimology, 10,* 539–559.

McFarlane, A.C. (1984). The Ash Wednesday bushfires in South Australia: Implications for planning for future post-disaster services. *Medical Journal of Australia, 141,* 286–291.

Mitchell, J.T. (1983). When disaster strikes: The critical incident stress debriefing process. *Journal of Emergency Medical Services, 8,* 36–39.

Mitchell, J.T., & Bray, G. (1990) *Emergency services stress.* Englewood Cliffs, NJ: Prentice Hall.

Raphael, B. (1984). Psychosocial aspects of disaster: Some Australian studies and the Ash Wednesday bushfires. *The Medical Journal of Australia, 141,* 268–270.

Raphael, B. (1986). *When disaster strikes.* London: Century Hutchinson.

Soloman, S.D. (1986). Mobilizing social support networks in times of disaster. In C. Figley (Ed.), *Trauma and its wake* (Vol.1, pp. 232–263). New York: Brunner/Mazel.

Taylor, S.E. (1983). Adjustment to threatening events: A theory of cognitive adaptation. *American Psychologist, 38,* 1161–1173.

Wilson, J.P. (1989). *Trauma, transformation and healing.* New York: Brunner/Mazel.

Post-Traumatic Stress Reactions in the Professional

CHAPTER FOUR

Michael Stewart and Peter Hodgkinson

THE word 'victim' is evocative — conjured up are images of bloodied faces, damaged bodies, and physical suffering. However, a wide range of people are affected when a disaster occurs. Among them are the rescuers and helpers, whose stress has often been unrecognised, leaving them as the 'hidden victims'. This neglect has one probable central cause — the popular stereotype of helpers as strong and resourceful (a stereotype often cherished by members of the emergency services) as opposed to the victims who are supposedly helpless and resourceless (Short, 1979). Helpers are simply not supposed to be at risk. It is crucial to consider some of the stresses involved in emergency service work, body recovery, and psychosocial support, and to look at strategies for mitigating the worst effects.

Stress reactions in emergency service workers

What is the typical scene greeting a member of the rescue services at the site of a disaster? The following descriptions of the aftermath of the 1981 Hyatt Regency Hotel skywalk collapse in the USA paint a vivid picture (Wilkinson, 1983). On the dance floor there was 'a huge pile of steel, concrete dust, and people ... then water flowing down from broken pipes on the fourth floor ... the blood and dust, and the water made a strange, penetrating odour that seemed to last forever'.

The frailty of the human body was pitifully exposed as 'bodies had literally exploded under the tremendous impact; limbs had been amputated; a foot, a leg, an arm independent of a body was not an infrequent sight'. One person was 'compressed into the shape of a letter Z. The stomach of one man protruded through his mouth, another man was cut neatly in half just below the thorax ... other bodies were split open and some were crushed beyond recognition. A few persons, still conscious, were partially pinned, while in other instances several were trapped together and often tried to console each other'.

Many rescue workers toiled for hours to remove the injured and dead from the devastation on the ballroom floor.

The firemen had a special burden to bear. They all knew that their fire chief had attended the tea dance and he was not found among the uninjured survivors. Hour after hour they worked ... constantly fearing that they might find their loved and respected commander under the rubble. Not until the next day did they learn that one of the first bodies extricated was that of the fire chief, who had been so badly mutilated that they did not recognize him (Miles, Demi, & Mostyn-Aker, 1984).

Fifty-four workers were followed up four months later (Miles et al., 1984), and reported the following reactions in the period just following the disaster:

- sadness and depression (60 per cent)
- frustration/irritability (40 per cent)
- vulnerability (38 per cent)
- numbness (36 per cent)
- dreams/nightmares (35 per cent)
- guilt (24 per cent)

Of these workers studied, 39 per cent sought mental health counselling.

One of the most harrowing aspects of rescue work is body recovery. The effects of this work were seen in those involved in 'Operation Overdue'. On the 28 November 1979, a DC10 airliner on a non-stop tourist flight crashed on the slopes of Mount Erebus in Antarctica. All 257 passengers and crew were killed. The body-recovery was undertaken by scientists, police, and federated mountain club climbers from New Zealand. Human remains were bagged and flown to an ice-strip, repacked, and returned to New Zealand, where police, dentists, and embalmers completed the 10-week job of identification.

Workers who had participated in these terrible tasks were followed-up by questionnaire at 3 and 20 months post-trauma (Taylor & Frazer, 1982). Stressors differed depending on where the person had worked:

Those on Mount Erebus found their frozen body recovery work arduous, visually offensive and somewhat hazardous underfoot.

Those on the ice-strip had to cope in short intensive bursts with heavy, thawing, slithering loads of ... flesh ... those in the mortuary found the ... work in overcrowded, overheated and malodorous conditions tiring, and some of the most experienced felt that the unrelenting procession of bodies deprived them of the regular breaks which might otherwise have helped them to cope with their pent-up feelings (Taylor & Frazer, 1982).

Several workers reported persistent intrusive images of disfigurements, body contortions, and fixed facial expressions, or dreams in which they were in aircraft collisions, trapped in claustrophobic situations akin to the mortuary, or experienced role-reversal with the corpses. A pattern of initial changes was reported, in several instances these were sustained over four weeks:

- sleep changes (80.5 per cent)
- appetite changes (76 per cent)
- feelings changes (50 per cent)
- talking changes (40 per cent)
- social activity changes (33 per cent)

At 20 months, only 8 per cent expressed a need to talk over their experiences and only 15 per cent had flashbacks. Eighty per cent felt they had overcome any problems satisfactorily. A few felt they had benefited from the experience, one them, 'very moved to find that by talking to his father about the debriefing he had inadvertently unlocked his father's experience from handling bodies in Concentration Camps in World War II' (Taylor & Frazer, 1982).

Stress levels, as measured by questionnaire, fluctuated over time. Immediately after finishing their work, 35 per cent were in the high-stress group. At three months, this group measured only 20.5 per cent, but included some workers who had reported this level of stress for the first time, showing a worsening of symptoms as they got further from the events. After 20 months, 23 per cent of workers were in the high-stress group. Those who were older and who had more experience of victim recovery work fared the best.

For emergency service workers, several variables exist which affect their reactions and which can influence the integration process after the initial impact.

Firstly, rescue and emergency personnel bring their personalities and previous experiences to the incidents they attend. These may be protective, or they may increase the likelihood of stress reactions. Secondly, there is the nature of the event itself and its particular stressors — a large number of badly damaged human bodies may be disturbing for the hardiest of workers, the bodies of little children particularly so. Thirdly, there is the support available in the social environment to which the worker returns, both at home and at work.

The following symptoms may occur in workers during the action phase of rescue and recovery operations (Alberta Professions and Occupations Bureau, 1989).

A PHYSICAL

1. Increased heart rate, respiration, blood pressure
2. Shortness of breath
3. Nausea, upset stomach, diarrhoea
4. Sweating or chills, hot/cold spells, clammy skin
5. Tremors of hands, lips, eyes
6. Muffled hearing
7. Headaches
8. Narrowed field of vision
9. Feelings of weakness, numbness, tingling or heaviness in arms or legs.
10. Feeling uncoordinated
11. Soreness of muscles
12. Lower back pains
13. Feeling a 'lump in the throat'
14. Chest pains (medical check required)
15. Faintness or dizziness
16. Exaggerated startle reflex
17. Fatigue
18. Appetite change

B COGNITIVE

All cognitive process are affected adversely by severe stress. The following symptoms usually follow the physical symptoms in acute stress situations.

1. Memory problems
2. Difficulty in naming objects, for example when asking to be given important equipment
3. Disorientation
4. Difficulty in comprehending, slowness of thinking
5. Mental confusion
6. Difficulty in making simple calculations, for example in relation to body counts.
7. Difficulty in using logic, making judgments and decisions or problem solving.
8. Loss of ability to conceptualise alternatives or prioritise tasks.
9. Poor concentration, limited attention span
10. Loss of objectivity

C EMOTIONAL

1. Feeling high, heroic, invulnerable
2. Euphoria, excessive gratitude for being alive
3. Anxiety (both anticipatory en route and post-incident), fear
4. Strong identification with the victim, perhaps enhanced by finding personal effects or photographs. As one doctor remarked during an incident: 'That guy's so much like me it was like working on my own body' (Mitchell, 1986).
5. Anger (with colleagues, officers, the media), blame
6. Irritability, restlessness, hyperexcitability
7. Sadness, grief, depression, moodiness
8. Recurrent dreams of the event or other traumatic dreams, sleep difficulties
9. Guilt feelings about not having done enough
10. Feelings of isolation, detachment, estrangement
11. Apathy, diminished interest
12. Denial of feelings, numbness
13. Excessive worry about the safety of others

D BEHAVIOURAL

1. Difficulty in communicating, verbally or in writing
2. Hyperactivity
3. Decreased efficiency
4. Outbursts of anger, frequent arguments
5. Inability to rest or relax
6. Periods of crying
7. Increased use of alcohol, tobacco and other drugs
8. Social withdrawal, distancing

The group of rescue workers who show no distress are probably those who make no identification with the victim. Identifying with the victim may lead to anxiety, not about oneself, but about the safety of one's loved ones. One worker involved in a rescue mission following an avalanche disaster (Dyregrov, Thyholdt, & Mitchell, in press) described the following:

> For a while following the disaster I often had to enter my daughter's bedroom to check if she was OK and if she slept. This happened many times during a night. While riding in my car my daughter once fell asleep. When I saw her sitting there quite limp and "lifeless", I was back at the disaster scene again.

Sixty per cent of fellow workers reported similar feelings.

The deaths of children pose particular difficulties for rescue workers. After the mass suicide in 1978 at the People's Temple at Jonestown, Guyana, military personnel had to recover bodies which had changed in both size and colour, were infested by insects, and had an intense odour[1]. The decomposing bodies of children made normal defences ineffective (Jones, 1985) and soldiers remarked: 'It was quite a shock to see three or four babies in a bag', 'The bodies of the children were of innocent victims and it shouldn't have been that way' and 'I can't sleep. Cannot get the small children out of my mind'.

However, it must not be assumed that all reactions are solely negative. Following their work on the mass suicide (Jones, 1985), workers felt they had made friends during the emergency, they matured, realised their mortality, and tried to improve their life and enjoy it more, as well as taking it more seriously. One soldier remarked, 'It made me aware of how beautiful life is. And, how ugly death can be'. Following the avalanche disaster previously mentioned (Dyregrov et al., in press), nearly half of the Red Cross workers reported a change in life values, with materialistic values de-emphasised, and non-materialistic values such as 'closeness to others' and importance of friends and family upgraded.

Rescue and emergency services everywhere are disciplined organisations whose members conceal personal sensitivities. 'Training directs them to focus upon their external performance, and to deny and suppress their feelings' (Taylor, 1983). It is difficult for such personnel to ask for help with painful feelings. Police officers carry with them the myth that they should be able to cope with anything. New recruits quickly learn from senior officers 'to bottle up their fears, sorrows and revulsion and to replace these at least publicly with a show of bravado and practical competence'. Officers are often more concerned with 'getting it right' and not making mistakes than they are about their feelings. Showing feelings is equated with weakness, which in turn is equated with incompetence.

After the 1985 Bradford City Football Stadium fire disaster in the UK[2], senior police officers became concerned that a week or so after the fire the officers who had been involved showed no signs of adjusting to their experiences. They set up a confidential screening and counselling program (Duckworth, 1986) and 399 officers were sent a screening questionnaire. Of the 59 per cent of officers who returned it, 15 per cent were 'likely cases' for psychiatric problems and 9 per cent 'likely serious cases'.

Just over half (57 per cent) of the 'likely cases' opted for counselling, and so did 65 per cent of the 'likely serious cases', totalling 33 officers in all. A third of the latter group qualified for a full diagnosis of Posttraumatic Stress

---

[1] In 1978, Jonestown was the site of the mass suicide of more than 900 members of an American religious cult called the People's Temple, led by Jim Jones. Jones ordered his followers to commit suicide with him by drinking a mixture of fruit cordial and cyanide

[2] The roof of a wooden stand caught fire during a weekend soccer match at Bradford City Football Club's ground. The entire stand burnt down within three minutes, resulting in the deaths of 56 spectators and injuries to many more. Most of the casualties suffered extensive burns to their heads and backs.

Disorder (PTSD). The 22 who did not opt for counselling gave two main reasons: firstly, confidentiality; and secondly, their problems not being connected with the disaster. Following assessment, officers who had opted for counselling had two or three treatment sessions, comprising cognitive, problem-solving therapy. Three weeks after these had ended they were reassessed: all but two now fell in the 'likely non-case' group. At nine months, one still showed evidence of disturbance.

Five different types of psychological difficulties could be detected among the officers who attended the fire: *performance guilt, reconstruction anxiety, generalised irritability, focused resentment,* and *motivational changes* (Duckworth, 1986).

PERFORMANCE GUILT

This was experienced in connection with rescue activities — the fire had developed so rapidly that decisions about what to do, and where to tell people to go, could easily, with hindsight, be seen as being wrong 'The guilt feelings seemed to be most intense in cases where bystanders had inadvertently "confirmed" an officer's imagined failings by their offhand comments'. Officers would go over events, thinking 'If only I'd realized how it was going to develop, then I would have ...' (Duckworth, 1986).

RECONSTRUCTION ANXIETY

Reconstruction anxiety involved the creation of alternative scenarios which became frightening when officers considered what might have happened. These constructions were so vivid that for some it was difficult to distinguish between them and reality. Many officers experienced this for only a short period after the events, while for others it became a more persistent problem.

GENERALISED IRRITABILITY

One of the most common and persistent changes, irritability showed itself both at home and at work, in relation to events which often had no connection with the fire. In turn, it made the officers feel bad, and in many cases had negative effects on relationships, eroding 'the officer's social support systems at a time when they needed them most' (Duckworth, 1986).

FOCUSED RESENTMENT

Bitter resentment was directed at the behaviour of certain journalists, the obstructiveness of young spectators, the football club itself, and the management of the compensation fund. 'Among other things, this set them up for furious and near violent exchanges if other people failed to agree with them.' (Duckworth, 1986)

MOTIVATIONAL CHANGES

Some officers felt that many aspects of their job were no longer important to them, and 'found great difficulty in bringing themselves to "perform" as required' (Duckworth, 1986). For a few officers, this difficulty with motivation extended to their homes.

So we can see that a significant percentage of rescue, emergency service and identification personnel experience short-term stress, and that a small percentage are affected over longer periods of time. Descriptions of symptom patterns reveal a 'mirror effect' with the reactions of the primary victims of disaster.

Although this chapter has focused on the effects of single major disasters, the stress of trauma may be cumulative in emergency service workers. One fireman attended several bad road accidents in which children were injured. He showed no ill effects. A week or so later he attended a house fire in a property believed to be empty. When the fire was extinguished he was the first to enter through the kitchen, to find a mother and daughter dead at the table. He went off sick and said he could no longer do the job.

Psychological debriefing of emergency service personnel

Providing support for emergency services personnel often runs into powerful resistance from both staff and their managers. Some have described a fear that opening a 'Pandora's box' — allowing people to explore their vulnerability, or to express their pain and bewilderment — may open the floodgates and inaugurate a model dramatically the reverse of the normal macho image. Leadership within organisations has a critical role to play in bringing about changes in this area.

Psychological debriefing, or Critical Incident Stress Debriefing (CISD; Mitchell, 1983), is a procedure that gained great impetus from work done with emergency service personnel. Three stages of intervention can be identified: *on-scene debriefing, initial defusing,* and *formal debriefing and follow-up.*

ON-SCENE DEBRIEFING

On-scene debriefing aims to identify acute stress reactions which develop in emergency service workers during an incident and intervene where necessary. An example of this process occurred during the recovery and identification of bodies from the Zeebrugge ferry sinking[3] (Quintyn, De Winne, & Hodgkinson, 1990). A military psychologist was attached to the Disaster Victim Identification (DVI) team to immediately detect any psychological disturbance arising in any team member. The individual would then be kept close to the building where the identification was proceeding so that they could be reintegrated into the task as soon as possible, following the principles of *proximity, immediacy* and *expectancy.*

---

[3] The passenger and vehicle ferry, *Herald of Free Enterprise,* sank in the English Channel off Zeebrugge in 1987, with the loss of 193 lives. The bow doors on the vehicle deck had been left open and the ferry capsized, sinking almost immediately.

The following conversation took place with a team member who left the building without reason on the second day of the identification process.

PSY: Aren't you feeling well?

X: No, it's too much.

PSY: What is going on?

X: Damn it, a child, a four-year-old ... Oh, God ...

PSY: Where are you working?

X: Internal autopsy.

PSY: That's bad, but you left your post.

X: (Irritated) That's not true — P has replaced me until they've finished with that child.

PSY: Will you go back afterwards?

X: Of course. What do you think I am? Do you have children?

PSY: No.

X: Then your psychology can't understand this. Now, damn it, you can go and tell the commander I'm a coward. I've got three children about that age.

PSY: You've got my word as an officer that no one will know anything about this talk.

X: You'd better be right. Can you go and see whether they've finished with that child?

PSY: (Returning) The child is done, there's an adult on the table again, what do you think?

X: I'll do as I said I would.

For the rest of the day this individual kept a suspicious eye on the psychologist, but that evening in the mess they had a long discussion and two months later the psychologist had supper with him at his home. There were approximately 10 interventions of this type for 150 personnel, and none required any follow-up treatment. Such interventions, as indicated here, may be viewed with suspicion by personnel, and good preparation for the presence of the person is essential.

INITIAL DEFUSING

Initial defusing, performed within a few hours of the incident, is most frequently led by a commander and its aim is to create an immediately supportive and positive atmosphere. Destructive criticism, which may develop at this stage, must be blocked, acceptance should be encouraged, and excessive sick humour contained.

FORMAL DEBRIEFING

Formal group debriefings aim to minimise unnecessary psychological suffering in emergency service workers, by enabling them to ventilate their impressions, reactions and feelings; to clearly understand both the event and their reactions to it (and thus decrease any sense of uniqueness of the event); and to prepare for reactions to come. These debriefings also help mobilise resources within and outside the group and increase group support, solidarity and cohesiveness.

Those carrying out a debriefing should be clear that it is just that — it is not 'counselling' and certainly not a therapy group in the traditional sense. Debriefings are not 'curative', either — they are an attempt to minimise the likelihood that psychological reactions will assume highly disruptive proportions. They cannot prevent reactions from arising, but they provide a framework for the individual to contain them, understand them, and take further action. They are, therefore, a method of crisis intervention, a preventative measure.

Those who carry out debriefings require a number of skills. They have to be familiar with group work, with anxiety-based problems and their management, and with trauma and grief. They also have to be confident and at ease with intense emotions.

Often, those involved will pass through a period of little reaction immediately after an event. A debriefing should be held about 48 hours after the event. Debriefings may be held any time after the event, of course, but the longer in time afterwards, the more hazy memories will be.

The ideal setting for a debriefing is a room away from interruptions. The group should be seated around a table rather than using the traditional group therapy model of a circle with an empty space in the centre. Most groups of people not used to the therapy group set-up will find the open space unfamiliar and may be threatened by it. The debriefing should have an identified leader and at least two co-leaders, though only one co-leader is acceptable.

Besides the leaders, 15 is probably a maximum number for a group, unless there are unusual circumstances. Anyone not involved in the incident or connected to it in some crucial way, should be excluded unless they are important to the group, such as a senior manager who may have a continuing and vital role in the group at a later date. The debriefing has seven identifiable phases.

1. Introductory phase

The introductory phase is very important — a clear introduction decreases the possibility that the group will malfunction in some way. The more time spent in introduction, the less chance that something will go wrong — a typical amount of time spent on an introduction might be 15 minutes.

The following issues should be dealt with in an introduction: the introduction of the debriefing team and the purpose of the meeting, creating the expectation that people are going to talk about thoughts and feelings, and that the participants are going to find it helpful.

The leader then lays down some rules for the debriefing, rules designed to minimise any anxieties that the participants may have. These rules include:

- participants' right to silence and confidentiality
- any discussion of procedural issues to be deferred (preventing a line of potential argument and blame from disrupting the expression of thoughts and feelings)
- people talk only for themselves (preventing unhelpful generalisations)

Participants are also made aware that feelings may get worse during the meeting before they improve.

Participants are reassured that they do, of course, have the opportunity to leave, but are requested to leave quietly and to come back if possible. They also are made aware that if they leave in distress, a member of the team will follow to be with them. The group is then given a brief outline of the structure of the meeting, and given the opportunity to ask any questions.

2. Fact phase

In this phase each person briefly describes what happened for them during the incident. Due to the scope of the incident or perceptual narrowing, each person tends to have a restricted view of events. They may simply have only experienced part of the events, or may have missed crucial aspects. If each participant describes their own experience, a clear and correct picture of the facts of the event becomes available for all.

Knowledge of all the events allows *formulation*, a sense of cognitive organisation. This is one of the main objectives of debriefing because it allows people the chance to think objectively rather than feel overwhelmingly. Having a picture of all the facts blocks speculation which, in turn, can fuel anxiety.

3. Thought phase

In the thought phase, the debriefing focuses on decisions and thought processes. First thoughts after an event may be important, but people are often reluctant to share them because they may be incongruous or bizarre, or reveal intense fear. However they may reflect what later becomes the core of any anxiety.

Further questions that should be asked during this phase are: What did you do during the incident? Why did you decide on doing what you did?. Answering this last question often brings out the need to protect others (to which first thoughts are often related). An example of this is the fire chief who ordered his men to stay out of the water following the crash of Air Florida 90 into the Potomac River in Washington[4]. His men were intensely frustrated that they could have been saving lives, and were angry with him. During the debriefing, the reason he gave for his actions was the fact that he smelled jet fuel and that two of his personnel had died of asphyxiation in a similar, earlier incident. He simply could not bear to put any of his men at undue risk again (Mitchell, 1986).

---

[4] This plane crash in 1985 killed all but five of the passengers on board.

Anger may similarly arise in emergency service personnel in response to commands they cannot understand and which appear to have nothing to do with protecting staff. Thus in the debriefing following a school bus disaster in 1988 at Mabodalen in Sweden, one of the commanders at the scene told how he was under pressure over the radio from his superiors. They demanded several times to know how many dead children and how many dead adults there were. He had to order one of his officers to look at all the bodies several times to get the exact numbers. This caused great stress on the officer carrying out the order and subsequent anger towards his commander for what seemed a pointlessly unpleasant action. Only during the debriefing did the officer find out why the commander had been forced to make such a gruesome request, affording the officer considerable relief.

At the end of this phase, participants' impressions from the scene can be explored. Questions that can be asked include: What were your impressions of what was going on around you as events took their course? What did you hear, see and smell? These sensory impressions form the basis of the intrusive images and thoughts which may be very disruptive in the post-event period.

Examples of these types of impressions include the following (Dyegrov, 1989):

'The stretchers were so light' (dead and injured children)

'Things such as life-vests, potatoes, teddybears and tape-recorders made it so alive, reminding us that it was people like you and me, and that it could have been my children'

'I can still feel the curls of a young child in my hand'

'The smell of burnt human beings was horrible, I will never forget it'

'A hand fell down on my back from a tree'

Verbalised and confronted, these memories become less powerful, and they intrude less often. This is because they are now located within a cognitive framework and therefore operate less randomly. Also, because they are shared, they take on less of a private, haunting nature.

4. Reaction phase

Questions about thoughts, impressions and actions lead to answers about feelings — the reaction phase, in which feelings are explored, is often the longest part of the debriefing. In order for this to be successful, the leaders have to be able to allow people to share their feelings, however painful. To cut them off may be extremely destructive.

When people describe reasons behind decisions they will often talk about fear, helplessness, loneliness, self-reproach, and frustration. The following comments are typical: 'I was so afraid of making a mistake'; 'I didn't know if I was saving lives or taking lives.'; or 'I had to shout that they should remain where they were, that we save them, but I knew inside I was lying'.

The process of sharing feelings establishes similarities and the normality of reactions. Questions which help establish the process include:

- 'How did the events make you react?'
- 'What was the worst of what happened for you?'
- 'Have you ever experienced anything in your life before that has made you so upset/frustrated/frightened?'
- 'How did you feel when X happened?

The question about the worst aspect of the experience is important because it is around these issues that difficulties may arise.

The leader of the debriefing must allow everyone the chance to participate and must intervene if ground rules are broken, or if there is destructive criticism. This is essential as one of the main therapeutic processes of the debriefing is modelling strategies of how the participants can deal with their emotional issues with each other, with families, and with friends in the weeks to come. Participants must learn that it is safe to express feelings and that they are not overwhelming, and to be assertive with others.

Leaders must watch for participants who seem to suffer a lot, who are silent or who have extreme symptoms. These may be the people who are most at risk. Sometimes other past events may surface for them, either related to work, stemming from previous incidents that have not been integrated successfully, or from more personal traumas such as bereavements.

5. Symptom phase

During the symptom phase, participants discuss certain reactions in more detail. They are asked to describe symptoms (emotional, cognitive and physical) that they experienced at the scene, when the incident was over, when they returned home, during the following days, and at the present time. Leaders may need to ask questions about any unusual experiences, and any difficulties in returning to work.

The familiar strands of post-trauma stress — re-experience phenomena, avoidance and numbing, and arousal — will no doubt appear. Fear may affect behaviour dramatically. Phobic reactions may begin to appear, such as people feeling unable to go back to where the event happened, which is a problem if it is their place of work.

One difficult area may be the impact on family life of the worker's involvement in a traumatic event. The person may feel that their family cannot understand what they have experienced. As one worker described, 'What I couldn't take was my wife's question on what we should do during the weekend. It was such a contrast to what I had been through, that I exploded in anger.' (Dyregrov, 1989). Such extreme reactions may then lead the spouse to question the worker's position ('Why on earth do you have to do such a risky job?'), leaving the worker feeling misunderstood and devalued. They may yearn to be back among their fellow workers who experienced the same things and understand their problems.

6. Preparation phase

The preparation phase aims to synthesise participants' reactions to make them understandable. Leaders need to emphasise the commonality of experiences while also putting value on the individual's reactions. By gathering together participants' examples and using material from other incidents or even research, the reactions become normalised. Using written material about reactions is helpful because it is a permanent resource. Participants must not be given the impression that they will or should experience reactions, only that they may do so.

Leaders will find it helpful to outline some of the experiences that participants may face in the coming weeks. Knowledge enables participants to form expectations and plan coping strategies. Explain that symptoms normally decrease with the progress of time.

7. Re-entry phase

In the re-entry phase, future planning and coping are discussed, particularly in terms of family and peer group support. Indeed, one of the main aims of the debriefing is to foster cohesion within the group. Experiencing a lack of understanding from fellow workers may be one of the most damaging aspects of post-incident stress.

It is helpful to discuss at what point participants might need to seek further help. Guidelines might be: (a) if symptoms do not decrease after about six weeks, (b) if symptoms increase over time, or (c) if workers are unable to function adequately at work or at home.

Identify avenues of further help The group may decide they need a follow-up to the debriefing or at least discuss the possibility of one: especially if the incident has been particularly traumatic; if an issue has not been properly dealt with; to meet for some specific action (such as commemorating the death of a fellow worker); or for further group solidarity (such as a meal out together); or for contact with other follow-up resources, perhaps within the organisation, such as occupational health.

The stress of psychological care

Very little is known about the effects of stress, immediately post-impact or in the long term, on those offering psychosocial care to victims of traumatic events. The pressure of crisis intervention may be extremely intense. After the 1977 Beverly Hills Supper Club fire in the USA (Lindy & Green, 1981), it was noted how 'a frequent cycle seemed to plague those of us working in outreach: resistance, zeal, overextension, frustration and anger'.

Three sources of extreme stress for helpers in disasters have been described (Raphael, 1986):

* the close encounter with death, which reminds helpers of their own vulnerability

- sharing the anguish of victims and families, and the close empathic identification that often results
- role ambiguity and conflict.

The immediate response to a disaster is to feel that something must be done to help, and one of the notable features of disaster aftermath is the landslide of offers of help — people want, almost need, to help. Those who do become involved often experience an elation, which may broaden into what has been called *counterdisaster syndrome.*

This 'high' is most rewarding and helps solve problems and frustrations, particularly in the immediate post-impact phase which requires the engagement of high levels of energy and involvement. Frequently, however, the helper can become over-involved, and may even experience the narcissistic belief that he or she is the only person who can, or really knows how to, help the victims. This can lead to overwork, which is not only unproductive and inefficient, but may be counterproductive in terms of the guilt and resentment that arises in fellow workers.

A sense of helplessness is also common, in which helpers feel unequal to the enormity of the task through lack of preparedness, training or other personal resources. This may lead to prolonged and guilty self-recrimination after the event, when helpers reflect on the supposed inadequacy of their performances.

TWO MAJOR BRITISH DISASTERS: STRESS IN SOCIAL WORKERS

In a study of social workers involved in disaster support work with victims of the UK's Piper Alpha oil rig explosion and the Clapham train crash[5] (Shepherd & Hodgkinson, in press), two major sources of stress were identified, both in the post-impact period and in the long term: the client's distress, that is the scale of distress and hearing accounts of disaster experiences; and uncertainty about role and anxieties about competence. During the first month of disaster support work, initial contact with clients was also listed as a major stress; over the long term, conflict with one's usual job or team was more frequently mentioned.

These sources of stress manifested in the social workers in four major ways.

Identification

Identification with victims' experiences was a major stressor, affecting almost the whole group in one way or another. Ninety-nine per cent had found themselves imagining how they would have coped if they had been a victim themselves, with 63 per cent imagining themselves as bereaved and 36 per cent as directly involved in the disaster. Eight-eight per cent found

---

[5] Both these UK accidents occurred in 1988. The North Sea oil rig explosion on Piper Alpha killed 167 of its crew, 62 survived. A commuter train crashed at Clapham, south-west London, killing 35 passengers.

themselves ruminating on the victims' experiences; mainly in terms of their clients' reactions.

Sixty-three per cent found that the disaster support work reminded them of earlier unhappy memories. This was mostly related to personal bereavement, but also to other loss-related situations such as divorce. However, identification is not problematic in its own right, in fact, the ability to identify with the victim may be one of the main tools the worker has to get close to comprehending the victim's experiences.

Role conflicts and organisational issues

Role problems were a major source of stress. Eighty-seven per cent reported confusion about what was expected of them in their role as a disaster support worker. For 51 per cent, this concerned role ambiguity issues such as unclear or unrealistic expectations on the part of the client, lack of professional boundaries, uncertainty about focus (whether therapeutic or practical help was required) and uncertainty about level of contact. For 14 per cent this stemmed from organisational factors such as the unrealistic expectations of managers and lack of information.

Personal impact

In terms of the personal impact of stress, indicated by reported changes in social life, use of drugs, involvement in accidents, or visits to their local doctor, 64 per cent reported no difference or a change in a desirable direction. In terms of more long-lasting changes, 61 per cent felt their attitude to life had changed. Thirty-four cent described a reprioritisation of values, a sense of gratitude for what they had, a new appreciation of life, or a determination to live for the moment. As with rescue workers, 27 per cent reported a heightened sense of their own and loved ones' mortality and vulnerability.

The involvement in disaster work, despite its stressful nature, was seen to be a positive experience as well. Eighty-five per cent believed they had benefited from their task resulting in a positive change in attitude to life. In addition, some felt more reflective and were more aware of their own shortcomings. Professional benefits perceived included seeing the work as useful experience for half the group, and increased confidence and job satisfaction for others.

Impact on well-being and psychological symptoms

Levels of symptoms (as measured by the Hopkins Symptom Checklist) were consistently higher than population norms, and the scores of 60 per cent of social workers fell in the high-stress group.

The study also researched the moderating effects of variables on the stress encountered by the social workers. The two external elements specific to the disaster support work which proved important moderators were role conflict (which moderated symptoms) and identification (which moderated well-being). The single most important moderator of both symptoms and well-being (measured by a scale of Psychological Well-being) was personal coping style, in this case hardiness (a coping style involving a strong sense of commitment to one's job, a sense of having control over what one does, and the experience of stress as a positive challenge). The second most important moderator was on-going life stress in the shape of immediately preceding life events. In particular, bereavement in the preceding year was a clear predictor of high stress in disaster support workers. The demands of disaster support work may therefore be broadly categorised into 'professional/external' and 'personal/internal'.

PROFESSIONAL/EXTERNAL: ROLE-RELATED DIFFICULTIES

Role-related difficulties included both role ambiguity, such as lack of established professional and time boundaries, and role conflict, such as difficulty in meeting the demands of both the disaster work and normal jobs.

This feature of disaster support work may distinguish those offering psychological support from other professionals working at the scene. Unlike the tasks of emergency personnel, those of support workers are often poorly defined, and it may be that this diffuseness of role is a core problem — not only is the individual worker incapable of making the task less diffuse, but the organisation's lack of familiarity with the situation means that it has no experience with which to aid the worker.

PERSONAL/INTERNAL: IDENTIFICATION

Victim contact may be stressful in both quantitative (exposure level) and qualitative (degree of identification) terms. The effects of identification may be mediated by individual differences in coping style; 'hardier' social workers appeared less likely to identify with clients. The true nature of identification has yet to be fully explored. Although, as we have indicated, it may be a necessary tool in therapeutic relationships with survivors, it may increase helpers' susceptibility to the impact of their clients' distress, interfere with other relationships, and create problems with disengagement.

MANAGEMENT OF STRESS IN DISASTER SUPPORT WORKERS

Management of stress in disaster support workers centres around two issues, good selection and good support.

Selection

One of the first ways of ensuring staff survival is to select appropriate staff in the first place. After one disaster, a member of staff was selected for some intensive work because she had suffered a spouse bereavement in the previous year and so selectors thought she would understand more of the situation. This led, of course, not to greater understanding, but to suffering for the worker.

As we have discussed above, managers should select workers who are hardy, that is, with a strong sense of commitment, challenge and control, and with low levels of recent life changes, particularly bereavement. But other than giving a paper and pencil test, how can hardiness be assessed in an interview? One disaster team manager made the following comments on selection (Hodgkinson, 1988): 'Looking back on what I discussed with candidates, I think I was looking for the following: (i) People who had a strong sense of work identity, not necessarily as a particular type of professional, but at the interface of personal strength/therapeutic ethos/appropriate identity as a helper. Theoretical perspective, I felt, was largely irrelevant. (ii) A strong sense of independence. (iii) Experience of loss related work.'.

What was being identified here was an indication of personal strength, simply to bear the onslaught of pain; and a therapeutic ethos, that is the ability to allow the expression of the pain, and see it as valuable, yet at the same time to have an appropriate identity as a helper, to see oneself as separate from the client's pain, and able to maintain a boundary. The strong sense of independence is particularly necessary to tolerate the loneliness of outreach work.

Supervision

Ongoing supervision is essential, and the role of social support for workers is clearly established as being a major buffer to stress (Bartone, Ursano, Wright, & Ingraham, in press). Some workers may only provide support in the immediate crisis — for them, debriefing as they return to their normal jobs is essential. Supervision of those who continue in long-term disaster support work should cover a number of areas:

* individual casework
* team process
* personal/professional boundaries

As these workers eventually have to finish their work, intellectual (what has been learnt) and emotional debriefing is highly necessary. Lack of such care with disaster workers means that they will run a strong risk of becoming victims too.

References

Alberta Professions and Occupations Bureau. (1989). *Critical Incident Stress Debriefing Training*. Alberta: Author.

Bartone, P., Ursano, R., Wright, K., & Ingraham, L. (in press). *Impact of a military air disaster*.

Duckworth, D. (1986). Psychological problems arising from disaster work. *Stress Medicine, 2*, 315–323.

Dyregrov, A. (1989). Caring for helpers in disaster situations: Psychological debriefing. *Disaster Management, 2*, 25–30.

Dyregrov, A., Thyholdt, R., & Mitchell, J. (in press). *Rescue workers' emotional reactions following a disaster.*

Hodgkinson, P.E. (1988, September). *Managing a disaster team.* Paper presented at the First European Conference on Traumatic Stress Studies, Lincoln.

Jones, D. (1985). Secondary disaster victims: The emotional effects of recovering and identifying human remains. *American Journal of Psychiatry, 142,* 303–307.

Lindy, J.D., & Green, B.L. (1981). Survivors: Outreach to a reluctant population. *American Journal of Orthopsychiatry, 51,* 468–478.

Miles, M., Demi, A., & Mostyn-Aker, P. (1984). Rescue workers' reactions following the Hyatt Hotel disaster. *Death Education, 8,* 315–331.

Mitchell, J. (1983). When disaster strikes ... The Critical Incident Stress Debriefing process. *Journal of the Emergency Medical Services, 8,* 36–39.

Mitchell, J.T. (1986). *Critical Incident Stress Debriefing workshop.* Richmond, VA.

Quintyn, L., De Winne, J., & Hodgkinson, P.E. (1990). The Zeebrugge disaster III: The disaster victim identification team — procedures and psychological support. *Disaster Management, 2,* 128–130.

Raphael, B. (1986). *When disaster strikes.* London: Hutchinson.

Shephard, M., & Hodgkinson, P. (in press) *Journal of Traumatic Stress.*

Short, P. (1979). Victims and helpers. In R. Heathcote & B. Tong (Eds.), *Natural hazards in Australia.* Canberra: Australian Academy of Science.

Taylor, A. (1983). *Hidden victims and the human side of disasters.* UNDRO News. March/April, 6–12.

Taylor, A., & Frazer, A. (1982). The stress of post-disaster body handling and victim identification work. *Journal of Human Stress, 8,* 4–12.

Wilkinson, C.B. (1983). Aftermath of a disaster: The collapse of the Hyatt Regency Hotel skywalks. *American Journal of Psychiatry, 140,* 1134–1139.

Developing Psychological Support Programs in Emergency Service Agencies

CHAPTER FIVE

Robyn Robinson

EMERGENCY service work has long been regarded as stressful. It combines general job stress (present to varying degrees in all occupations), shift work with its known negative effects on sleep and health (Cox, 1981; Everly & Feldman, 1985), and exposure to traumatic situations. Workers may witness gruesome sights, large-scale disasters and the intense suffering of human beings. They are frequently responsible for the lives and well-being of others, and may have their own safety threatened. Occasionally emergency service workers lose their lives protecting or rescuing members of the public.

Workers who regularly experience traumatic situations do not necessarily get used to them. For example, repeated exposure to loss of life on the roads may not lessen the emergency service worker's sense of anger, sadness or empathy for family members on each and every occasion. Familiarity does not necessarily dull a person's reactions or emotions. Professional competence in coping with these kinds of situations does not protect the worker from the consequences of caring for others.

The development of support programs in Australia

Attention has been given to the effects of trauma on emergency service workers in Australia since the late 1980s, and as a result many programs of psychological support have been introduced to assist staff and their families. The impetus for this development derived from the work of Dr Jeffrey Mitchell who systematised a debriefing procedure for assisting emergency service staff to deal with traumatic or critical incidents (Mitchell, 1983; Mitchell & Bray, 1990). Debriefing involves gathering staff together after a traumatic incident and, in a supportive, confidential forum, discussing the impact of the situation on them and how they are coping.

Mitchell's method and general approach was widely adopted by Australian emergency services following his visits to Australia in 1986 and 1988. Similar developments also occurred about this time in Canada and Norway.

At the same time, the Mitchell model, as it came to be known, was adopted by, and adapted to, many other occupational groups and work settings such as hospitals, defence force services, institutes of correction, banks, government education and welfare departments, industries with potential for industrial accidents (e.g. mines) and even recreational groups, such as parachuting clubs.

Australia is still in the process of developing Mitchell's model and adapting it to circumstances which are specific to this country. For example, the role of peer support personnel — specially trained emergency service workers — has been expanded so that peers often provide front-line counselling support to colleagues. This development suits our outback geography, with its sparse resources of professional counsellors.

Implementing support programs in this country has not always been easy. Opinions persist that workers who react to traumatic events are psychologically weak and unsuitable for the job; that talking makes people 'soft', and that these 'new support programs' were not needed before and are not needed now (Lawler et al., 1990). These attitudes can make it difficult for programs to be accepted and used. Ongoing educational campaigns are needed in order to enlighten staff and encourage some to develop a more tolerant attitude — especially to those workers who seek peer or professional counselling assistance.

Despite the challenges outlined above, the introduction of support services in Australian emergency services has been very rapid. Within three years of Mitchell's first visit in 1986, nearly every emergency service in Australia had established at least a rudimentary debriefing/peer support program.

Why have psychological support programs?

The main rationale for work-based psychological support programs derives from the understanding that all human beings can be affected by exposure to

traumatic events. While employment selection and post-employment training may assist employees to cope with traumatic situations, it is an essentially
human condition that even the most skilled and experienced employee can
be affected by or have a reaction to a particular traumatic event. These
reactions are seen as a normal response to an abnormal event (Mitchell &
Bray, 1990). If a work place exposes an employee to trauma, then that organisation has a responsibility to undertake both preventive and remedial
measures to assist the worker.

The second rationale for psychological support programs is economic.
Money is lost through sick leave, early retirement, staff replacement, and
training of new staff. Further, stressed staff who remain at work may show
low morale or anger, and disrupt others. There may be personal costs in
terms of family dysfunction, anxiety, depression, or alcohol or other drug
abuse, which in turn will become hidden costs to the organisation.

Cost-benefit studies on support programs are being developed. These
will test the commonsense view that happy, healthy employees work more
productively and stay in the workplace longer than their more stressed
colleagues.

What are traumatic situations?

Mitchell and Bray (1990) have defined critical incidents as 'any event which
has a stressful impact sufficient enough to overwhelm the usually effective
coping skills of either an individual or a group' (p. 5). Such an incident can
cause an acute stress reaction experienced immediately or some time after
the incident. It may or may not develop into patterns of symptoms which
can be classified as Posttraumatic Stress Disorder (PTSD; American
Psychiatric Association, 1980).

The following events are identified by emergency service workers as
stressful (Robinson, 1984, 1993):

- death or severe mutilation of children
- death of any person
- dealing with relatives of deceased or injured persons
- death or serious injury of a colleague in the line of duty
- suicide of a colleague
- threats to the life or safety of a worker or their colleagues
- dealing with body parts
- attending disasters
- responsibility for the lives or well-being of others
- multiple casualty incidents
- dealing with situations where the victim is known to the worker or
  reminds him/her of a loved one

Some incidents are fairly readily recognised as traumatic, whereas others may be more subtle but no less disturbing. For example, seeing the distress of staff can itself be traumatic. Further, workers do not have to be present at a traumatic event to be affected by it. For example, communications staff who have dispatched crews to a dangerous situation may be concerned for those crews. Even when the crews are known to be safe, the concern which was aroused may remain. Off-duty staff may feel distressed that they were not there during a major event. All of these groups need to be considered in planning support services after a critical incident.

When assessing the seriousness of a critical incident, it is important to consider the size of the event, the intensity of the situation, its duration over time, the number of workers involved, and the uniqueness of the event. Careful assessment may help in understanding the aspects of a situation which workers found unusual or difficult.

Response to an event will also be influenced by idiosyncratic and histori-cal factors. Traumatic situations often cause a person to recall memories of a prior traumatic experience. While the reasons for this phenomenon are not entirely clear, there is an argument that significant experiences (trauma, grief, etc.) are stored in physical proximity in the brain and can be reactivated by a similar new experience (Eye movement desensitisation and reprocessing: Shapiro, 1989). Thus any work situation may cause a worker to recall either a similar prior work experience or a personal memory (e.g., attending the death of a child when the worker has lost his or her own child).

Peer support

Peer support personnel have played a unique role in Australian work support programs. Traditionally, psychological support in the workplace has been provided by professional clinicians. However, the emergency services programs in Australia and overseas have have offered support to employees by both professional clinicians (such as psychologists and social workers) and peers or specially trained emergency service workers (such as ambulance officers, firefighters and police officers) (Robinson & Murdoch, 1990).

Peer support programs began in public service organisations in Chicago in 1955, as a way of dealing with employees with alcohol and drug problems. The concept was developed further by emergency service organisations; initially by the Los Angeles Police Department which developed a program in 1981 following a shooting incident. Peers were integral to the debriefing procedure introduced by Mitchell, though their role centred on participation in debrief-ings. In Australia, in the late 1980s and early 1990s, that peer role was expanded to encompass one-on-one counselling as well as group interventions.

The value of peer involvement probably comes from the fact that peers have experienced similar situations to their troubled colleagues and so can readily understand that person's plight. Importantly, they are perceived by the worker in that light and to be people who have 'been there'. While research is needed in order to gain a better psychological understanding of the importance of peers, preliminary findings indicate that talking to others who understand is very therapeutic (Robinson & Mitchell, 1993).

Peer programs emphasise the preventive aspect of such programs. Peers are on site and can often identify problems in the early stages. Less stigma may be attached to discussing problems with peers than professional clinicians, and the problem-solving process is more likely to be seen as 'talking' rather than counselling.

Since most peer support programs work on a voluntary basis, they are an extremely cost-effective way of managing occupational health. However they are not cost-free, and training and supervision of peers needs to be maintained at all times.

Peers can undertake many functions:

- to provide basic counselling to staff
- to refer staff, where appropriate, to professional clinicians
- to provide information to fellow employees on stress, trauma and coping
- to form debriefing teams with professional clinicians to assist staff following a major incident

Selection of peers is usually one of the most difficult aspects of peer programs. It is often the responsibility of a specially formed committee comprising the most senior peer support person, the most senior professional clinician, and sometimes a professional clinician who is independent of the particular organisation but knowledgeable about emergency service peer programs.

Selection criteria should be well advertised before the process begins. Criteria should include clinical skills (such as good listening skills, good communication skills, desire to help people, and capacity to work collaboratively with professional clinicians) and field credibility (in particular, perceived ability to maintain confidentiality). Peers need to be acceptable to their own colleagues and judged as being trustworthy.

The selection process may begin with written applications in response to a call for interest with applicants required to supply names of referees (who are contacted by the selection committee). Applicants may be interviewed as well.

The subsequent training programs may vary in length but are usually at least three days long and cover topics such as critical incident stress, basic helping skills, stress, coping, crisis intervention, debriefing, defusing, spouse support programs, and helping the helper. Some applicants may leave the program after training if they or the clinicians deem them unsuitable for the role. In many programs, peers are appointed on a yearly basis and need to meet minimal requirements such as attendance at training updates.

Early peer programs were cautious about using 'unqualified' persons as counsellors. For example, the Royal Canadian Mounted Police program limited peer roles to 'listen and refer'. However, as programs have developed, it is my experience that emergency service peers are now recognised as being highly skilled in their roles and extremely responsible in referring colleagues to professional clinicians when appropriate. Nevertheless, it is important that peers work closely with clinicians who supervise on a regular basis. The ultimate responsibility for peer programs must lie with a competent and skilled professional clinician.

Peer programs are still in the formative stages in Australia. Most reports on development and progress come from papers presented at the series of conferences organised by professional groups with interest in this area, such as the Australasian Critical Incident Stress Association (ACISA). Undoubtedly, publications and program evaluation will be forthcoming in the years ahead. (For details of training programs see Los Angeles Fire Department, 1989; Robinson & Murdoch, 1990; Royal Canadian Mounted Police, 1989; Tunnecliffe & Roy, 1993.)

Components of support programs

Many of the current support programs in emergency services are made up of a variety of components. The earliest programs emphasised debriefing following major incidents: these circumstances were probably the easiest case to argue for. Nevertheless, workers in emergency services and other workplaces, may experience an accumulation of stress from several 'lower intensity' critical incidents, or traumatic stress may combine with general work stress. A recent survey of ambulance officers in Victoria identified most stress as accumulating from multiple sources and only 14 per cent from the experience of a single major incident (Robinson, 1993).

Debriefing major critical incidents is one piece of the occupational health jigsaw. If an organisation cannot implement a comprehensive program, then a multifaceted blueprint can be developed, and priorities assigned to components. Without this planning, mismanagement can occur. For example, it is inappropriate to apply debriefing, as it was originally conceived, to all stress problems in an organisation.

The central components of psychological support programs are given below.

EDUCATION

Most programs emphasise the role of education. Education can assist people to recognise stress and trauma in themselves as well as others. Employees can be encouraged to manage stress in its earliest stages and information can be given on how to access established support services. Also, education is a key preventive strategy which can reduce the problems associated with cumulative stress/trauma responses.

ONE-ON-ONE COUNSELLING

Employees should have access to one-on-one support, either from a professional clinician and/or a peer support person. Many organisations report that employees value rapid access to counselling (via pagers or a list of telephone numbers) and suggest that this be a 24-hour year-round service.

Where first-line response is provided by a peer team, back up by professional counsellors should also be available so that peers can check their initial assessment if they are unsure and refer quickly if necessary. Peers are not equipped, for example, to deal with staff with severe psychiatric problems or who become actively suicidal or homicidal.

A counselling system also needs to develop a protocol to facilitate immediate hospitalisation or protective care for workers in the event of an immediate threat to the worker's life, for example from suicide. Access to hospitals can be difficult, especially outside office hours or on public holidays. Contracts with particular hospitals may minimise delay in hospitalisation.

GROUP INTERVENTION FOLLOWING MAJOR INCIDENTS

A cluster of interventions has been developed by Mitchell and others (e.g. Mitchell & Bray, 1990). These are fully described elsewhere and include the following.

Defusing

Defusings are brief discussions held within eight hours of an incident. Involved personnel are gathered together and given the opportunity to share information, express initial reactions to the incident, and receive some education on how best to cope in the next 24 hours. Defusings may eliminate the need for a debriefing. Defusings are usually conducted by peers.

Debriefing

This is a problem-solving, educational group process lasting for two to three hours and ideally conducted 24–72 hours after a traumatic incident. Debriefing provides an opportunity for workers to share their experiences, consider the impact which the event has had and is having on them, and to examine ways of coping. Members of the group offer support to one another. Debriefings are conducted by a team of peers and clinicians.

Demobilisation

Following very large-scale incidents where staff have worked for exhaustive periods of time (sometimes days), they are brought together for some food, a short rest and 10 minutes' information on coping over the next 24 hours. This is a bridge between release from duty and returning home. It will always be followed by a debriefing at a later and more appropriate time. In most instances, professional clinicians conduct these sessions and deliver previously prepared information to workers.

Follow-up

All group interventions require follow-up of participants. Further debriefings may be held, some individuals may be referred for individual counselling or no further action may be taken.

Family support

Families of workers should not be neglected. Spouses and children are also affected by the critical incidents to which workers are exposed (Robinson & Mitchell, 1993). As well, spouses often seek information on how best to help their partner after a critical incident. Family support offers individual counselling and group debriefing, depending on the circumstances. Spouse support programs can take many forms. They may function as self-help groups or peer groups in which peers are trained in the same way as workplace peers.

Case study: Ambulance Service Victoria

Ambulance Service Victoria has a crisis counselling unit (established in 1986) with 24-hour access to clinical psychologists and a team of approximately 60 peer support personnel. This system was activated some years ago after a particularly distressing incident in which an off-duty ambulance officer and his wife were killed by a stolen car as they walked their dog late one night. The car went out of control and mounted the footpath, killing the couple instantly. The ambulance crew who attended the couple were from the same station where the deceased officer had been in charge.

The Service clinician was notified very shortly after the incident and, together with a peer support person, went immediately to the station where they talked to the attending crew for several hours.

The crew were particularly concerned that all 18 staff from their station be notified personally of the tragedy, and not hear it on the early morning news. It was therefore decided that a team of peers would contact the homes of staff between 7 a.m. and 8 a.m. that morning. The crew selected, from a total list of about 12, those peers who they wanted to assist in this task. Three peers were phoned, briefed and subsequently undertook the house calls. All staff then met at 12 noon for a brief information and support session (defusing). Relieving staff had already been organised so that rostered crews had a choice as to whether or not they wished to go on duty that day.

The clinician/peer team met together after the defusing for several hours to plan individual follow-up of people over the next few days, taking into account that some staff had been close personal friends of the deceased officer and his wife. The peers subsequently gave much support to this staff group over the three days leading up to the funeral. Staff were also reminded that they could access clinicians through the 24-hour ambulance crisis line.

After the funeral, two debriefings were held: one for the staff (to help them to prepare for the grieving ahead) and one for the spouses (to help them with their grief and also in coping with their partners). Individual contact with staff and their partners continued for many months as required.

The debriefing team also kept in contact with and supported one another, because it had been a difficult time for them too. Some of the peers had known the deceased, and therefore excluded themselves from active peer involvement, but remained in close contact with the team.

The partnership of clinicians and peers worked well. The clinicians maintained responsibility for the psychological aspects of interventions and timing considerations. The peers were essential in encouraging colleagues to talk about the situation and also in facilitating the necessary organisational changes such as rostering and relieving. It was indeed a team effort.

Organisational framework for support systems

Support programs in emergency services operate under a variety of organisational frameworks. These include:

- welfare or psychology departments, staffed with psychologists, social workers and/or welfare officers
- contracted counsellors such as industry counsellors; for example, Inter-Church Trade & Industry Mission (ITIM) or Employee Assistance Programs (EAPs)
- contracted debriefing services to manage critical incidents

Whereas in-house counsellors can gain a good knowledge of the workplace and its employees, employees may be concerned that counselling contacts are recorded on employees' files or reported to management. These counsellors may also experience a conflict of interest or division of loyalty between their employer (management) and employees.

External counsellors may be trusted to maintain client confidentiality and impartiality but they may have problems being truly accepted by an industry (especially by those industries with strong professional identity). Counsellors may also lack the influence to change policies within the organisation (e.g., to increase welfare for employees) or be found by management to provide insufficient feedback or accountability about the counselling program they provide.

The importance of counsellor impartiality and client confidentiality led the debriefing movement to initially advocate that the debriefing team (of peers and clinicians) remain relatively independent from the organisation. However, a recent development in Australian and Canadian psychiatric hospitals is the training of senior staff in conducting defusings following a critical incident. The on-duty senior staff member is responsible for this meeting and for assessing the need for further support. He or she may activate a debriefing team as a follow-up. Involving senior staff in critical incident management may raise concerns that management will judge employees' capacity to cope but this approach also involves senior management more closely into the handling of critical incidents and makes them more involved in the psychological welfare of employees. This direction is sure to generate debate and illustrates how Australia has pioneered establishing the most effective ways to provide support services in the workplace.

Steps for setting up a psychological support program

The following guidelines may be useful in setting up a support program within emergency service agencies.

1. Determine the need for the program and its support
An adequate number of management and field personnel must support the development of the program. Conduct awareness-raising sessions to inform all personnel about the nature and purpose of the program.

2. Determine policy and kind of service required
Policy needs to be developed and resources allocated; for example, the role of peer support and the balance between internal/external clinicians needs to be discussed. Call-out protocols must be developed and made known to all personnel, because in times of intense demand (when support services also are most likely to be needed) there can be competition for resources.

3. Establish potential peer and clinician members
A call of interest should be issued for people to be trained as peers. Some organisations have clinicians on staff or contracted to the organisation; if not, there can be a call of interest for assistance from external clinicians. Clinicians need to be selected and trained; do not assume that their general psychological training is sufficient preparation for working in the trauma area or with emergency services.

4. Conduct a training program and develop a team
It is important to train all team members together. The initial training (usually three to five consecutive days), is followed by regular update and review sessions (about four half-days or its equivalent per year). Many programs ask team members to serve on a yearly basis and review membership after this time.

5. Evaluate the program
Evaluation serves two purposes: (a) to improve the performance of team members and the general program following field feedback, and (b) to assess the value of the program as a measure of accountability to the funders, supporters of the program, and the recipients of its services. If possible, evaluation needs to be planned at the outset. Any records or means of obtaining feedback data must be sensitive to the issues of confidentiality. Information about the program can be collated and group data disseminated throughout the agency.

Summary

The last ten years have been exciting ones and have seen a vast development of support systems emerge within many workplaces, not only the emergency services. These programs now need to be evaluated carefully. Anecdotal information and early evaluation studies (Robinson & Mitchell, 1993) indicate that, at least in the emergency services, these programs have been widely accepted and are highly cost-effective to organisations. Many evaluation studies are now in progress or awaiting publication. They will add to our knowledge of these programs, guide our future directions and help us to understand how best to undertake program assessment in the years to come.

As organisations become more comfortable with the notion of psychological support following traumatic incidents, it will be possible to plan systematic enquiry into the effectiveness (or otherwise) of these interventions. To date, developments have mainly come from the field knowledge of clinicians and peers, often shared at the growing numbers of seminars and conferences on this topic. A research base will add to this very valuable pool of knowledge.

The emergency services can be particularly proud of the role they have played in promoting this movement. Much has been learnt and adapted to other work settings as a result of their pioneering efforts. Perhaps the most important message to be learned, however, is the commonness of response to trauma irrespective of occupation. In the end we are all, first and foremost, human beings.

References

American Psychiatric Association. (1987). *The diagnostic and statistical manual of mental disorders.* (3rd ed. rev.) Washington, DC: Author.

Cox, T. (1981). *Stress.* London: The Macmillan Press Ltd.

Everly, G., & Feldman, R. (1985). *Occupational health promotion.* Baltimore, MD: Chevron Publishing Co.

Lawler, G., Lidgard, C., Murdoch, P., Pittman, S., Roy, O., Smith, M., Westerink, J., & Wood, S. (1990, November). *CISD teams in Australia: The state of the art.* Paper presented at the Third International Conference on Managing Stress and Trauma in Emergency Services, Victoria.

Los Angeles Fire Department. (1989). *Peer support training manual.* Los Angeles, CA: Author

Mitchell, J. (1983). When disaster strikes: The critical incident stress debriefing process. *Journal of Emergency Medical Service, 8*(1), 36–39

Mitchell, J., & Bray, G. (1990). *Emergency services stress.* Englewood Cliffs, NJ: Prentice-Hall

Robinson, R. (1984). *Health and stress in ambulance services: Part I.* Melbourne: Social Biology Resources Centre.

Robinson, R. (1993). *Follow-up study of health and stress in Ambulance Service Victoria, Australia.* Melbourne: Victorian Ambulance Service Crisis Counselling Unit.

Robinson, R., & Mitchell, J. (1993). Evaluation of psychological debriefings. *Journal of Traumatic Stress, 3,* 367–382.

Robinson, R., & Murdoch, P. (1990). *Guidelines for establishing peer support programs in emergency services.* Melbourne: Waterwheel Press.

Royal Canadian Mounted Police. (1989). *Handbook for members assistance program referral agents in the Royal Canadian Mounted Police.* Canada: Author.

Shapiro, F. (1989). Eye movement desensitization: A new treatment for post-traumatic stress disorder. *Journal of Behaviour Therapy and Experimental Psychiatry, 20*(3), 211–217.

Tunnecliffe, M., & Roy, M. (1993). *Emergency support: A handbook for peer supporters.* Perth, WA: Bayside Books.

The Psychology of Working With Victims of Traumatic Accidents

CHAPTER SIX

David J. de L. Horne

RESEARCH into the psychological consequences of trauma has developed considerably since the late 1980s, and the more that is learned, the more complex the picture becomes. We now have substantial relevant reference works, for example, Figley (1985), Raphael (1986), and Wilson and Raphael (1993). This chapter focuses on practical and conceptual matters to take into account when contemplating how to assess and treat people who have been involved in accidents or disasters and who appear to be suffering from adverse, long-lasting psychological reactions.

There is no uniform consensus about what should be done for such people. Debate can become heated and the issues are complex. Important factors in such debates are the different orientations, experiences, expectations, knowledge, and theoretical assumptions of the professionals concerned. Complete agreement between clinicians, counsellors, researchers, and clients might seem to be an important aim, but would actually be counterproductive because healthy debate stimulates curiosity and increases efforts to more fully understand the nature of post-traumatic stress reactions. Some argument may be due to lack of consensus about operational definitions and a failure to listen to what others are actually saying. However, regardless of their differing theoretical orientations, most therapists who work with trauma victims recognise that any psychological intervention has to be highly, but appropriately, active, and involve, somewhere along the path to recovery, symbolic re-exposure (e.g. talking about, reviewing audio or videotapes, etc.) to the trauma-inducing stimuli or events. Certainly, valid arguments do then arise about how this should be done and what psychological mechanisms or processes are involved in the recovery process.

Asking the right questions

This chapter discusses the help that psychology can offer people who have experienced severe trauma, particularly when they first present to a busy hospital doctor or nurse, and asks and answers questions that are important in any discussion of the psychological aspects of the treatment of post-traumatic stress reactions. In spite of undoubted limitations, the definition of Posttraumatic Stress Disorder (PTSD) provided in the *Diagnostic and Statistical Manual of Mental Disorders* (DSM-III-R) of the American Psychiatric Association (1987), is useful:

> The person has experienced an event that is outside the range of usual human experience and that would be markedly distressing to almost anyone, eg. serious threat to one's life or physical integrity; serious threat or harm to one's children, spouse, or other close relatives and friends; sudden destruction of one's home or community; or seeing another person who has recently been or is being, seriously injured or killed as the result of an accident or physical violence. (p. 247)

But what constitutes an event that is 'outside the range of usual human experience'? The most crucial issue may be an individual's own perception of what has happened. For example, in a serious motor vehicle accident, is whether the victim had warning of the impending disaster and believed their life was about to be violently terminated a critical factor in the development of post-traumatic stress reactions? Research data is just not available to answer this kind of question, but it is important to detect the person 'at risk' after an accident.

PTSD: What is the extent and nature of the problem?

THE EXTENT OF THE PROBLEM

The medical practitioner, nurse, or social worker in a busy casualty department, outpatient clinic, community health centre, or general practice, has a real problem; namely, the number of patients seen within the time limits of these situations. Unless a presenting psychological problem is obvious it may well be overlooked. Physical injury often has an identifiable, tangible problem to focus upon. But, even then, there are physical disorders which health professionals have difficulty in dealing with effectively. Physical injuries associated with trauma include soft tissue damage, neck and back sprains, and minor head injuries — even these 'minor' injuries can have severe long-term repercussions. For example, Porter (1989) showed that

15–30 per cent of occupants of road vehicles involved in an accident initially reported neck sprain symptoms (he strongly argued against the use of the term 'whiplash injury' on the grounds it is not an accurate diagnostic term) but, somewhat later after the accident, this had risen to 60 per cent. Of this majority, 40 per cent were significantly disabled, with chronic pain, depression, and other psychological complaints, two years after the accident.

It is, of course much easier for both victim and helper to focus upon the physical injuries after an accident, and, in the short-term, this is entirely appropriate and saves lives. However, the significance of their physical injury to a victim is complex. For example, a young woman may cope with a permanent facial scar from an accident very differently compared to a man of the same age who already has scars from sporting injuries. This kind of response becomes even more complex when injuries are more covert and the sufferer seems superficially 'normal'. If a health worker mishandles such people, however inadvertently, the victims' feelings of anger and frustration can be increased so much that recovery may be hindered. For example, in this author's experience, people with a blow to the head but no skull fracture or overt evidence of brain damage are often told, after cursory investigation, that there is nothing wrong with them and they are fine. Yet they may present months later with memory and concentration problems, mood changes, lack of energy and so on.

Thus, one problem militating against quick and easy detection of those at risk is that the range of psychological complaints after being involved in a traumatic incident is considerable and the individual's pattern of symptoms may vary over time. Unfortunately, it does seem that the longer a person's problems continue without being detected, assessed and treated, the more complex and entrenched their presenting complaints may become.

Of course, some people (perhaps the majority) will cope very well without professional help. One American survey (Helzer, Robins, & McEvoy, 1987) found that the incidence of full-blown PTSD was very rare in the population as a whole, except among Vietnam veterans and, apart from this group, the only others reporting it were people who had been physically attacked or had experienced severe individual psychological trauma. Natural disasters accounted for no cases of PTSD. However, other psychological stress reaction symptoms did occur in about 15 per cent of those in this study who had experienced significant trauma. One important development is the realisation that major post-traumatic stress reactions do occur in a variety of people, such as women who have experienced rape, people who have been assaulted, burned, or involved in accidents at work or while travelling (e.g. Pilowsky, 1985).

Thus, at a conservative estimate, it could be said that at least 15 per cent of people involved in a major traumatic event will experience significant long-term psychological stress symptoms even when their physical injuries are relatively minor. Nothing like this percentage would appear to receive the help they merit at present.

THE NATURE OF THE PROBLEM

Disasters can be small, medium or large, and can also be local, national or international in their ramifications. People who have been involved in a large-scale disaster, such as a train or plane crash, or bushfire, and so on, are more likely to have societal resources mobilised to help them than are victims of a small-scale disaster, such as the majority of road accidents and personal assaults. A paradox is that it is the small, local disaster victim who most frequently presents to the busy clinician or health professional. Theirs is the kind of disaster that receives least attention, yet it is these victims who are disadvantaged psychologically. As one patient of mine, who had been in a car accident, said in the early stages of therapy, 'To the doctors and lawyers I am just another crash and bang case'. Basically, any person who has been involved in any disaster is a person at psychological risk.

What affects people's responses to disaster?

A disaster victim's own perception and interpretation of what happened is important. This will undoubtedly be influenced by such factors as their personality, prior experience of traumatic events (e.g. recent sudden death of close associates), whether they were alone or with others at the time, whether they felt they had an influence over the event or not, and so on. Thus, in order to provide a proper assessment and management program, more than just the medical aspects have to be heeded.

The sufferer is a member of society, as are all the health, legal and government professionals involved in 'helping' them. Therefore, the sufferer may be confused not just by their actual symptoms but because of the social system within which we all find ourselves. For this reason, even in the early stages of detection and management, we must acknowledge the significance that medical, legal, financial, and other social systems (such as family and work) have on the victim. These systems in themselves can either augment or ameliorate the victim's complaints. For example, a person who has experienced rejection and denial of the validity of their complaints and symptoms by an ill-informed and non-empathic doctor or lawyer will feel confused and angry. This will affect how they present to future professionals.

Much of the inappropriate treatment that does occur is usually due to professionals' lack of adequate knowledge and skills. Although formal instruction in psychology or behavioural science occurs in most medical, nursing and other health sciences courses, detailed information about extreme, abnormal psychological reactions, or even about the range of normal but disturbing reactions to trauma, is not widespread. For example, one general teaching hospital gives accident victims a list of symptoms that might occur after their discharge from hospital, but this list does not mention psychological reactions, such as phobic anxiety, panic, irritability, disturbed sleep, and depression. Yet, all of these are well-known responses to traumatic injury.

Working with trauma victims is not easy and dealing with them in a high-pressure outpatient setting is particularly difficult. A good example of how things can go wrong is history taking. With the best of intentions, each professional, upon first having contact with an accident or disaster victim, will almost certainly take a history. However, asking a person to go over a traumatic experience repeatedly can keep reminding them of it and even cause uncontrollable flashbacks. This incidental re-exposure can increase the victim's confusion and anger. Repeated exposure to traumatic stimuli, usually symbolic, is part of therapy, but this exposure is deliberate and controlled, accompanied by carefully planned help in learning to cope with the trauma and to deal constructively with the powerful emotions that arise in the therapy session.

Psychological and emotional support should also be provided for professionals working with traumatised clients or patients. Working with medical practitioners and nursing staff in general hospital settings, I have found that such emotional support is generally inadequate and unreliable. This can lead to frustration and anger, without staff realising why they are experiencing these feelings. In turn, this can lead to disturbing behaviours, such as bickering and arguing among the staff.

What should the busy doctor or nurse lookout for?

The first important thing is to recognise that any trauma victim, however minor their physical injuries, is at risk psychologically. Therefore, the patient must be encouraged to return for further assessment and help if those psychological symptoms occurring in the few weeks after the accident do not resolve themselves fairly quickly. Giving patients simple, factual information on what to do and where to go in this early stage of contact could well reduce long-term morbidity. For example, reassure someone who has been in a casualty department that it is fine to re-contact the hospital, or that a letter will be sent to their local doctor, and that they should feel comfortable about getting in touch if they have any queries.

Phobic anxiety is a very common, and often unrecognised, complaint after an accident or trauma. Thus, if a patient finds they are avoiding things they used to do without any difficulty they should be encouraged to seek help. Fortunately, many post-accident phobias (even severe ones) can be quite quickly and successfully treated using specific psychological interventions (either with or without adjunctive medication) (Horne, 1988, 1993).

Other psychological and psychiatric complaints are depression, sleep disturbance (including nightmares), memory and concentration difficulties, chronic pain, hyperalertness and excessive vigilance, avoidance of cuddling and lovemaking, feelings of irritability, being on 'a short fuse', and so forth. If any of these symptoms or complaints persist then referral for further help is warranted.

To summarise, the DSM-III-R criteria for PTSD (American Psychiatric Association, 1987) lists trauma-related psychological symptoms under three broad categories of symptoms. The first concerns the person re-experiencing the trauma in a variety of ways; for example, nightmares, flashbacks, and uncontrollable intrusive recollections. The second concerns the avoidance techniques used by the person. These are always maladaptive in the long term, although usually they bring an immediate sense of relief because they reduce the need for facing painful reality; for example, avoiding situations that trigger recollections of the event, blocking off all feelings (known as *psychic numbing*), and feeling detached and estranged from others. Another distressing symptom sometimes reported is the feeling of a foreshortened lifespan, or of premature ageing. The third group of symptoms concerns excessive arousal seen in sleep difficulties, poor concentration and memory, being hyperalert, vigilant, and easily startled.

ASSESSMENT BY THE FRONT-LINE PROFESSIONAL

To detect these psychological symptoms and problems, the patient has to be asked about them. Patients will not spontaneously raise these matters and, in most instances, they need permission and encouragement to talk in order to overcome their reticence to disclose information about which they may feel embarrassed, or ashamed. This can be a hard thing to do for any doctor or nurse who does not feel confident in their communication skills or their ability to cope with disturbing emotions, and they may feel out of their depth. In any case, under pressure, they may feel that there is no time for lengthy listening and discussion with a patient. Unfortunately, failure at this stage can increase the patient's morbidity and either more therapy will eventually be needed or the patient will opt out and become a chronic, untreatable case. Skilled questioning and listening is not actually time consuming, especially if the questioner is aware of resources to which the patient can be appropriately referred after initial assessment. But it does require professionals to have some insight into their own emotions and to have developed a healthy ability to cope with stress. As mentioned above, staff denial, or lack of awareness, of their own emotional reactions to stress and trauma, can lead them to inappropriate and damaging behaviours.

Most important, at this stage, is accepting the validity of the patient's complaint, regardless of what theories or speculations might be held about the reasons for them. All people involved in traumatic incidents are likely to experience at least short-term mental, emotional, and physical complaints. Patients must be reassured that the psychological symptoms they are experiencing are an understandable and normal reaction to the trauma and that help is available through appropriate counselling and therapy. Often these people feel they are going insane, so this reassurance is important at an early stage. As well, they may feel their complaint is not 'a real one' and is 'all in their mind'. They may even have been told this by someone they perceive as being in authority, such as another doctor or nurse.

The patient with post-traumatic psychological symptoms may require the services of more than one specialist. In some places, specialist psychological trauma clinics, centres or services have been developed, but for most hospitals and clinics such specialist resources are not readily available. The question then becomes: to whom should a further referral be made? At this stage it is appropriate to consider the next question.

What psychological assessment is useful before therapy should commence?

The first requirement to optimise a patient's response to subsequent treatment will probably be further, more refined assessment than has been possible so far. There can be dangers in proceeding with therapy prior to detailed assessment being carried out. For example, therapeutic attention might be focused quickly on obvious phobic anxiety without realising that the major problem is depression, panic disorder, or fully developed PTSD. These raise more complex treatment issues, often including dealing with grief reactions. If such issues are not dealt with effectively, progress in therapy can be hindered.

All people with disturbed psychological reactions to trauma are confused; their safe and predictable world has been shattered, at least temporarily. This confusion should not be aggravated by the treatment they receive from the system. Thus, whatever the role of the multiple professions dealing with a trauma patient, the need for coordination between them is crucial. Unfortunately, the legal system (with its emphasis upon the adversarial method of establishing truth), the insurance implications of disaster-induced psychological trauma, and the complexity of the health services system(s), means it is often difficult to achieve the desired degree of communication and coordination between the relevant professionals.

Good arguments can be made for having one person as the main coordinator and reference point for the patient to turn to. This person adopts a form of advocacy-counsellor role, in addition to their own particular professional expertise. As a clinical psychologist, I have found this role to be quite crucial for certain patients, in order to collate all the investigations and reports carried out so far in their case, to explain the processes of the systems operating in society, to answer their queries (if possible), and to plan further assessment and therapy.

Patients who present for psychological help are most usually referred by a medical practitioner who requests further assessment, and, often, the provision of relevant psychological therapy. However, a lawyer may also make a referral for a psychological report for court purposes. Some lawyers are occasionally so concerned about their client's mental state, that they ask if help can be made available as well.

Before embarking upon more refined psychological assessment using formal psychological tests, etc., it is best to conduct a structured, open-ended interview over one or two sessions (one-and-a-half to two hours total duration). Giving patients permission to talk and to be listened to, while accepting their version of what has happened to them without necessarily agreeing with their interpretations or attributions of causes, establishes trust and rapport. Thus, hearing them out without passing judgement is the first step to more intensive psychological assessment and therapy.

A course of formal psychological testing may follow, possibly with a further referral for additional physical investigations, for example, a thorough neurological examination, perhaps including a CAT scan of the brain. Explain to patients the rationale for each investigation, and to significant others who come along to the consultation (e.g. spouse, offspring, etc.). Encourage questions about the explanations and rationale, both to verify that the information has been comprehended and to discuss and allay any misconceptions and anxieties.

THE USE OF PSYCHOLOGICAL TESTS

Psychological tests can serve at least two important functions in the overall treatment and management of trauma patients. Firstly, they clearly specify the nature of the psychological problems resulting from trauma, allowing the diagnosis to be refined, and they provide data upon which to make decisions about the kind of therapy required.

A specific aspect of psychological assessment that should be mentioned here is *neuropsychological investigation*. When there are significant changes in intellectual functions and/or in mood, and there is indication of some head trauma, even of a minor nature, neuropsychological investigation can clarify the acquired deficits and indicate which cognitive (perception, memory, learning and thinking) functions remain unimpaired. Where there is obvious head injury and brain damage, such assessment is crucial both for diagnostic purposes and also for providing a baseline for comparison over time. At present, neuropsychological investigations are more sophisticated for cognitive and intellectual functions than they are for detecting changes to emotions and personality. However, frontal lobe damage is a problem for quite a number of road accident victims and neuropsychological testing can be effective in evaluating frontal lobe dysfunction that may not be clinically overtly apparent. (e.g. Walsh, 1978).

The second purpose of psychological tests is to provide some baseline measures of psychological functions such as the patient's cognitions (thoughts), certain actual behaviours (e.g. avoidance reactions), and associated feelings. These measures can be repeated at various points during treatment and serve to provide some reasonably objective feedback about therapeutic progress, or the lack of it. Such measures can be in the form of standardised psychological tests or individually tailored measures. Specific questionnaires are now available for assessing and evaluating the reactions of people who have experienced trauma, for example, the Impact of Event Scale (Horowitz, Wilner, & Alvarez, 1979). For personalised measures, behaviour checklists are useful for quantifying the frequency and setting of particular behaviours and can be completed by patients themselves or by prepared observers (e.g. spouse), or by a combination of both. Various forms of analogue scales are also useful as simple, robust measures of degrees of distress, anxiety, etc. (e.g. McCormack, Horne, & Sheather 1988). Generally, patients rate themselves by placing a mark along a 100 mm line which runs between extremes, for example, a mark at 0 mm denotes 'no anxiety at all', while a mark at 100 mm denotes 'the worst anxiety attack I can imagine'. Alternatively, the patient may simply learn to rate a particular feeling state with a number from 0 to 10 or, 0 to 100.

WHAT HAPPENS NEXT?

Once a thorough psychological assessment is completed, sensible formulations can be made about treatment requirements. These may include medication from a psychiatrist, or other medical practitioner; or rehabilitation, including physiotherapy, occupational therapy, etc. However, psychologists have particular skills to offer which can either be used as the primary therapy or as complementary treatment, depending upon the particular case.

The topic of counselling and psychological treatment is, of course, an enormous area and the following section highlights some important principles of therapy and provides one or two illustrative clinical vignettes.

What psychological interventions are available and appropriate?

LEVELS OF INTERVENTION

Without debating what counselling and therapy are, it is useful to be aware of their different levels of intervention. Generally, counselling is a more universal phenomenon than therapy and involves a wider range of both practitioners and clients. At a very basic level, counselling involves providing accurate and appropriate information that will help someone solve a problem; in this case, the person who has been in a bad accident or disaster and is experiencing post-traumatic reactions. Counselling skills involve both knowing how to obtain reliable information from the patient (often referred to as 'empathic' listening skills) and how to present information in a form that makes sense and is appreciated by the patient. In addition, some simple interventions may be used, such as a range of relaxation techniques, to help the sufferer cope better. However, counselling is limited in the extent and the depth of its intervention. Psychological therapy, often referred to as *psychotherapy*, goes much further in both the analysis of the sufferer's (patient's) problems and in the range of interventions used. Therapy tends to go beyond the surface presentation of the problem and involves intensive intervention over time.

PHOBIC ANXIETY

A good example of intervention beyond counselling is given below in a case study of phobic anxiety — perhaps the most common post-traumatic stress reaction response. A phobia is an irrational anxiety, accompanied by an unrealistic perception of the probability of danger of some event, situation, or object in the environment, with a consequent avoidance of that thing. For example, after a motor vehicle accident many people apparently experience varying degrees of phobic anxiety (Mayou, 1992). One example of a phobic reaction to a road accident is feeling very tense, even panicky, when going near the site of the accident and going to great lengths to avoid ever going past the site, even if that means travelling via an intersection that is actually more dangerous than the location of the accident. Other examples are avoiding all travel by car on wet roads because the accident happened on a wet day, or refusing to travel in the model of car that was involved in the accident. For most people, these phobias are relatively mild and have few adverse social and personal consequences. Indeed, some degree of post-accident phobic anxiety may make the victims drive more carefully in the future (Mayou, Simkin, & Threlfall, 1991). However, in some cases the phobic anxiety becomes so severe that the person's ability to go out or socialise is incapacitated.

Mrs. B.L., 34, was the driver of a car involved in a night-time head-on collision. Miraculously, no-one was seriously injured. The driver of the other car admitted to being on the wrong side of the road. Both cars were wrecked beyond repair.

By the time Mrs. B.L. was referred for treatment by her local doctor it was 17 months after the accident and she complained of the following symptoms:

1. Hyperalertness whenever in a car and more difficulty in driving than in being driven by her husband (before the accident she had thoroughly enjoyed both driving and looking after her own car).

2. Always tensing involuntarily at oncoming headlamps.

3. Loss of interest in cars but able to drive herself to and from the local railway station in order to go to work.

4. Some intermittent depression after the accident had resolved. Her sleep, appetite, energy, concentration, memory, and relationships were all normal.

Her treatment comprised six 45–60 minute sessions over a five-month period. The main therapeutic interventions were:

1. Self-monitoring of anxiety levels associated with imagined and real driving situations by rating herself on a 0 to 100 analogue scale of experienced anxiety (sometimes known as using a *fear thermometer* or *subjective units of distress*).

2. Training in relaxation, using guided imagery (floating on a small raft in clear tropical water, on an island with white sand and palm trees).

3. *Systematic desensitisation* to the phobic anxiety using the acquired relaxation skill to both dampen down general levels of anxiety-associated arousal and as a counteractive response to anxiety, specifically associated with imagined and real exposure to car travel scenes.

The results for this particular case are summarised in Table 6.1. What this meant in real-life was that she could drive a car, or comfortably be a passenger, and travel anywhere without being constantly reminded of the accident.

TABLE 6.1
Results of therapy using guided imagery in relaxation and systematic desensitisation for Mrs B.L.

Rank Ordered Car Travel Phobia Scenes	Subjective Units of Distress (0–100) Pre-therapy	Post-therapy
1 Travelling to parents' place by car (a two-hour journey including passing through the centre of Melbourne)	90	0
2 Travelling to a favourite seaside resort 70 kilometres away	80	10
3 Night-driving in rain	70	10
4 Shopping centre car park	60	0
5 Going through a local, five-road intersection	50	0
6 Travelling to and from her local station	40	0
7 Travelling to local shops	30	0
8 Driving to sister-in-law's	20	0
9 Reversing out of home driveway	10	0

From my own experience with road accident victims, severe phobic reactions are often inadequately detected and treated. As a result many people probably suffer quite unnecessarily over a number of years. Severe phobic anxiety, especially when not accompanied by other significant psychiatric problems such as depression, can respond rapidly (within six to nine sessions) to psychological intervention using such techniques as systematic desensitisation, as illustrated in this case.

It is perhaps pertinent to mention here a new form of psychological treatment that purports to produce rapid desensitisation to traumatic experiences. It is known as eye movement desensitisation and reprocessing (EMDR), a technique developed in the USA that has become rather popular with a number of psychiatrists and psychologists in a range of countries, including Australia. In simple terms, it involves asking a patient to bring a memory or image of a traumatic event into their mind and then to label and focus on the emotions associated with the experience while being required to move their eyes rapidly from side-to-side. It is argued that this quickly reduces the hyperarousal and disturbing emotions associated with the memory (Shapiro, 1991) but, as yet, the evidence for its effectiveness is largely anecdotal and the underlying mechanisms for its purported effectiveness remain unknown.

PANIC ATTACKS

Panic attacks are commonly seen as a post-traumatic stress response. They need to be dealt with early on because if they continue, patients adopt maladaptive avoidance techniques. Certainly, some kinds of medication do seem to reduce panic symptoms but recently developed *cognitive therapy* psychological intervention can be equally as effective. Since many people prefer not to take medication, it is worth using a cognitive intervention first (e.g. Clark, 1986). Basically, this involves helping the patient understand the nature of their panic attack and learn not to misattribute its significance. In other words, they learn to recognise that their frightening symptoms do not indicate a heart attack or major physical illness, and they learn not to hyperventilate and that if they ride out the panic attack the symptoms will go away, with the consequent return of feelings of being in control.

OTHER PROBLEMS

Sophisticated psychological interventions have a major role in dealing with chronic pain (Peck, 1982); sleep disorders, especially nightmares; mood irritability and anger control; and concentration and memory difficulties. The following case study illustrates some further interventions, specifically anger management.

This patient was a 33-year-old married man with two daughters (aged 6 and 9 years). He had been involved in a motorcycle accident, resulting in severe bruising to his neck, shoulders and back and in a large wound to his right leg, requiring hospital treatment. He was referred 18 months after the accident suffering from a number of psychological symptoms that could be directly attributed to his traumatic experience. He had marked phobic anxiety and he was also depressed and irritable, and prone to uncontrollable acts of violence against his family. This behaviour had not existed at all before the accident and was causing him great distress. He was confused and overwhelmed by it and always regretted his actions after the event. Nevertheless, it was having severe effects on his family, with a breakdown in family relationships appearing imminent because his wife was seriously considering leaving him.

Treatment of this particular aspect of his problems was urgent, so he and his wife were seen together. The nature of his behaviour changes was discussed openly and ideas about what could be done explored. His wife was very cooperative and treatment was highly successful. Specifically, he was instructed to keep a diary of his feelings of anger and to record when and where they occurred in order to see if he could detect any early signs (feelings) that he was building up to an aggressive outburst. He had thought they came 'out-of-the-blue', but his self-monitoring showed this was not the case. There were definite periods in the day when he was more prone to them, for example, on arriving home from work. He was also taught relaxation, using progressive muscle and guided imagery techniques, and encouraged to use this early in the day to prevent tension building up. After a two-week baseline of self-monitoring his anger, which led to him successfully detecting early warning signs, he was instructed to tell his wife and children if he felt an anger outburst was imminent and to immediately remove himself from the situation, for example, to go into the garden for 'time-out'. As soon as he calmed down he had to return and resume communication with his family. This was important because it prevented avoidance habits developing. This strategy worked extremely well and within three weeks the problems with anger outbursts had gone and never again recurred. He was followed up one year after treatment had finished and was going very well. He continued to successfully manage his residual psychological symptoms, using the coping skills he had learned during therapy.

Intrusive thoughts, with associated feelings of uncontrollability, are also an important aspect of reaction to trauma. Compulsive, uncontrollable flashbacks, images, and nightmares can be extremely distressing. Sufferers often work out complex techniques for avoiding these intrusions which are nearly always, ultimately, unsuccessful. Nightmares can be treated with night sedatives and in the short-term these can help patients sleep, but they do not prevent nightmares. Sometimes sufferers are afraid to tell others about the nightmares, intrusive thoughts, or hallucinations they have, for fear of appearing ridiculous, mad or insane, or burdening others.

One patient reported being confronted with a vision of the face of the young woman driver whom he had seen seconds before she ran into his stationary truck while she was chatting away to a friend in her car and driving on the wrong side of an otherwise deserted road, and immediately after the accident when he tried to rescue the two women. When he descended from his truck, despite multiple injuries to his right leg and back, and went to the wrecked car, he was confronted with sight of the decapitated young woman driver with pretty blonde hair, whose eyes were still open. He subsequently alternated between closing-up and refusing to talk about this experience (he felt very numb and cold inside), to compulsively talking about it to his wife but failing to be soothed or reassured by her attention.

Treatment was complex but eventually successful. Two key elements in its success were obtaining police photographs of the accident and his ability to return to the scene of the accident without being overwhelmed by dread. This could only be achieved after many hours of preparation involving discussion; training in relaxation to dampen hyperarousal; encouraging participation in normal life events, such as his son's soccer club; and allowing him to talk about his visual hallucination without feeling he would be labelled as 'mad' or 'crazy'. Eventually, he was able to resume truck driving and lead a normal life.

One of the key elements to successful therapy in trauma does seem to be the re-exposure of the sufferer to the traumatic event in a way that is controlled and allows the development of new, more adaptive ways of coping without the use of denial or avoidance.

This can be an extraordinarily difficult, demanding and time-consuming process for both patient and therapist. As a general rule, the more the intrusive thoughts and images can be made explicit and externalised, the easier they can be dealt with. Thus, by encouraging the patient to deliberately focus on the image of the dead young woman in therapy, and to allow himself to feel his sadness and anger while being in control, gradually decreased both the frequency and intensity of the image. This process of exposure to the trauma also allowed him to develop a more constructive framework within which to interpret what had happened to him.

Conclusion

Questions concerning 'why me?' and one's own inevitable mortality are important themes in trauma therapy. These themes are pertinent to both therapist and victim. What is heartening is that psychological assessment and intervention does appear to be becoming more clinically sensitive and effective. It is hoped that this chapter has demonstrated this and that it has proved to be informative and helpful through offering some practical ideas and strategies for those busy professionals who are not experts in the psychology of trauma but who do from time to time, meet and have to deal with traumatised clients and patients.

References

American Psychiatric Association (1987). *Diagnostic and statistical manual of mental disorders* (3rd ed. rev.). Washington DC: Author.

Clark, D.M. (1986). A cognitive approach to panic. *Behaviour Research and Therapy, 24*, 461–479.

Figley, C.R. (Ed.). (1985). *Trauma and its wake: The study and treatment of Post-Traumatic Stress Disorder*. New York: Brunner/Mazel.

Helzer, J.E., Robins, L.N., & McEvoy, L. (1987). Post-Traumatic Stress Disorder in the general population. *The New England Journal of Medicine, 317*, 1630–1634.

Horne, D.J. de L. (1988). Post-Traumatic Stress Disorder: Unresolved stress. *Patient Management, 11*(2), 113–124.

Horne, D.J. de L. (1993). Traumatic stress reactions to motor vehicle accidents. In J.P. Wilson & B. Raphael (Eds.), *The international handbook of traumatic stress syndromes*. New York: Plenum Press.

Horowitz, M.J., Wilner, N., & Alvarez, W. (1979). Impact of Event Scale: A measure of subjective stress. *Psychosomatic Medicine, 41*, 209–219.

McCormack, H.M., Horne, D.J. de L., & Sheather, S. (1988). Clinical applications of visual analogue scales: A critical review. *Psychological Medicine, 18*, 1007–1019.

Mayou, R. (1992). Psychiatric aspects of road traffic accidents. *International Review of Psychiatry, 4*, 45–54.

Mayou, R., Simkin, S., & Threlfall, J. (1991). The effects of road traffic accidents on driving behaviour. *Injury, 22*, 365–368.

Peck, C. (1982). *Controlling chronic pain.* Sydney: Fontana.

Pilowsky, I. (1985). Cryptotrauma and "accident neurosis". *British Journal of Psychiatry, 147*, 310–311.

Porter, K.M. (1989). Neck sprains after car accidents: A common cause of long term disability. *British Medical Journal, 298*, 973–974.

Raphael, B. (1986). *When disaster strikes.* London: Century Hutchinson

Shapiro, F. (1991). Eye movement desensitization and reprocessing procedure: From EMD to EMD/R — a new treatment model for anxiety and related trauma. *The Behaviour Therapist, 12*, 133–135

Walsh, K.W. (1978). *Neuropsychology: A clinical approach.* Edinburgh: Churchill Livingstone.

Wilson, J.P., & Raphael, B. (Eds.). (1993). *The international handbook of traumatic stress syndromes.* New York: Plenum Press.

The Impact of Major Events on Children

CHAPTER SEVEN

Ruth Wraith

THE media often report disasters and traumatic events in terms of physical destruction, financial consequences, and the number of people killed or injured. While these are the immediate and obviously devastating impacts, other consequences of the disaster can have subtle, intense, and frequently long-term negative effects on individuals, be they children or adults; on families as a unit; and on the communities in which people live. This chapter is about the impact of traumatic events on children.

Less than a decade ago, the professional health and welfare communities took little interest in the impact of psychological and developmentally damaging experiences on children. These experiences may be as diverse as being witness to assault, murder, or accidental death; or direct experience of actual or perceived life threats from abuse, illness or medical treatment, disaster or other social upheaval; or the sudden death of a significant other such as a parent or sibling.

As recently as 1987 the *Diagnostic Statistical Manual of Mental Disorders* (DSM-III-R) of the American Psychiatric Association (1987) referred for the first time to Posttraumatic Stress Disorder (PTSD) symptom manifestation in children. We are only now recognising the impact of trauma on the neuro-biological, psychological, cognitive, and social functioning of children. (Pynoos, 1990, 1992).

While their responses to trauma may be similar to an adult's, children's development, age-related needs, and levels of maturity make the impact of trauma qualitatively different for them. Consequently there are specific requirements for management and treatment of the trauma reaction in children.

The following vignette illustrates the responses of a child to a major incident.

CASE STUDY ONE At the time of a bushfire, Michael was almost five years old. He was the youngest of four children of a busy and absent father and an equally busy, highly organised, and community-minded mother. The family were trapped by the fire and had to flee, fearing for their lives. Their home was one of the few not burned down in a vast area of almost total destruction. A few weeks prior to the fire, Michael had started primary school. Three years after the fire, the mother made contact, wondering if an appointment could be made for Michael because he was failing at school, experiencing severe peer problems, and was clingy in his relations with her. The mother presented with these problems at a time when the father had lost his job. On assessment, Michael presented as an intellectually competent boy who, in his play, communicated that he experienced his world as potentially overwhelming and destructive and that he was helpless in the face of it. In treatment, two major issues emerged. Michael had not been able to successfully negotiate separation issues from his mother at the time of school entry because of his overwhelming fear, based in the reality of the fire experience, of dangers in the outside world away from home and mother. These combined with a pre-existing vulnerability about separation. His experience of the fire, and the accompanying fears, had not been worked through to become integrated into his internal world and so interfered with his ongoing tasks of independence, development of social skills, and engagement in intellectual activities.

Children, including young infants, are sensitive to the environment around them, react to it, and are dependent on it for physical and psychological survival and growth. The environment is the nurturing cocoon of the young child and if it is disrupted or compromised and consequently is not able to meet the needs of the child there will be an impact on the child. Therefore, an incident causing adverse effects upon the emotional, psychological and physical environments of the child has the potential to cause negative changes within the child. This is particularly the case if key people, particularly the parents or other primary care givers who form the child's cocoon are traumatised. The cocoon of protection and nurturance becomes threatened and the child is placed in a situation of psychological and developmental risk.

These reactions give the lie to a number of myths, frequently entrenched in cultural attitudes, about children's reactions to trauma.

Myths about the responses of children to trauma

Wraith and Gordon (1987) described the myths which abound, even among professional people and workers in children's services, about the impact of major incidents on children.

An implication in the mythology, which is also overtly stated, is that children do not need assistance integrating their experiences, nor do they need assistance with their recovery process following trauma and major incidents. The following discussion shows that the existing mythology is incorrect.

- *'Children are too young to be aware of or
appreciate what is going on around them.'*

This myth applies particularly to pre-verbal and pre-school children: that if a child is too young to talk about an experience, or to fully comprehend significant factors (as identified by adults), the experience does not have an impact upon them. It is often assumed that cognitive immaturity provides an immutable barrier of protection.

Even though children may not understand the total context of what is happening to them and around them, they are nonetheless sensitive to and aware of changes in their world and respond to changes in significant people, to changes in the familiar environment, to changes in routine, and to changes in the emotional climate. Research evidence is accumulating which supports clinical experience that parents' attitudes, and emotional and psychological responses to disaster, influence their children's understanding of the experience and their responses to it. McFarlane (1987) found that separation from parents in the days immediately after the Ash Wednesday fires, continuing maternal preoccupation with the disaster and changed family functioning were more powerful determinants of post-traumatic phenomena in the children than were exposure to the disaster or the losses sustained.

Pre-school children are cognitively and socially mature enough to need some understanding of their world. Because their knowledge is limited, their capacity for logical thinking is immature, and because at this age their imagination is very active, they will frequently construct their own idiosyncratic explanations to make sense of their confusing world. Relying on imagination to interpret their environment and to ascertain their own place in it can lead children to hold wildly inaccurate and often disturbing beliefs. For example, children may attribute blame to themselves for adverse events in their surroundings.

A four-year-old child whom I saw clinically was held hostage for 20 minutes by an excited and angry man who threatened her life and the lives of 17 other children at a siege in a Melbourne kindergarten in 1989. The child believed that if she had taken action more promptly to open a door to escape, four other children who subsequently were held for seven hours would have avoided this ordeal. This was not the situation, but until she became aware of and accepted the facts, she assumed total responsibility in the event and the disturbing outcome for her friends. This was indeed a burden for her.

Misperceptions and attributions of causal effects, if not corrected, will be carried by children into adulthood and distort their adult perception of their own experience and also of reality. So we must assist children to gain an accurate perception of events and appreciation of the outcomes, even at a very young age.

- *'The effect, if any, on children of a major incident will be short-lived.'*

The facts of the event, the emotional and psychological changes within the child's environment, including a loss of the sense of safety, and the engagement of imagination provides the basis for the child's interaction with the present. This interaction can have the potential to be carried forward into the future. If these repercussions are negative and cause any of a range of *maladaptive responses* (patterns of behaviour likely to cause psychological distress or dysfunction), the effect on the child will certainly not be short-lived. McFarlane, Policansky, and Irwin (1987) have identified morbidity in children eighteen months after a national bush fire disaster.

The following case indicates the influence a traumatic event may have on the unfolding life of a child and the potential for the repercussions to carry through into adulthood and beyond.

A 64-year-old man stated after a lecture on normal psychological reaction to disaster, that when aged sixteen years he had been called a coward through experiencing what he now knew to be normal anxiety reactions in the face of a very large fire. He had believed that he was a coward all his life and had brought up his sons within this belief and frame of reference. He now felt able to begin developing a new understanding of himself, and one would also expect, a new sense of identity.

- *'Children are resilient and will naturally recover from any effects by forgetting the experience, getting over it, or growing out of it.'*

Lack of cognitive capacity to retain memories is part of the natural inheritance of early childhood. However, one does not only have to understand or consciously remember something for it to have an impact. Any major event, be it happy or sad, good or bad, becomes part of the child. Just as good experiences may be forgotten but are nonetheless less important in the long-term life of the child, so difficult and bad experiences can also become part of the growing child and constantly challenge healthy adaptation and development. The challenges affect cognitive life, emotional life, social life, and behavioural life.

The notions of 'getting over it' and 'growing out of it' are part of the myths of the child not being aware of events they are nonetheless engaged in; 'forgetting' the experience comes from the child appearing to manage well enough.

The discrepancy between adult perception of children's vulnerability and the child's report of their own reactions, has been described following man-made disaster events. (Yule & Williams, 1990). Clinically, it is frequently found that two contradictory sets of attitudes and expectations exist side by side. Adults generally are sensitive, deeply concerned, and anxious about the welfare of children involved in major incidents. However, simultaneously, adults are often unable to recognise behaviours and symptoms which indicate stress in children. They have powerful co-existing needs to not recognise, in fact, to deny children's symptoms of disorientation, anguish, confusion, and pain; instead they focus on superficial behaviours which they interpret as indicating that everything is normal. Assessment of children's reactions, distress, vulnerabilities and needs must be based on a sensitive, astute, and knowledgeable appraisal of children's self-reported feelings, attitudes, behaviour, and general functioning.

Adult incapacity to recognise distress in children is shown in the following example.

CASE STUDY TWO	Five months after a severe bushfire I visited a kindergarten where the teacher, a warm, caring, and sensitive lady, said that all the children had settled down and were now back to normal. As I stood talking to her I noted that recent paintings on the walls contained scenes of unhappy experiences of the fires, and that one group of boys were playing an 'evacuation from fire' game with components of an intense struggle for mastery of their frightened feelings. On commenting on these observations to the teacher and focusing her attention on the distress that was about us, she was at first surprised and then somewhat amazed that it should continue to exist. She became distressed that the children were still suffering and that she had not recognised it.

- *'A lack of obvious behavioural or psychosomatic response means that the experience has not negatively impacted upon the child.'*

Relying on overt signs of distress to indicate whether a child has been influenced by their experience means that the child's inner world of thoughts, feelings, and ideas may not have been recognised. The child is, in fact, left to cope alone. Lack of observable behaviour or symptoms does not mean the child has come to terms with the trauma.

Exposure to an incident can initiate major physiological responses expressed in behaviours such as hyperarousal, hypervigilance, and stress-induced analgesia, as described by van der Kolk, Greenberg, Boyd, and Krystal (1985). These can be extremely frightening and frequently overwhelming to the point of traumatisation in their own right. If the biochemical changes persist, the child will be come even more vulnerable.

In fact, rather than not displaying symptoms, children who are confronted with traumas which induce physiological responses, or who are in a state of constant hyperarousal anticipating a traumatising experience (for example, witnessing violence or being the subject of physical, sexual or emotional abuse), may have subsequent changes in their physiology. (Pynoos, 1990; Ornitz and Pynoos, 1989). The question has been raised that traumatised young children may even suffer permanent damage to the brainstem because they have lost the normal inhibitory modulation of the startle response. The complexity of psycho-neuro-biological responses to PTSD are being explored (Davis, 1986; Friedman, 1990; van der Kolk et al., 1985).

What is trauma for children?

Laplanche and Pontalis (1973) describe trauma as:

> ... an event in the subject's life defined by its intensity, by the subject's incapacity to respond adequately to it, and by the upheaval and long lasting effects that it brings about in the psychical organiza-tion ... the trauma is characterized an by influx of excitations that is excessive by the standard of the subject's tolerance and capacity to master such excitation and work them out psychically. (p. 465)

Children's responses to trauma rarely manifest as clearly defined psychopathology, but as problems in behaviours, relationships, academic performance, emotional changes or somatic symptomatology. Clinical inter-ventions mainly focused on the presenting problems, or responsive only to evident psychopathology therefore are inappropriate.

The significance of a major incident for children arises from the impact it has upon any of a number of facets of the child's life. Children's develop-ment may be affected as they try to deal with the trauma. They may divert energy away from the natural developmental progress, even channel it into maladaptive behaviours, all while trying to cope with the experience (Gordon & Wraith, 1992).

Whether an experience traumatises an individual child or not is predi-cated by a number of factors. An event which appears more or less benign or marginally disturbing to adults may be highly significant and disturbing for a child because of its affect on their inner life of feelings, fears, wishes, imagination, ideals, conscience, and defence mechanisms.

PROXIMITY

Pynoos, et al. (1987) and Gleser, Green, and Winget (1981) demonstrated that proximity to an event broadly correlates with the impact of the event on the individual. Being at the epicentre of the event may include experi-ences of life threat, physical injury, witness to death or injury of another, abuse, torture, or the destruction of the environment. Physical or psycholog-ical distance from the epicentre (as an on-looker, or absent member of the family or community) generally correlates with diminishing reactions.

Therefore, children who are at the epicentre of an event are more likely to have more intense responses than children who are more distant from it or who were not there. However, increasing distance does not confer correlated or automatic immunity from impact (see case study below).

EXISTING CONDITIONS

Proximity to the event is only one of the determining factors in the potential for a major response to a situation. Other factors which render a child more vulnerable to trauma include existing factors such as ill health, existing psychopathology, or areas of dysfunction (such auditory difficulties). Previous experiences the child has had can also make them more vulnerable; for example, if they or their family or community has sustained losses or experienced traumas prior to the current event, particularly within the preceding year.

An incident may impact upon a child through interacting with pre-existing problems, concurrently interacting with new issues in the short- to long-term, or re-awakening past issues and undoing previous adaptions and defences. The following case study demonstrates how the potency of a previous experience affected a child, even when he was not at the centre of events.

CASE STUDY THREE — Steven, aged five, was returning from holidays with his parents when the family farm was extensively burned. Almost all the stock was lost, but their home was saved. The family watched the fire for 30 miles as they approached their home, wondering what they would find. Subsequently, Steven became aggressive and restless, and began having nightmares. His parents became worried about him because they sensed, rightly, that he might be vulnerable because of a previous episode at three-and-a-half years when he had been lost for 18 hours in the bush and they feared he had been abducted. Found safe and well after an extensive search, Steven had never spoken of these experiences and it seemed that he had made a healthy adaptation and was progressing in all areas. However, the fire awoke the experience of being lost and it become enmeshed within his fire experience so that they became one experience for him. Over a period of months both incidents were addressed in individual therapy with me, along with concurrent work with his parents.

RELATIONSHIP TO A VICTIM

Children, like adults, are more vulnerable if a victim is known to them, or if they are worried about the present or future safety of a person important to them. This factor may be made worse if the child, its family or community have been threatened or experienced loss in the recent past (see 'Existing conditions', page 107).

The quality of a traumatising experience is also affected by how the child's family, peer relationships, social context, and community environment cope with the trauma. Many of the factors which influence individual responses also apply to these systems; degree and type of exposure to the incident, pre-existing psychopathology, previous losses or traumatisations, levels of development, maturation, coping skills, and current stresses.

A community disaster may exacerbate the reactions because the wider social context has also become destabilised and engaged in its own reactions and tasks. Friends, activity groups, and schools may also, to varying degrees, be dysfunctional and unable to support and help the child and their family.

DEVELOPMENTAL STAGES

The stage of development of a child is a key factor to be taken into account when working with a child's direct or indirect exposure to trauma. Thus it is obvious that a potentially traumatising event will impact differently according to developmental stage — infant, pre-school, primary school, or puberty. Events may also impact differently upon different children according to any maladaptive adjustments they may have already made in earlier phases of development.

IMPACT ON PARENTS

A major incident and the impact it has on parents profoundly influences the meaning children struggle to give to their experiences, the coping style they will develop, and their capacity to integrate the experiences. An important component in the quality and style of a child's response is the child's experience of his or her parents' experience. This may include the parents' behaviour and management of the actual impact and recovery phases, but is frequently determined by the quality of the parents' psychological availability to the child after the event. A parent's trauma becomes, to a lesser or greater extent, part of their child's psychological reality. This process is described in the section 'Children of emergency service workers' on page 112.

Responses of children to traumatisation

Children's responses to events in their external world may interact with their inner emotional and psychological worlds to cause internal stress. They use resources in the world around them — parents, friends, activities, or their own inner strengths and capacities — to deal with these stresses aroused by traumatisation and to support the integration of the experience. Without those resources being available, in the way they are needed at that time, children's development may be temporarily or more permanently diverted or arrested. This process is described as the *traumatic response.*

Responses may present immediately, months, or even years post-event. A child may respond to an incident or a series of incidents by regressing to earlier behaviours such as thumb-sucking or bed wetting. The young child may become clingy within their important relationships and the older child and adolescent may develop separation problems. Other common reactions are nightmares, withdrawal from family and social relationships and activities, poor concentration, forgetfulness, fears, mood changes, vulnerability, disobedience, headaches, stomach aches, or illness.

SHORT-TERM RESPONSES

In the short-term, from immediate impact to weeks after the event, children may show newly emergent fears and insecurities. These may be related to the trauma experience or unconnected issues. Children may have nightmares about what happened to them or about seemingly unconnected topics and engage in frequent talk and play about the experience. Emotional changes may show themselves in withdrawal, sadness, irritability, anger, moodiness, demanding behaviours, conflict, and fights. Children may regress and become disorganised in their behaviour, their habits and skills may deteriorate; they may appear confused and disoriented. Their autonomy may deteriorate also, with reduced self-care, restricted interests and activities, and increased comfort seeking. Their confidence and intiative may decrease. Separation problems may present or re-present.

Even very young children may develop a precocious awareness of the circumstances surrounding the experience, an awareness that leads to thoughts, questions, concerns, and comments which are beyond their capacity to deal with. Children may also take an increased responsibility for themselves, siblings, friends, and parents which is inappropriate for their age. They can become protective towards their parents, colluding with parental denial and so minimising their own difficulties and needs for help. These responses may settle down after a number of weeks and constitute only an interruption in the child's life.

MEDIUM-TERM RESPONSES

If a child's responses continue to persist and are present up to a year after the event, they are described as *medium-term effects*. As well as the short-term effects persisting, additional factors may become evident which can be related to the traumatising experience.

Medium-term effects include stress, poor health, emotional instability, and reduced concentration. Problems may emerge at school in academic performance and peer relationships. There may be more permanent mood and personality changes, expressing themselves as bad behaviour, outbursts, negativism, tantrums, destructive behaviours, and entrenched conflicts. Children may avoid engaging in new challenges appropriate for their age-group and also have difficulty learning from experience. They may become depressed, and start stealing and lying. A child's development and state of well-being are significantly interfered with by these changes.

LONG-TERM RESPONSES

Sometimes short- and medium-term effects persist indefinitely and carry forward as children mature, consolidating these disordered functions within their characters and personalities. These long-term changes may show up as a sense of changed or foreshortened future and postponed life issues, as described by Terr (1983), and avoidance of challenges and new experiences. Children who fail to develop skills compromise their skill bases and maturational profiles, resulting in patterns of disordered functions in one or any number of areas. Character changes may include entrenchment of chronic anger, depression, distrust, bitterness, and pessimism, as the following example shows.

CASE STUDY FOUR After a presentation on normal reaction to disaster, a senior professional woman in her mid-fifties told me that when she was aged about five she had been with her father when they were trapped in a fire, close to death, and he became overwhelmed with fear. She had hitherto felt completely safe in his competent and protective aura, but her sense of safety and trust in his capacity to care for her dissolved during this experience, never to return in the same way. She said she came to realise during the lecture that she had not trusted men since, and wondered if that was why she had never married.

Very occasionally, a child may appear to cope in the short and medium-term. The effects may only appear later when the child is thrown into overload by another crisis, perhaps of similar nature to the original incident; for example, illness, death, or other major life-event change. The original incident may be reactivated in a new phase of development which challenges the coping skills employed to adapt to the earlier traumatisation. For instance, the move into puberty and adolescence, when children grow as individuals and transfer their attachments from family to peer relationships may activate latent separation vulnerabilities which have a core within an earlier trauma.

Table 7.1 summarises examples of negative outcomes from traumatisation which may be found in children. Depending on developmental stage and levels of maturity attained, some responses are more likely to occur or be predominant than others. They may present in the individual or family and interfere, over time, with developmental process, communication, relationships, identity, and psychodynamic constitution. Together, these factors form the life continuum of the child, which trauma compromises or breaks (Gordon & Wraith, 1992).

TABLE 7.1
Traumatic impact on the child's life continuum: Examples of negative outcome

	SHORT-TERM INTERRUPTION first weeks	MID-TERM INTERFERENCE months to first year	LONG-TERM DISORDER second year and thereafter
INDIVIDUAL	Fracturing of stimulus barrier	Short-term difficulties continue interacting with other factors in child's life	Short and medium responses consolidate or appear
	Changed physiological functioning	General stress signs	Poor physical health
	Regressed, disorganised behaviour	Loss of developmental pathways	Developmental dysfunctions or deviations
	New, intense emotional responses	Relationship, mood, attitude changes	Defence mechanisms overactivated
	Sudden changes in patterns of relating	Peer relationship changes	Personality changes
		Discharge behaviours	
	Fear, insecurity	Avoidance of new experiences and challenges	Chronic peer problems
	Disorientation, confusion	Pseudoneurotic symptoms	Cognitive functioning compromised
			School failure
	Perceptual disruption	School performance problems	Identity changes
	Vulnerability		Neurotic systems engaged
	Precocious awareness		
			Preoccupation with traumas
	Preoccupation with other traumas		Postponement of life issues
			Philosophical Review
			Changed life goals
FAMILY	Previous communication patterns not adequate	Short term difficulties continue	Acceleration of pre-existing or newly emergent difficulties
	Misunderstanding of own and other's reactions, behaviour, attitudes	Changes in relationship patterns	Chronic family and marital problems
		Daily routines disordered	
	Pre-existing conflict and vulnerabilities increase	Decreased ability to respond to life's demands	Divergent philosophy and goals in members
		Family tensions	Narrowing of focus
			Family breakdown

Children of emergency service workers

All children are vulnerable to the negative effects of their parents' work. Children of emergency services workers are particularly vulnerable because of the nature of the parents' work experiences and the demands it makes on the worker and/or spouse. The personal stress responses a parent brings into a family, knowingly or unconsciously, immediately become active in the environment in which a child lives and grows, and may influence that child's functioning and development (see 'Impact on parents', page 108).

An emergency worker-parent's stress may be brought into the experience of a child along a number of pathways identified by Gordon and Wraith (1987) as *transmission effects*, *repercussion effects*, and *induced effects*.

TRANSMISSION EFFECTS

CASE STUDY FIVE   A volunteer fire-fighter reported that his toddler cried whenever he saw him and did not want anything to do with him for some weeks after a fire. The child had also become a fretful sleeper. The father had been engaged in mopping-up duties for several days following fire duty in a major bushfire and would return home intermittently, blackened, red-eyed, exhausted and rushed, to eat, bathe, and sleep for a short time and then disappear again in a flurry of activity. The parents were distressed by the newly present fear in their baby, wearied by his disturbed sleep, and were becoming estranged from each other over how to manage the problems.

This example of transmission effects shows the direct result on the family of changes in the emergency worker's behaviour and emotional state. The effects are usually direct and clearly related to work experiences and may be dated from the event. The family may have high tolerance for these changes because they can identify the causes which are seen as something imposed from outside the family. They may even bring the family closer together as they try to understand the problems and help each other.

In the above example, we can see early patterns in the father/child interaction which have the potential to evolve into permanent disruption of the relationship between them and also the establishment of potentially permanent disruptions in the relationship between the parents.

REPERCUSSION EFFECTS

Repercussion effects are reactions generated in the family as a result of the worker incorporating work stress and unresolved issues into his personality and behaviour. They may result from the alteration over time, of self-image, lifestyle, life values, work habits, or mood of the worker, with consequent changes in behaviour, emotional state, or relationships in other family members. They are secondary to transmission effects and may resolve or become permanent characteristics within the family member or the family system.

CASE STUDY SIX   Another fire fighter was almost killed along with his crew when the fire front engulfed their truck. The danger was so great that he and the other fighters prepared themselves for death by farewelling each other. The father was deeply affected by the experience but was unable to share it with his wife because of her long-standing anxiety and opposition to his membership of the fire service. Over the ensuing months he felt deeply cut off from her by this gulf in experience and the changes in his life values as a result of his being so near to death.

    The change in the quality and balance in the relationships in the family system was expressed principally by an adolescent daughter who became difficult, rude, disruptive, angry, and uncooperative, while the rest of the family appeared on the surface to continue with life as previously. The parents thought the changes in their daughter were 'normal adolescent behaviour'.

Changes brought about by repercussion effects are often accommodations to what is experienced, frequently unconsciously, as a permanent alteration in the parent. The link to the work experience is not obvious and the problem is seen as internal to the family and belonging to one or more members of the family. The changes are frequently difficult to identify and are often expressed by members other than the worker-parent. In this case study, the daughter was responding with behavioural expressions of uncertainty to deep changes in her father and the changes in the relationship between her parents. However, the link between the disaster and her behaviour was obscure and her actions were seen as a typical teenage stage of development. She was a sensitive and perceptive young person who, because of the usual uncertainties associated with the early adolescent phase of development, was particularly vulnerable to the changes introduced into the family as a consequence of her father's experience.

INDUCED EFFECTS

The third process which introduces the emergency worker's experiences into the family is induced effects. These are not directly attributed to the impact of work stress and are also difficult to identify. They are emotional, behavioural, or relationship changes produced in other family members as a result of their fantasies being activated or their past traumatic experiences being reawakened. The only connection with the worker's experience is the emotional demand it makes on the family member.

CASE STUDY SEVEN   Kathy was a happy, healthy eight-year-old girl whose father, an active member of a combat service, was required to work away from home for an extended period and was frequently engaged in highly dangerous work. During one of his absences, the family experienced a major incident within their local community and were significantly but marginally involved. These events caused Kathy to regress, to have terrifying nightmares, bed wetting, problems separating from her mother, and deteriorating school grades. Although she was seen for psychotherapy over a period of time and her symptoms improved, they did not disappear. Eighteen months later the mother told the therapist how, at the same age as her daughter, she had been terrifyingly sexually assaulted. As she spoke, she became aware that the important component for her in her relationship with her husband was that he was to be an effective protector of her and the children. However, because of his work, she was concerned for his safety and had active fantasies that he would be killed while away from home on the job. With the traumatic event in the local community her fears became in one sense a reality. She and the children were confronted with a possibly overwhelming, life-threatening experience and her husband, their means of protection and therefore safety and survival, was absent in a dangerous situation himself. This conjunction of events brought about a significant emotional change in the mother. Kathy sensed her mother's fear and as a result lost her sense of safety, expressing fear for both of them through her behavioural expressions of anxiety. The mother's strengths enabled her to overcome her own vulnerability. However, Kathy was vulnerable because of her youth, her stage of development, and her sensitivity to her mother's feelings. This led to her expressing the stresses of the whole family. Responding to these issues of which the family was unconsciously aware, at the height of the family distress the father considered changing jobs. When the factors were identified, both mother and daughter were able to settle and the father continued successfully in his job.

Changes wrought by induced effects take time to become identifiable and usually families are not able to connect their distress to changes induced by the workers' experience. If the reactions are misunderstood, they may lead to long-term consequences for family life. Because they are linked to powerful underlying psychological issues, the induced effects settle very slowly or may give rise to permanent, often maladaptive, adaptations.

Adding to the complexity of understanding the impact of any of these modes of worker's stress on children, is the fact that they may all impact together in varying complex and dynamic ways, and rarely present as discrete and readily understood processes.

The above cases from personal clinical practice represent examples in which the work experiences of one family member caused significant changes in individuals within the family, or in the family as a unit. They included changes in child/parent relationships, marital relationships, lifestyle, and changes in children's developmental pathways. In a number of other cases, the effects lasted some years and continued to unfold. It is not difficult to see these responses as the start of far-reaching alterations in the fabric of the life of the child and of the family.

The next section, which discusses managing and treating children's responses, makes some specific suggestions for the families of emergency services workers.

Management and treatment of children's responses

An incident may impact upon a child through direct experience of the event or its aftermath; indirectly through the traumatic experiences of a parent, family member or other significant person, or through the destruction of their physical environment. Traumatisation obstructs the developmental process in the child and can prevent them attaining age-appropriate skills such as independence and social acumen. It shatters contexts and beliefs about life, oneself and other people. All these threads need to be re-established and re-connected into the previously held systems and beliefs and also incorporate the changes and new realities provoked by the event to provide a sound basis for movement to the future.

Pynoos and Nader (1988) have identified a schematic structure in which life threat and witness to injury can lead to post-traumatic disorder responses; the experience of loss can lead to grief reaction; worry about another may lead to separation anxiety symptoms; and reminder of previous life experience may lead to exacerbation or renewal of symptoms associated with that event. As there may be a combination of these components within a child's experience, management must be responsive to individual and family issues, circumstances and requirements.

FAMILY TREATMENT

First and foremost, the child needs to feel safe, physically and psychologically. Parents provide the core of the recovery sheath for their child. Raphael (1986) described the interrelationship of the trauma experiences and their aftermath for a child, their parents and family, and how these relationships affect a child's responses to trauma. Parents may need assistance to understand the child's experiences and responses. In turn, this will support their confidence in their parenting. Increased understanding of the child's responses and ongoing reactions will assist the parents to be emotionally available in the way the child needs. For instance, the need for comfort following a distressing experience, even for a considerable period, needs to be understood as an appropriate reaction not as pathological regression or an indication of over-dependency in a child.

When helping a stress-impacted family, it is frequently necessary to assist parents to deal with their own issues either before or concurrently with the assistance being provided to the child. This enables parents to be more available to their child and so more able to meet their child's needs. The child and their family may also need assistance to identify the physiological responses and develop means to manage them.

Family members need to feel safe within themselves and to understand each other's experiences at the time of the trauma and afterwards, each other's current feelings about the event, and the processes the event set in train for the family and its members. The need for this type of sharing frequently becomes apparent perhaps months or years later, when other seemingly unrelated problems emerge. Family members can isolate themselves and become distanced from one another. Integrating the family through understanding each other's experience can ameliorate or prevent this. Without this understanding, a secondary series of negative and often destructive experiences can be set in train and the family, as a unit, may need to have some or all of these issues identified and worked with, often with a person outside the family as a facilitator.

In the early stages of treatment, the establishment of a sense of safety is also supported by post-incident contact between the child, their parents, family, friends, and services, such as school, to provide factual information, assess current status of the incident, clarify errors, and provide an opportunity for the child to give a definitive account of their experience.

COMMUNICATING THE EXPERIENCE

Like adults, children need opportunities to communicate frightening, worrying, or confusing experiences. But they may want to protect parents from further distress or parents may not recognise the distress in their child. Children frequently deny or repress untoward experiences and unless adults are alert to the more subtle changes in children, they may not be aware of their underlying struggles. In situations of stress it can be difficult for parents and children to find opportunities to communicate their experiences and to establish new ways of understanding and talking to each other. This may be because of the nature of the personal experience arising from the event, the intensity of the feelings associated with it which are often beyond words, a perceived need to protect members of the family from personal distress, or the fear of the impact of the knowledge on others.

Stress within a family confronts, often overwhelmingly, children's strengths, their style of attachment to their significant others, and their capacities to deal with developmental tasks. When a child changes in any of the principal parameters of cognitive, emotional, social, psychosomatic functions in response to a traumatic experience and the changes become fixed in time, increase in severity, or change in quality, it can be assumed that the child is experiencing difficulty and needs help.

UNDERSTANDING THE IMPACT

The stress event or process, regardless of the cause, can bring to the fore earlier traumas in a child's life which now also need to be addressed in the context of the current experience. It can also exacerbate previous difficulties and non-coping styles in children. These factors, combined with the totality of stress-inducing experiences within the family, can cause significant problems for families and their members.

Throughout the recovery phase and for an indefinite period, a child may need frequent opportunities to continue the exploration and the telling of their trauma story. Children need assistance to develop an understanding of the impact and meaning of this major experience in all facets of their lives. This includes the impact it has had upon their behaviours, feelings and fears; on the requirements of their relationships; of their understanding of the world, and their understanding of themselves, their history and their life in the present and also the future that they envisage for themselves.

To help a child integrate their experiences it is, of course, important to establish a warm, caring, secure rapport with the child and to listen with ears, eyes and empathy to what the child tells you about themselves and their experiences in their own words, play, relationships, gesture, facial expression and body language. One is then able to understand the overt and the covert feelings and issues in the child and help them make sense of their experiences by assisting them to identify, define, focus and express them in their own particular way and time.

In developing strategies to help children who have been traumatised by one or a number of experiences, Gordon and Wraith (1992), emphasised the importance of working with children to assist them to identify the actual nature of the experience they have had and to understand the nature and quality of the traumatising components within the experience. Children need to construct a clear and factual story of the whole of the experience they have had, and identify fantasies which have developed in an attempt to provide completion. They need to know the facts of the event so that they can develop understanding of the experience and take the opportunity to orient themselves to the reality of the events. The work has to be done within the context of the developmental stage of the child, their skill and maturity levels, and the strengths and vulnerabilities within each child and their family.

Interventions

PROCESS INTERVENTION

A model of intervention called process intervention has been developed which responds initially to the incident, to the unfolding stages of integration of the event, and recovery from it; supports a planned response to anticipated events in the aftermath such as anniversaries; and also responds to developmental changes and other significant and often unplanned events such as illness, accidents, and family upheaval. Within the process intervention model the services provided at different stages following the event are tailored to the specific requirements of that phase.

PSYCHOLOGICAL FIRST AID AND DEBRIEFING

Pynoos and Nader (1985) developed strategies for psychological first aid which help children understand their experience, clarify errors and ambiguities, gain factual information, and assess the current status of the incident.

Debriefings may need to be provided individually, or within the family or the group which shared the experience. The different forums provide the opportunity for different issues to be addressed. The debriefings should be provided by skilled personnel as soon as the emergency is over and the children have emerged from reactive shock. This is usually within the first two to three days. Any debriefing or psychological first aid must be designed to accommodate children's needs for physical and psychological safety, their developmental and emotional needs for engagement with their primary care givers, and their requirement for and capacity to understand and integrate information. Thus the format and style of the intervention will vary according to the specific incident. The emotional environment must be sensitively and skilfully managed, with opportunities for communication of feelings and experiences carefully balanced with containment, support, and appraisal of the need for further, more specific help.

BRIEF INTERVENTIONS

Brief interventions, individually focused, help children grasp their trauma experiences more comprehensively and to begin to explore their needs. It provides an opportunity to deal with the trauma impact, the current crisis they are experiencing, and the matters it raises. At this stage it is important that children have support networks which are informed and educated about post-traumatic responses and management strategies; where they are ensured access to people, assistance and services that will be able to meet their needs and enable their healthy development to continue. Integrating their new experiences will be easier for children if their peer groups and adults at school, and in the wider community, are able to support the recovery process. Any negative aspects which may work against the recovery process must be identified and worked with. The support system should also be assisted to monitor any changes and identify new needs and issues that may arise for the child.

LONG-TERM THERAPY

Long-term therapeutic interventions of a more traditional kind may be required if the child experiences changes in life values and expectations, behaviours or other responses which begin to affect normal functioning, or if the continuation of symptoms becomes unacceptable.

Future intervention may also be necessary if subsequent events relating to the trauma, such as anniversaries, inquests, seasonal changes, or normal developmental transitions, negatively impact upon a child.

FAMILY SELF-HELP

In conjunction with the above, the impact of a parent's own traumatisation or distress on a child may be modified by parents taking some active steps to manage their own response. Acknowledging their own personal stress, frequently difficult for adults, provides parents with the opportunity to identify their own repercussions and styles of coping. Parents who are alert to the impact of these factors on their family can become active in the management of their effects. To help this process, parents should be active in their own stress management, open to assistance through the reflections of family and friends about changes in attitudes and behaviour, and accept assistance from agencies and the personal network of family and friends. Many organisations provide critical incident stress services and counselling for workers, as well as education and support for spouses. If properly conducted by skilled and experienced staff, this counselling gives workers and their families the opportunity to address issues which may arise for them.

Summary

In providing a responsive management and treatment process it is necessary to step outside the confines of the traditional clinical-pathology model, to take a preventive approach and support ongoing development and coping skills while being responsive to vulnerabilities and difficulties in children and their world. Thus services required for children, their parents, families, schools, and communities require skills in individual, family, group, and community work. An understanding of the biological, psychological, and sociological parameters and of the recovery process all need to be integrated in the trauma recovery program.

References

American Psychiatric Association. (1987). *Diagnostic and Statistical Manual of Mental Disorders.* (3rd ed., rev.). Washington. DC: Author.

Davis, M. (1986). Pharmacological and anatomical analysis of fear conditioning using the fear potentiated startle paradigm. *Behavioural Neuroscience 100*, 814–824.

Friedman, M.J. (1990). Biological approaches to the diagnosis and treatment of Post-Traumatic Stress Disorder. *Journal of Traumatic Stress, 4,* 67–91

Gleser, G.C., Green, B.L., & Winget, C.N. (1981). *Prolonged psychosocial effects of disaster: A study of Buffalo Creek.* New York: Academic Press.

Gordon, R., & Wraith, R. (1987). Workers' responses to disaster. *The Macedon Digest 2*(4) Australian National Disaster Organisation.

Gordon R., & Wraith R. (1992). Responses of children and adolescents to disaster. In J. Wilson & B. Raphael (Eds.), *International handbook of traumatic stress studies.* New York: Plenum Press.

Laplanche, J., & Pontalis, J.B. (1973). *The language of psychoanalysis.* New York: Norton and Co.

McFarlane, A.C. (1987). Post-traumatic phenomena in a longitudinal study of children following a national disaster. *Journal of the American Academy of Child and Adolescent Psychiatry, 26,* 794–796.

McFarlane, A.C., Policansky, S.K., & Irwin, C.P. (1987). A longitudinal study of the psychological morbidity in children due to a national disaster. *Psychological Medicine, 17,* 727–738.

Ornitz, E.M., & Pynoos R.S. (1989). Startle modulation in children with post-traumatic stress disorder. *American Journal of Psychiatry, 147,* 866–870.

Pynoos, R. (1990). Post-traumatic stress disorder in children and adolescents. In B. Garfinkel, G. Carlson, & E. Weller (Eds.), *Psychiatric disorders in children and adolescents.* Philadelphia, PA: W.B. Saunders & Co.

Pynoos, R.S. (1992). Violence, personality and post-traumatic stress disorder: Developmental and political perspectives. In A. Kales, C.M. Pierce & M. Greenblatt (Eds.), *The mosaic of contemporary psychiatry in perspective* (pp 53–65). New York: Springer Verlag.

Pynoos, R., Frederick, C., Nader, K., Arryo, W., Steinberg, A., Eth, S., Numez, F., & Fairbanks, L. (1987). Life threat and post-traumatic stress in school-age children. *Archives of General Psychiatry, 44,* 1057–1063.

Pynoos, R., & Nader, K. (1988). Psychological first aid and treatment approach to children exposed to community violence: Research implications. *Journal of Traumatic Stress, 1*(4), 445–474.

Raphael, B. (1986). The young, the old and the family. In B. Raphael, *When disaster strikes: How individuals and communities cope with catastrophe* (pp 149–175). New York: Basic Books.

Terr, L.C. (1983). Chowchilla revisited: The effects of psychic trauma four years after a school bus kidnapping. *American Journal of Psychiatry. 14,* 1543–1550.

van der Kolk, B., Greenberg, M., Boyd, H., & Krystal, J. (1985). Inescapable shock, neurotransmitters, and addiction to trauma: Towards a psychobiology of post-traumatic stress. *Biological Psychiatry, 20,* 314–325.

Wraith, R., & Gordon, R. (1987). Myths of response to disaster of individuals and communities. *Australian Child and Family Welfare, 12*(3), 26–28.

Yule, W., & Williams, R. (1990). Post-traumatic stress reactions in children. *Journal of Traumatic Stress, 3*(2), 279–296.

Long-Term Repercussions of the Trauma of Sex Abuse in Childhood

CHAPTER EIGHT

Denise Brunt

THE long-term repercussions of sex abuse in childhood is a very large topic to discuss in a single chapter. Hence I will aim to focus on some specific issues involved in treating an adult who presents, for the first time, with a history of significant abuse in childhood. This chapter poses a series of questions and answers them with a discussion of the timing of presentations and specific repercussions of the trauma. The answers also describe a conceptual framework for understanding the experience and the implications of involvement for the helper.

Finkelhor (1984) has argued that much of the debate over the effects of childhood sexual abuse upon adult behaviour is a kind of ethnocentrism on the part of adults. Adults may become preoccupied with the experience of adults who had been abused as children. However, this preoccupation can overlook or ignore the immediate effect of this kind of trauma on children, while they are still children.

Moreover, children may present to a health professional with any type and number of problems, such as truancy, physical complaints, depression, aggression, substance abuse, and so on, which may disguise an experience of trauma of this nature. These childhood symptoms may disguise the experience of sexual trauma. The effects of such an experience are then compounded by the lack of recognition and/or protection of the children, even by well-meaning adults. This may even compound over time and influence the entire psychosocial adjustment of the child. This was certainly my experience when I worked for a long time in a community health service as a clinical child psychologist. I had many female and male children who were sexually abused who presented directly with this problem and/or indirectly with behavioural and educational problems. Child-based services must receive enough funding to provide an available and skilled service.

Significant misconceptions are that sexual abuse only happens in poorer, or disorganised families; that sexual abuse is by strangers; that it is fabricated by children; that child-adult sexual behaviour does not harm the child; that children 'invite' it; that children would say when to stop; that male-child sex abuse is perpetrated by homosexuals; and so on. These are myths which minimise or justify child sexual abuse. They should be recognised and debunked whenever possible.

Question 1: When might the clinician be consulted?

The situation is relatively straightforward, of course, when someone presents or is presented as 'This person has been sexually abused as a child, please treat'. More often, however, the presentation is obscured. As the title of this chapter implies, the time of disclosure to the clinician may be many years after the abuse. Childhood sexual abuse may become problematical for the clinician treating an adult client who originally presented with depression, interpersonal difficulties, and/or borderline features. Childhood sexual abuse may become an issue for an adult who thinks that a child, probably their own, has been sexually abused. It might become problematical when the drawings and other projective material from a child assessment is examined. Also, the subsequent interview with the parent may reveal that she (usually) had been sexually abused as a child. The client may not disclose at all but the clinician needs to be alert to the possibility when certain features are present, in clinical settings, mental health and addiction centres, or the courts. Some of these features are addressed below.

AMNESIA

Amnesia about aspects of childhood itself are especially common in patients who also have a history of sexual abuse. This type of amnesia is correlated with more stigmatising events such as the abuse involving a close relative, sexual penetration, or disbelief from others about the traumatic event.

Another feature of amnesia is that such experiences seem to be stored kinaesthetically (for example, revealed in body movements) rather than verbally. This feature should alert the clinician to what are, perhaps, hidden causes of somatic complaints. These are the symptoms which may bring the adult client to seek professional assistance, so careful history taking is important. Clinicians may need to ask explicit questions about sexual abuse in childhood; such as, 'Were there times when you felt unsafe?', or 'Who did you go to when you felt unsafe?'.

Even when the client can recall the events, the clinician may be perplexed at the amount of time that has elapsed between the occurrence of the sexual abuse and the client's presentation to the clinic. Phenomenologically, for traumatised individuals, the concept of time does become distorted (Ellenberger, 1958). For example, after two years of weekly therapy, one woman disclosed a most traumatic incident that had occurred 20 years previously. She was amazed to realise that the last 20 years of her life (since the incident) were like a very small part of her psychological life, and that, subjectively, she had hardly lived them at all. Yet the time span of the traumatic event (a couple of weeks) had subjectively expanded to such an extent that it felt as if most of her life had been lived in the place where the event occurred.

Question 2: What is the range of presenting problems?

The range of presenting problems is broad because there are many variations on the nature, frequency, intrusiveness, duration, etc., of childhood sexual abuse.

THE RANGE OF RISK FACTORS

Variations in presentation may be due to the age of the child when the abuse occurred, the relationship of the child to the offender, the sex of the child, and the sex of the offender. There are variations in the ways in which disclosure came about, if at all; the ways in which subsequent interventions occurred, and the sensitivity with which these were conducted; and the degree of resolution of the practical aspects of the disclosure.

The risk factors in child sexual abuse have been identified and summarised succinctly by Hunter (1990, cited by Polkowski, 1991):

> ... the sexual abuse pattern that would probably have the least impact on a victim's life would be this one: a single, violent encounter at a later stage of childhood, with a complete stranger, combined with a family and a society that noticed that something undesirable had been done to the child, believed the victim, and provided him with support and guidance. At the other end of the continuum would be a pattern of ongoing, frequent, violent abuse that started at a young age and was perpetrated by numerous close family members, combined with a hostile attitude toward the child from society when the child attempted to gain assistance.

The risk factors depend upon the age of the child. For the young child, risk factors seem to include the sex of the child; the qualities of the major caregivers, such as hostility and sexual problems in the mother; a susceptibility to misreading the signals of the child; and poor impulse control in the male figure (father). For the older child, some of the risk factors include a very immature mother who may abdicate some of her duties to the daughter in the presence of a dominant and controlling father.

Even though the risk factors can be identified, the offender must still bear full responsibility for the abuse.

Child sexual abuse, when linked with neglect (and psychological and physical abuse and family disorganisation), seems to be a strong risk factor for the development of adult psychiatric illness. This is especially so for border-line and multiple personality disorders, and affective, panic, and somatoform disorders. Bessell, van der Kolk, and Glenn Saxe (1992) studied 100 consecutive admissions to a state hospital, 18 per cent of whom had a dissociative disorder. Every person in this subgroup had a history of sexual abuse and severe neglect.

Knowledge of the long-term repercussions of childhood sexual abuse has been increased by research of both clinical and non-clinical samples. Some writers have produced lists of common clinical characteristics found in adults who have experienced childhood sexual abuse (e.g. Powell, 1991). In my experience, such lists have limited use when taking into consideration the enormous variations in individual presentations. However using such a checklist to give clients feedback on their symptomology may help them to feel normal and reassure them that what they are experiencing is an under-standable reaction to events.

PROBLEM RANGE

Self-injury may be a feature (van der Kolk, Perry, & Herman, 1991). It may take the form of suicide attempts, self-mutilation (especially if abuse was early in life), self-injurious behaviour, such as risk-taking (especially if neglect is in the history), bingeing, anorexia (if abuse later in childhood or adolescence), and/or risk-taking behaviour.

Clinicians need to explore with the client the meaning of their self-injury. Such behaviour may be self-punishment because of perceived blame for the abuse or for the consequences experienced by the abuser. For example, a 16-year-old girl who cooperated with her siblings in reporting her father to the police subsequently tried, on several occasions, to cut her hand off. Van der Kolk and Saporta (1991) also argued that such behaviour may be an effect of physiologically conditioned distortions (for example, long-term stress-induced analgesia) of arousal mechanisms. Sufferers may really feel numb, describe themselves as dead, and may attempt to injure themselves in order to feel something. Rather than feel numb, sufferers may experience chronic physiological arousal, including chronic pain.

Question 3: What is the nature of the traumatic response to sexual abuse?

Post-traumatic stress is defined succinctly, in DSM-III-R (American Psychiatric Association, 1987), as having the features of the persistent reexperiencing of the traumatic event, the persistent avoidance of stimuli associated with the trauma or numbing of general responsiveness, and the persistent symptoms of increased arousal. The duration of these symptoms are to be of at least one month and may have delayed onset and/or chronic manifestation. Ochberg (1988) advises, as a rule of thumb, that those who work with victims of crime should think of victim status in psychological terms and PTSD in physiological terms. Both approaches have important contributions to helping the client manage the symptoms and work towards resolving the issues.

But do the features, signs, and symptoms observed in 'survivors' (perhaps a more acceptable and useful word than 'victims'), conceptually or diagnostically relate to the diagnostic category of post-traumatic stress? This constitutes a debate in the literature where reference is made to (usually) 'unresolved' post-traumatic stress (e.g. Lindberg & Distad, 1985), or the 'post-sex abuse' trauma (e.g. Briere & Runtz, 1987), since the symptoms were felt to overlap but not be synonymous with PTSD. Donaldson and Gardner (1985) studied, in a clinic sample, whether or not adult women who have experienced childhood incest could correctly be described as having delayed or chronic post-traumatic stress. They decided that it was a relevant concept, at least in this sample, and the reader is referred to their paper for the full argument.

There is increasing concern over problems associated with the use of PTSD to describe the effects of child sexual abuse; particularly because of its overuse and misuse, especially in forensic matters.

Van der Kolk and his colleagues at Harvard Medical School support the notion that there is need for a separate category for developmentally based PTSD, to adequately describe the symptoms of those adults who present with a history of early and chronic trauma. They recommended adopting a subcategory of 'PTSD with Personality Change' after their analyses of the Disorders of Extreme Stress (DESNOS) data (B. van der Kolk, personal communication, June 14th, 1992). Adults who present with a history of prolonged repeated (sexual) abuse have experienced a state of captivity, and of disrupted parental care, especially the lack of a protective and secure attachment. This is the origin for many adults of their self-destructive behaviours (van de Kolk et al., 1991).

Moves to have this category included in DSM-IV have not been successful. Readers are therefore referred to this paper and others for a fuller discussion of the criteria. However, in order to understand the process involved in recognising traumatic responses resulting from abuse, both the stressor and the disclosure procedure need to be discussed.

THE STRESSOR EVENT

The trauma (for diagnosis of PTSD) is usually considered to be outside the range of usual experience. But this is not so, if statistics on the level of sexual abuse of children in our communities are any guide. Statistically, and regrettably, the experience is not outside the range of usual experience. Finkelhor (1984) reported the results of a number of random sample surveys of the general population. While reported rates varied, Finkelhor concluded that 3–9 per cent of males and 12–22 per cent of females had been sexually abused as children by a person at least five years older than themselves. These figures are 10 years old but other studies have provided similar statistics. If the rates were 10 percent, this is a large number of abused children each year. Even though the trauma is not outside the range of usual experience, the experience is nevertheless 'traumatic'!

THE DISCLOSURE

The actual experience of abuse is not the only traumatic event. Practising clinicians in the field of sex abuse know that the disclosure and subsequent events are often very traumatising for the client. Many cases report a child, or teenager attempting to disclose who has been met by adult disbelief or failure to take effective action, either to have the abuse stopped, or to protect the child from the repercussions of disclosure, such as removal from the family home or protection from public knowledge and ostracism by the peer group, and so on. To disclose, a young person has to make a considerable effort in the first place because of fear of ridicule, disbelief, and implied or explicit threats by the offender.

The questions of why disclosure occurs at a particular time is important. The aim of disclosure is almost always to stop the abuse, if not for the victim then for others, by any means possible. Did the teenager disclose because the offender had access to other victims? For example, has the former de facto of the mother moved into a household where there are other children of the same age as themselves when they were abused? Or, was an offender barred from the family and the abusive events pushed below consciousness, only for him to reappear when a younger sibling reached a vulnerable age?

Had the person attempted to disclose in the past and been ignored, not heard, let down, etc.? Did the disclosure lead to denial or disbelief by the discloser's significant adults?

In what way has the system perpetuated and exacerbated the abuse? For example, did the disclosure lead to intervention by the police, who may have done an assessment but then left the victim in ignorance about the results? Going to court or taking legal action is a complex and stressful event in its own right. It can be a source of 'system abuse'. Discretion is often exercised by police, government departments, and the legal system about whether or not, and how, cases are brought to court, and whether in the Children's, Family, and/or Criminal Court. This discretion is necessary when dealing with the myriad issues in child sexual abuse cases. Even so, that discretion may also cause a number of problems, such as the delays caused by adjournments. For example, one of the problems that may arise was seen in one family where a group of siblings were abused over a long period by the father/stepfather. They had to suffer two years of repeated adjournments caused by lack of preparation of the case. Whenever there was an adjournment, the children were left unsure as to whether or not they would have to give evidence of an explicit nature against their father. One teenager would run away and hitchhike with truckies at each adjournment, acting out self-destructive wishes. The family's mother was hospitalised with acute asthma during this period. Meanwhile, the father continued to have access to the mother via routine domestic tasks, their joint social network, and so on.

Another simple example of inadvertent system abuse was a mother whose child presented as having been sexually abused. This mother reported that, in the assessment interview with a social worker, her own history was taken. She had been raised in a series of foster homes and in one she established a close relationship with another boy in the home. She was 12, he was only 14. But the worker taking her history (allegedly) said, 'Oh, so you were sexually abused too'. The mother was considerably distressed as this relationship was one of the few warm memories that she had held onto from her otherwise deprived life.

As this chapter is focusing upon the adult who is now retrieving memories, the question of 'Why now?' has to be answered. Does it relate to the age of the survivor's own children ? This can act as a reminder cue for critical stages in the survivor's own life span. Or, it may be that the intimacy created through an effective therapeutic relationship has uncovered past repressed memories. Taking careful note of how disclosures and attempted disclosures were dealt with in the past will also alert the clinician to possible implications for current management. History should not repeat itself in therapy, but lead to new ways of resolution.

Although features of legal and social system abuse can lead to inappropriate disclosure and reinforce the traumatic experience, this does not mean that these systems should only operate for the benefit of the survivor. Due social and legal processes need to be adhered to in the pursuit of justice. However, there is also a need to work on developing more informed and humane systems to respond to abused people's needs.

Question 4: What are the specific features of post-traumatic reaction to childhood sexual abuse?

I consider that the features subsumed within the DSM-III-R classification of PTSD, should be further divided into separate dimensions. I have summarised these divisions below.

AVOIDANCE

This dimension, which is covered in the DSM-III-R (American Psychiatric Association, 1987) classification of PTSD, needs modifying including elaboration of the mechanisms underlying 'flight' from the trauma. Anna Freud's (1966) ideas are particularly useful in accounting for how victims may identify with the aggressor, resulting sometimes in the reenactment of the traumatic incidences and the brutalisation of the personality of the victim.

EMOTIONAL NUMBING

Emotional numbing (freeze) can restrict the experience of all emotions, including joy, and may require special understanding and handling for optimal results (Tracey, in press). Indeed, emotional numbing may play a role in cases where the victim withdraws from treatment, even in those instances where their distress is detected by those around them, such as their spouse or children, but where the numbness is so strong it blocks out awareness in the self that something is seriously wrong. Withdrawal from treatment may possibly be a manifestation of difficulties with the intimate nature of the helping relationship and the experience of high arousal levels.

TRUST DESTROYED: IMPAIRED CAPACITY FOR INTIMACY

Sex abuse within the family constitutes an abuse of trust in others and in one's own perceptions and judgements. This is over and above the aspects of physical hurt and degradation.

The client may not even trust the clinician. The client may miss appointments, cancel at the last minute, or simply fail to attend until the next crisis occurs. This is likely to occur just when the clinician feels that the work is 'getting somewhere'. Avoidance like this is an important clue and, when appropriate, understood and shared with the client.

SELF-ESTEEM AND ESTEEM OF OTHERS

Feelings of being understood, respected and taken seriously are profoundly affected by sexual abuse. Negative self-esteem, irrational feelings of guilt, shame, self-loathing, self-fragmentation, and self-destruction may be in evidence. More specifically, self-esteem in the sexual area may have been dramatically impaired. Finkelhor (1984), using a scale of sexual self-esteem, found that victims, male and female, do have significantly lower sexual self-esteem. Detailed analyses of the results from this study indicated, 'that sexual victimization made a contribution to negative sexual self-esteem, independent of family income, emotional deprivation, family sexual practices and other variables' (p. 193).

The client's perception of others could be affected such that others are perceived as bad, malicious, or uncaring. Hence the survivor may manifest chronic anger, bitterness, and cynicism, and be isolated and despairing (McCann, Pearlman, Sakheim, & Abrahamson, 1988).

POWER/CONTROL

Sexual abuse in childhood or adulthood is a crime of abuse of power, not sex. One way to operationally define this abuse of power is by defining it in terms of how much older the abuser is than the victim. An accepted age differential is five years, however, this is a guideline, not a rule. For example, a boy in Year 4 was found in a 'rape' position with a Year 3 girl while other boys looked on. The power resided in this instance not just in the boy but in the social context of being the object of attention of the crowd. At another extreme, a father/stepfather, over a long period of time, coerced his male and female children to perform sex with him, with each other, and with inanimate objects.

Adult clients must examine the consequences of moving from victim to survivor on their current relationships, particularly with partners. The changes in power balance in the relationship can have profound effects and be so uncomfortable that their partner may be resist or sabotage the move.

SEX DIFFERENCES

Sexual abuse happens to male and female children. Although much research has been done on its effects on adult women, adult males, who generally use health services much less frequently than females, may suffer as much.

Sexual abuse of male children has attracted increasing attention recently (the work of Briere and Runtz (1988), Grubman-Black (1990), and Lew (1990) discuss this issue in detail). Briefly, some of the effects on men have been noted by Quina and Carlson (1989):

• Men may not label their experience as abuse
• Men may be expected by male cultural norms to 'tough it out'.
• They may experience a fear of latent homosexuality or attention-seeking (if homosexual) because of the confusing experience of an erection at the time of the assault.

In summary, male survivors have many similar experiences to female survivors, and also are subject to cultural pressures which may prevent them being able to approach counselling resources.

When both males and females present for treatment, a careful history needs to be taken, probably over more than one session, to establish the presence or absence of sexual abuse in those who appear to be at risk. Certainly, I cannot recollect treating a family for incest with a female child where there was not also incest with a male sibling if there was one in the same family.

Little is known about how boys are socialised into sexual behaviours. The Year 4 boy referred to above was seen by me in family interviews. His (step) father described how he himself was introduced to sex — by raping (along with a number of other boys) a girl from a more junior grade while at primary school. The father also described how he had a tattoo on his backside and the boys in the family also had been tattooed. The rape and the tattoo were part of the sexual initiation of the boy to manhood, for both the father and the son. Neither showed any remorse for the girl. It was as though their own rituals of sexual initiation had been intruded upon by the referral process.

Question 5: How can we understand
victims/survivors of sexual abuse?

How can we conceptualise trauma reactions to childhood sexual abuse succinctly and in a manner which might make sense of the variety of presentations and the timing of the presentations by adult men and women?

I recommend adopting the *life span developmental model*. The reason for adopting such a model is the well-established phenomenon of symptoms reappearing at transition points in the individual's life span and the repercussions this has on their capacity for intimacy and protection of their own children from similar traumas (e.g. Dolan, 1989).

The life span developmental approach should be combined with knowledge of the *flight/fight/freeze* reactions to intense stress, from arousal theory.

The combination of these two conceptual approaches provides a framework for understanding the person who presents at any significant phase of their life: at entry to school, at puberty or in young adulthood and when forming a long-term sexual relationship, or after the birth of children, and/or at middle-age.

This combination also helps to account for how some victims may present as an activist in welfare work or an activist of another, less socially condoned kind, for example, manifesting criminal behaviour. Other manifestations include exhaustion, depression, dissociative or fugue states, or multiple personality disorder. Adults presenting with these symptoms may also have problems of intimacy, no apparent growth in psychological wholeness or integration, and an inability to take on adult responsibilities. For example, they present with conversion disorders or somatoform disorders, where affect is denied (that is, they have poor insight) and are found to be unable to play the essential role of mediating between psyche and soma (McDougall, 1986).

Moreover, details of this conceptual approach have yet to be fully developed, but the theory is supported by the work of researchers such as Danieli (1985). In his study of Holocaust survivors and their children, he noted that they had flashbacks (which led to them being referred for therapy) at developmental life span transitional points. Apparently, the consequences of their trauma impinged upon their parenting of the next generation. The work of van der Kolk and his colleagues has supported this life span development perspective.

The evidence that women who are victims of childhood sexual abuse become victims in later life also supports the life span developmental model, and takes account of the intergenerational effect (Finkelhor, 1984; Sgroi, 1988). Finkelhor (1984), in particular, claimed that having a mother who frequently punished sexual curiosity or masturbation made a woman vulnerable to both early and later sexual victimisation. The dynamics of this kind of reaction are complex and need to be explored carefully. For instance, these behaviours may be representative of others which, in total, constitute the development of individual identity. Impaired identity may result in non-assertive or masochistic characteristics. Alternatively, punishing the behaviours could result in a rebellious preoccupation with sexual matters. Another effect might be that a punitive mother may be unable to provide a nurturing environment, so the deprived child may seek the solace which may accompany the sexually abusing adult.

Question 6: What are the options for treatment and the implications for the clinician?

Since most symptoms of childhood long-term abuse in adulthood can be viewed as survival strategies which may no longer be useful, treatment can focus on better adaptive control through anxiety management, relationship negotiations, and so on.

PROTECTION OF THE CLIENT

In the past, when disclosure of sexual abuse occurred, the health professional may have adopted different treatments depending upon whether or not the offender was inside or outside the family. Family systems theory applied in the former and criminal and adult psychopathology in the latter. However, this approach failed to do justice to the problem. Increasingly, clinicians recognise that the essential thing is the crime has occurred, regardless of the relationship of the offender to the victim. Moreover, a significant percentage of paedophiles, when assured of complete confidentiality, stated that they have offended against children inside and outside their family (Abel, Becker, Cunningham-Rather, & Mittelman, 1988; Abel & Osborn, 1992), and have raped adult females, and even males, who probably do not report the offence.

Clinicians, police, and legal officers should adopt an inquisitive stand in order to identify other children who are at risk and actively protect them. For example, an adolescent disclosed that the de facto of her grandmother had sexually abused her, yet no action was taken because the family had become aware of the abuse and planned to keep the adolescent away from the offender. Later, however, the de facto reappeared in the family when a sibling reached a similar age to her sister's age when the abuse had occurred. What was this man doing in the interim?

DEFINING CURRENT LIFE ISSUES

Where is the client in terms of his or her life span development? What are the physiological corollaries? How might what is happening in the client's life now be reminiscent of the degree of resolution of the trauma of their experience of childhood sexual abuse? How can the health professional help the client resolve current life issues so that they experience a different outcome?

The recovery process, which a clinician facilitates and guides, is based upon empowering the victim/survivor and creating new connections with others. The locus of control needs to be returned to the survivor. Therapists assist this process but are not the agents of it. The proper role of the therapist is as a witness, consultant and ally.

The recovery process has been conceptualised in three stages (Herman, 1983):

- The first stage involves the establishment of safety. The initial therapeutic alliance forms around the common goal of securing the patient's self-care and self-protection.
- The second stage involves the work of remembrance and mourning when the traumatic experience is explored in depth. The purpose of this work is integration rather than exorcism of the trauma.
- The third stage involves the reconstruction of present social relationships, including those with the client's children.

These stages are not always sequential: the client may move back and forth and, at any point in the process, may prefer to focus on current issues.

Not all victims develop psychological symptoms that impair their capacities. Many people are able to work through much of the trauma of their experience within their usual social support and lay counselling networks. There may even be positive consequences, often overlooked, perhaps, because the dramatic symptomatology and psychopathology found in those who do present for therapy is so riveting to society. However, even severe symptomatology may reflect a kind of positive adjustment to an horrific experience, for example, extraordinary memory, profound religious ideas, development of the intellect, or activity in social issues. People may involve themselves in caring for other people in need and never present for treatment.

MODELS OF INTERVENTION

Clinicians need to guard against the stereotyped notion that all victim/survivors behave the same. They should aim to match appropriate therapeutic interventions to particular forms of reaction, either on an individual basis (e.g. Dolan, 1989), through group therapy (e.g. Donaldson & Gardner, 1985; Sgroi, 1988), or by self-help (e.g. Ochberg, 1988), or through preventive program models (Brunt, 1988).

Group work helps survivors overcome the feeling that nobody who has not undergone similar experiences can 'really understand' what has happened to them. Identification with 'their group', initially based on common background alone, facilitates change as individuals have the opportunity to discuss and share their current concerns and past experiences. As Foulkes suggests, 'the deepest reason why these patients ... can reinforce each other's normal reactions and wear down and correct each other's (pathological) reactions, is that *"collectively they constitute the very norm, from which, they deviate*"' (Foulkes, cited in Danieli, 1985, p. 310-311, author's italics).

Regardless of which approach the health professional and client adopt, Ochberg's (1988) words seem an apt reminder, 'That the impact of human cruelty is experienced with a recognisable pattern of personal and interpersonal disruption and does not confer 'patienthood' per se' (p. vii). The cognitive reframing evidenced by this motto also clearly puts this position:

> I have been victimized.
> I was in a fight that was not a fair fight.
> I did not ask for the fight. I lost.
> There is no shame in losing such fights, only in winning.
> I have reached the stage of survivor and am no longer a slave of victim status.
> I look back with sadness rather than hate.
> I look forward with hope rather than despair.
> I may never forget, but I need not constantly remember.
> I was a victim.
> I was a survivor. (p. vii)

PROTECTION OF THE HEALTH PROFESSIONAL

Acknowledgment of these dimensions leads psychologists, and other health professionals, to play key roles in public policy making and community education, improving the effectiveness of treatment programs, and participating in evaluating existing management strategies (e.g. Brunt, 1987). This is also one way to prevent professional burnout, that is, to be active at levels of intervention other than with individual clients, such as writing submissions, assuming an advocacy role, and so on.

Child protective service workers receive little if any specialised training to cope with the emotional demands of intervening in child maltreatment cases. They usually have high case loads and inadequate support, so it becomes even more important for other clinicians to develop good consultation skills (not just principles, but practice), in order to make a valuable contribution in this field of work.

SELF-AWARENESS/COUNTERTRANSFERENCE IN THE TREATING PROFESSIONAL

Psychological naivety, and even active avoidance of these types of referral, has been a feature of many clinicians in the past. This can no longer be condoned. Childhood sexual abuse has affected too many patients to be ignored by clinicians in the aetiology of a range of disorders, especially when accompanied by neglect or even hostility.

There are a range of practical books to guide the clinician (e.g. Sgroi & Bunk, 1988; McCann et al., 1988; Ochberg, 1988). Sgroi and Bunk (1988) offer these suggestions:

- Be reliable, be honest, and do not require clients to trust you
- Encourage them to describe the abuse

- Demonstrate limit setting and consistency
- Negotiate a time limited therapy contract, and so on.

Psychoanalysis developed a bad name (e.g. Masson, 1984) and was considered inappropriate and even harmful to those who had experienced abuse such as prolonged sexual abuse. However, modern theories are more flexible and practically oriented and can accommodate patients who do have a history of deprivation or abuse. An important step on the way to healing is to come to know what these experiences mean for the patient (Malcolm, 1984), for their life as it is now, and for their current relationships.

This here-and-now approach is apparent in most contemporary major theories. Particularly useful is the range of cognitive reframing and cognitive-behavioural interventions derived from modern cognitive-behavioural psychology. Short-term therapies are being developed which emphasise that the 'child', even presenting as the adult, is not to blame and that actively working with the strengths of the survivor is extraordinarily important.

More knowledge of clinician reactions (e.g. Eisenberg, 1989; Hoxter, 1983) will assist the professional to provide the best possible assistance to victim/survivors (and help prevent secondary traumatic stress disorder). Often therapists' difficulties in treating victim/survivors may have their roots in the nature of the victimisation. For example, a female lesbian victim of long-term sadistic and multiple abuse by a stepfather, asked her therapist to read her statement to the police. In classical psychoanalytical therapy, the therapist could ask her what was there about reading the statement that was important to her. To know the horror can be victimising for the therapist by imposing the trauma upon her or him, or it may be that if the therapist can 'take it', then the client might learn to bear it, and so on. One thing is certain, such requests should be accepted as a valid expression of need on the part of the patient but should not necessarily be accepted at face value. The meaning of such a request must be worked through before any action should be taken.

SOCIALISATION OF PROFESSIONALS

Competing professions do not necessarily view the problem of sexual abuse in the same light. A variety of philosophies about the nature and handling of the problem have developed. Those who emphasise it as a crime see punishment as the main objective with, perhaps, the secondary aim of treatment of the offender to reduce their impulse to repeat. Others may see the abuse of others as primarily a mental illness and seek to provide treatment. Some might see it as evidence of a patriarchal society and attempt to change society by increasing power to women (although this would ignore what is known about the victimisation of males). Again, others might see that children need to be taught protective behaviours at school. Each of these perspectives has an important role to play, but not to the exclusion of all the others.

References

Abel, G.G., Becker, J.V., Cunningham-Rather, J., & Mittelman, M. (1988). Multiple paraphiliac diagnoses among sex offenders. *Bulletin of the American Academy of Psychiatry and the Law, 16*(2), 153–168.

Abel, G.G., & Osborn, C. (1992). The paraphilias: The extent and nature of sexually deviant and criminal behaviour. *Psychiatric Clinics of North America, 15*(3) 675–687.

American Psychiatric Association. (1987). *Diagnostic and Statistical Manual of Mental Disorders* (3rd ed. rev.). Washington, DC: Author.

Bessel, A., van der Kolk, B., & Glenn Saxe, M.D. (1992, June). *Trauma and dissociative disorders* (Abstract poster no. 385). World Conference of International Society for Traumatic Stress Studies, Amsterdam.

Briere, J., & Runtz, M. (1987). Post sexual abuse trauma: Data and implications for clinical practice. *Journal of Interpersonal Violence, 2*(4), 367–379.

Briere, J., & Runtz, M. (1988). Symptomatology associated with childhood sexual victimization in a nonclinical adult sample. *Child Abuse and Neglect, 12*(1), 51–59.

Brunt, D. (1987, August). *Evaluating a primary (protective) prevention programme*. Paper presented at the 27th Annual Conference of the Australian Psychological Society, Townsville, Queensland.

Brunt, D. (1988, June). *Prevention as treatment and vice versa: A progress report on establishing a secondary prevention program for sexually abused children, adolescents, and their families.* Paper delivered at 1st Victorian Conference on Child Abuse, Melbourne.

Danieli, Y. (1985). The treatment and prevention of long-term effects and intergenerational transmission of victimization: A lesson from holocaust survivors and their children. In C. Figley (Ed.), *Trauma and its wake: The study and treatment of post-traumatic stress disorder* (pp. 295–313). New York: Brunner/Mazel.

Dolan, Y. (1989) "Only once if I really mean it": Brief treatment of a previously dissociated incest case. *Journal of Strategic and Systemic Therapies, 8*(4), 3–8.

Donaldson, M.A., & Gardner, R., (1985). Diagnosis and treatment of traumatic stress among women after childhood incest. In C. Figley (Ed.), *Trauma and its wake: The study and treatment of post-traumatic stress disorder* New York: Brunner/Mazel.

Eisenberg, N. (1989). Attitudes of health professionals to child sexual abuse and incest. *Child Abuse and Neglect, 11,* 109–116.

Ellenberger, H.F. (1958). A clinical introduction to psychiatric phenomenology and existential analysis. In R. May, E. Angel & H.F. Ellenberger (Eds.), *Existence: A new dimension in psychiatry and psychology* (pp. 92–124). New York: Touchstone.

Figley, C. (Ed.). (1985). *Trauma and its wake: The study and treatment of post-traumatic stress disorder.* New York: Brunner/Mazel.

Finkelhor, D. (1984). *Child sexual abuse: New theory and research.* New York: The Free Press.

Freud, A. (1966). *The ego and the mechanisms of defense.* New York: International Universities Press.

Grubman-Black, S.D. (1990). *Broken boys/mending men: Recovery from childhood sexual abuse.* New York: Ivy Books.

Herman, J. (1983). Recognition and treatment of incestuous families. *International Journal of Family Therapy, 5*(2), 81–91.

Hoxter, S. (1983). Some feelings aroused in working with severely deprived children. In M. Boston & R. Szur (Eds.), *Psychotherapy with severely deprived children* (pp. 125–132). London: Routledge and Kegan Paul.

Lew, M. (1990). *Victims no longer: Men recovering from incest and other sexual child abuse.* New York: Perennial Library.

Lindberg, F.H., & Distad, L.J. (1985). Post-traumatic stress disorders in women who experienced childhood incest. *Child Abuse and Neglect, 9,* 329–334.

Malcolm, J. (1984). *In the Freud archives.* London: Jonathan Cape.

Masson, J.M. (1984). *The assault on truth: Freud's suppression of the seduction theory.* Toronto: Farrar, Straus and Giroux.

McCann, L., Pearlman, L.A., Sakheim, D.K. & Abrahamson, D.J. (1988). Assessment and treatment of the adult survivor of childhood sexual abuse within a schema framework. In S.M. Sgroi (Ed.), *Vulnerable populations: Evaluation and treatment of sexually abused children and adult survivors* (Vol. 1, pp. 77–101). Toronto: Lexington Books.

McDougall, J. (1986). *Theatres of the mind: Illusion and truth on the psychoanalytic stage.* London: Free Association.

Ochberg, F.M. (1988). *Post-traumatic therapy and victims of violence.* New York: Brunner/Mazel.

Polkowski, M. (1991, September). *Unresolved post-sexual abuse trauma: Notes from a workshop.* Annual conference of the Australian Psychological Society, Monash University, Adelaide.

Powell, M.B. (1991). Investigating and reporting child sexual abuse: Review and recommendations for clinical practice *Australian Psychologist, 26,* 77–83.

Quina, K., & Carlson, N.L. (1989). *Rape, incest and sexual harassment: A guide for helping survivors.* New York: Praeger.

Sgroi, S.M. (Ed.). (1988). *Vulnerable populations: Evaluation and treatment of sexually abused children and adult survivors. Volume 1.* Toronto: Lexington Books.

Sgroi, S.M., & Bunk, B.S. (1988). A clinical approach to adult survivors of childhood sexual abuse. In S.M. Sgroi (Ed.), *Vulnerable populations: Evaluation and treatment of sexually abused children and adult survivors* (Vol. 1, pp. 137–186). Toronto: Lexington Books.

Tracey, N. (in press). The psychic space in trauma. *Journal of Child Psychotherapy.*

van der Hart, O., Brown, P., & van der Kolk, B. (1989). Pierre Janet's treatment of post-traumatic stress. *Journal of Traumatic Stress, 2*(4), 379–395.

van der Kolk, B., Perry, J.C., & Herman, J.L. (1991). Childhood origins of self-destructive behaviour. *American Journal of Psychiatry, 148,* 1665–1671.

van der Kolk, B., & Saporta, J. (1991). The biological response to psychic trauma: Mechanisms and treatment of intrusion and numbing. *Anxiety Research, 4*(3), 199–212.

Cultural Issues in Posttraumatic Stress Disorder

CHAPTER NINE

I. Harry Minas and Steven Klimidis

AUSTRALIA'S population is characterised by cultural and linguistic diversity (Jupp, 1990). Over 21 per cent of Australia's population in June 1986 was born overseas. Two-thirds of this population were born in non-English speaking countries (Castles, 1989), and speak more than 60 different languages. This diversity is a product of Australia's migration program, which has experienced major shifts in the countries of origin of Australia's immigrants (Jupp, 1990). Our large migrant population is a major issue when discussing Posttraumatic Stress Disorder (PTSD) in Australia.

Between 1981 and 1991 the number of refugees worldwide more than doubled, from 8 to 17 million, with a further 15 million people displaced from their homes by war, famine and other natural and human-made traumatic events (Lombard, 1993). Australia has accepted large numbers of refugees as part of its immigration program; in fact, among the largest proportion in the world on a per capita basis. Between 1983 and 1986 approximately 59,000 immigrants to Australia were classified under the refugee and humanitarian migration programs (Castles, 1989).

Refugees are one of the largest groups of potential sufferers of PTSD. As well as dispossession and displacement, many refugees have experienced death of or injury to loved ones or friends, imprisonment, assault, and enduring uncertainty. A substantial proportion of people who enter

Australia as refugees have been tortured (McGorry, 1988; Stanton, 1993). Although these people have a high prevalence of PTSD (Ramsay, Gorst-Unsworth, & Turner, 1993), they do not commonly come into contact with the mainstream health system. In a study of Vietnamese refugee adolescents conducted by the Victorian Transcultural Psychiatry Unit (Minas, Klimidis, Ata, & Stuart, 1993), a substantial proportion reported traumatic events experienced either by themselves or by close members of their family. Figure 9.1 shows the frequency with which such events were experienced by these people before they left Vietnam. This group of refugees experienced further significant traumas during the voyage from Vietnam and during their stay in overseas refugee camps.

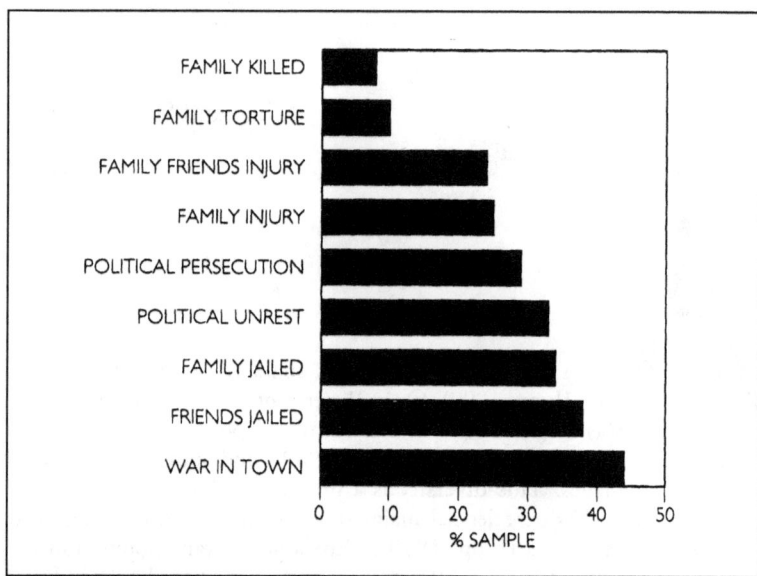

FIGURE 9.1
Experience of traumatic events by Vietnamese refugee adolescents

In addition to the refugees' traumatic personal history, their migration and resettlement in a foreign and culturally unfamiliar environment create difficulties and stresses which may contribute to the delayed onset or maintenance of PTSD (Hierholzer, Munson, Peabody, & Rosenberg 1992; Lin, Tazuma, & Masuda, 1979; Masuda, Lin, & Tazuma, 1980; Van Dyke, Zilberg, & McKinnon, 1985). Events which evoke meanings and reactions similar to those of the original traumatic experience are most likely to result in appearance or recurrence of the disorder (Christenson, Walker, & Ross, 1981). In addition, the severity and course of PTSD may be influenced by concurrent life stresses (Friedman, Schneiderman, West, & Corson, 1986;

Hierholzer et al., 1992). Kinzie and Fleck (1987) noted that, 'Even the possibility of the loss of housing or income caused patients to panic as if these were actually severe threats to their lives, thus reactivating their constant fear of death' (p. 83). Interactions with authority figures and institutions, and even apparently benign questions (such as, 'What is your name?'), may activate or reactivate the disorder, particularly in those who have experienced torture or have had to hide their identity for fear of being killed (Kinzie & Fleck, 1987). Media reports and popular films depicting war scenes bring up memories of traumatic experiences for refugees and aggravate PTSD or cause it to recur.

What is culture?

The theme of this chapter is the role of people's culture in their response to traumatic stress. The sense in which we use this term *culture* is that outlined by Goodenough (cited in Ramondo, 1991):

> A society's culture consists of whatever it is one has to know in order to operate in a manner acceptable to its members. Culture is not a material phenomenon; it does not consist of things, behaviour or emotion. It is rather an organisation of those things. It is the form of things that people have in mind, their models for perceiving, relating, and otherwise interpreting them. Culture consists of standards for deciding what is ... for deciding what one feels about it ... for deciding what to do about it, and ... for deciding how to go about doing it. (p. 70)

Culture consists of shared ideas, rules and meanings (Keesing, 1981), a largely unconscious code which enables individuals within a community to communicate, live, work, anticipate and interpret behaviour. Culture is the lens through which people see the world and how they function within it. Culture informs, influences and shapes fundamental beliefs and values, and thereby shapes attitudes and behaviours. Although culture is commonly identified with ethnicity, they are not synonymous. The range of beliefs, values and practices within any ethnic community is broad, so uncritical use of terms such as Italian or Vietnamese or Lebanese culture may mislead as much as it might inform.

The experience of migration, swapping a known culture for an unfamiliar one, encompasses a complex set of factors (Minas, Klimidis, & Stuart, 1993; Nicassio & Pate, 1984) which can increase general psychological and emotional distress over an extended period (Murphy, 1977) and activate or aggravate PTSD in those who are vulnerable (Kinzie & Fleck, 1987; Kroll et al., 1989). These factors are listed below:

- Socioeconomic status — working below educational level, unemployment, substandard housing
- Changes in the social milieu — re-structuring of the social network, family separation, loss of contact with significant others, isolation

- Lack of necessary skills for the new environment — inadequate knowledge of English or of the manner in which the new society and its institutions operate
- The need to adapt successfully to the pressures of acculturation, both at the personal level (Berry, 1990) and in response to differing rates of acculturation in family members (Ranieri, 1992).

This set of factors may influence the course of PTSD in immigrants, as will whether they seek treatment or not, the timing of treatment-seeking after the onset of the disorder, and their ability to participate fully in any treatments offered.

Experience and expression of illness varies cross-culturally

The early work of Zborowski (1952) and others on pain in various ethnic groups, the World Health Organisation's multi-centre studies of schizophrenia (Jablensky, 1988; Jablensky et al., 1992), and the work of Kleinman (1980), Marsella (1988), and others on cross-cultural aspects of depression have demonstrated cultural variation in the experience and expression of psychiatric illness. Such studies confirm the clinical experience of working with people from a variety of cultural backgrounds.

An illness episode begins with the perception that something is wrong (is both abnormal and undesirable), with perceived physical or psychological dysfunction, pain or discomfort, or disturbed behaviour. The perception of such experience as abnormal, its naming and the evaluation of its meaning for the person are cognitive processes which are deeply embedded in a complex family, social and cultural matrix (Good & Good, 1980). Illness is constructed from knowledge which is available to the person about illness (that is, popular medical culture) as the sufferer draws on culturally prevalent theories, beliefs and networks of meaning to interpret and communicate his or her distress. Each culture provides distinctive understandings of human suffering and of healing. Each provides explanations for the occurrence of illness, models of bodily structure and function and personality, and forms of dealing with illness. These understandings are grounded in a culture's cosmology, epistemology and set of beliefs and values. The illness and its symptoms condense multiple meanings and expected consequences for the sufferer — life stresses, personal traumas, fears and expectations concerning the future, and social reactions of friends and authorities (Good & Good, 1980). Such a process of illness construction is important in the development and maintenance of an illness such as PTSD, which occurs as a consequence of exposure to particular environmental events, the attribution of meaning to those events, and the cognitive, affective and physiological consequences of the particular attributions of meaning. A patient's degree of distress, illness behaviour, pattern of help-seeking, and extent of engagement in recommended treatments all stem from the meaning which those external events and internal experiences have for the individual. The sufferer's construction of the PTSD experience will reflect social class, cultural beliefs, education, occupation, religious background, and past experience of illness and health care. It will also reflect the specific circumstances in which the disorder has developed.

The development of PTSD and the role of culture

To help us examine culture's role in PTSD, Figure 9.2 delineates the necessary conditions for the development of the disorder. The necessary conditions are:

1. *Exposure of the individual to a particular class of events which are outside the range of normal human experience and which will produce distress in virtually anyone who experiences them*
The likelihood of exposure to traumatic events is obviously greatly influenced by the social, economic and political circumstances prevailing in the country/region where the person lives. As well as political and economic factors (which are also closely related to culture), broad cultural factors will influence the probability of exposure by influencing the occurrence of war or social strife, the prevalence of crime against the person and domestic violence, attitudes towards and treatment of women and children, and so on.

2. *The person must perceive the event as traumatic, that is, as a threat to the integrity of the self*
The perception of events as being outside the range of normal human experience will obviously be different depending on where the sufferer comes from. Events which would be regarded as extremely traumatic in Melbourne may be so common in Somalia, Belfast, or Bosnia as to have achieved the status of normality. It is important to remember that conceptions of the self, and what constitutes a threat to the integrity of the self, will also vary widely in different cultures.

3. *There must be the characteristic set of cognitive, affective, and physiological reactions to the event*
The socio-cultural context will be a powerful determinant of the nature and severity of reactions to adversity. The predominance of cognitive, affective, or somatic (physiological) components of such responses are also, to a large extent, culturally shaped.
Angel and Thoits (1987) cite evidence that cultural groups differ in the extent to which they teach their members to monitor bodily and emotional states. Kleinman (1980), in his analysis of Chinese culture, suggests that an external, sociocentric rather than individualistic focus in this group, along

with socio-cultural unacceptability of overt expressions of emotions and the stigma of psychiatric disorder, promote somatic rather than psychological expressions of distress.

Initial attention to, and subsequent selection of, information from altered internal states is, to a substantial extent, concept driven ('top down' processing). Cross-cultural variability in internal representations will influence the processes determining which information is attended to for cognitive elaboration. Angel and Thoits (1987) propose that once detection of change in somatic or emotional state has occurred, further cognitive elaboration will determine whether the experiences are regarded as normal or abnormal. This will be based on one's knowledge of the prevalence of, and attitude towards, such experiences in one's own cultural group (see also Kirmayer, 1989). Further cognitive elaboration will result in classification of the experience as physical, psychological, or spiritual in nature, and judgements will be made as to its seriousness, cause, and probable course. Such elaborations are part of the transformation of chaotic reactions to trauma into an identified illness, such as PTSD, and are culturally shaped. The core of such cognitive processing is attribution of meaning to the somatic or emotional state and to the expected consequences of this state. The meanings attributed will have wide-ranging effects on the perceptual selective processes, the pattern of distress, the forms of remedy which will be mobilised or sought, and on the course and outcome of the disorder. Such an approach to an understanding of the development and persistence of PTSD allows consideration of the interplay of biological, psychosocial, and cultural factors.

4. The reactions are construed by the person him/herself (or others, for example, family or health professionals) as constituting illness rather than as some other class of human problem

Whether personal suffering is construed as illness or as some other class of human problem will depend on culturally derived conceptions of illness, on religious and other views about the causes and meaning of suffering in human life, and on the availability of medical solutions to problems of suffering. In our own culture, much human suffering which was previously conceptualised in other terms, has become medicalised.

Assessment

The clinician assessing a patient with PTSD requires all the usual clinical skills and the specific knowledge relevant to an understanding of this disorder. In addition, the clinician will need to systematically explore the patient's culturally derived beliefs, values, knowledge, and attitudes if he or she is to understand the patient's experiences and their consequences.

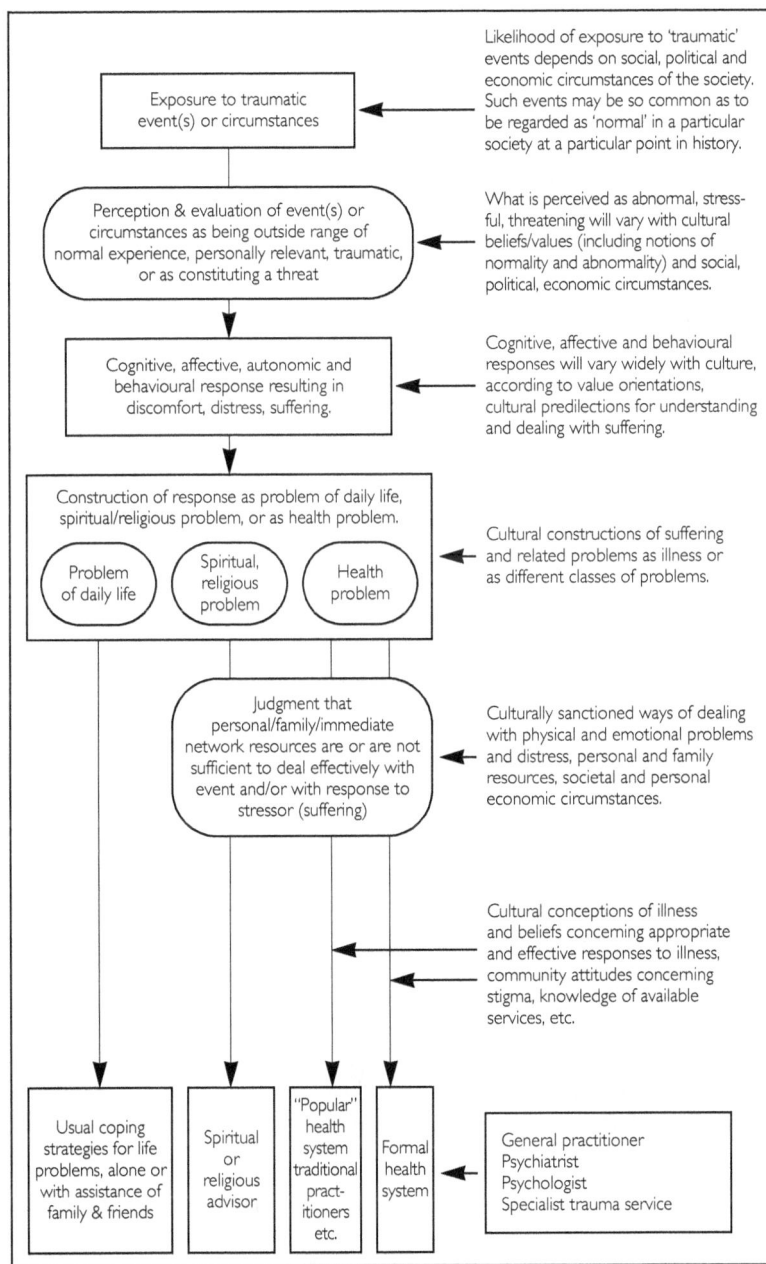

FIGURE 9.2
Cultural influences on PTSD

COMMUNICATION

The first requirement for assessment is adequate communication between clinician and patient. Language is the core instrument, although non-verbal communication is also very important. When the patient comes from a different cultural background and does not speak the same language as the clinician, the two must be able to communicate adequately—probably by using a professional interpreter. There is an abundance of evidence of difficulties in clinician-patient communication, even when they speak the same language. One of the problems, of course, is that they do not always, in fact, speak the 'same language'. If their respective meanings are not examined and clarified, there is room for interpretive error and mis-communication. In a clinical encounter where clinician and patient do not have a common language, adequate communication is especially difficult, even when an interpreter is present. Even patients who appear to have a reasonable knowledge of English may have a limited knowledge of vocabulary, grammar and syntax and use of idiom in English. With a significant psychiatric disorder, the patient's ability to communicate adequately in a second language frequently deteriorates (Marcos et al., 1973; Peck, 1974).

A well-trained and skilful interpreter can provide the necessary bridge between clinician and non-English speaking patient. However, the use of untrained interpreters is still a common practice in many clinical settings. This practice, which demonstrates a gross underestimation of the difficulty of the interpreting task (Demetriou, 1991), results in problems in assessment and disadvantages the patient. The ability to work effectively with interpreters is a skill which must be learned, since the presence of the interpreter inevitably changes the nature and structure of the interaction between patient and clinician. Deviations from the ideal pattern of interaction (Baker & Briggs, 1975) can diminish the effectiveness of communication between clinician and patient and can cause difficulties in both assessment and treatment.

Special problems may arise in the interpreted interview with refugee patients (Kinzie & Fleck, 1987). An interpreter (and indeed clinical staff) may have undergone traumatic experiences which are similar to those of the patient. This may precipitate strong emotional responses in the interpreter during the session. Interpreters may need recognition, support, and debriefing to enable them to continue to work effectively with the patient. The possible importance of gender differences between members of the patient-clinician-interpreter triad should be considered since such differences may obstruct the development of a therapeutic relationship and may substantially inhibit disclosure. An additional difficulty is patients' frequent concerns about confidentiality when an interpreter from the patient's community is involved, particularly if the community is small and divided along political, religious, and other lines.

DIAGNOSIS

Diagnosis in a cross-cultural context poses considerable problems. The main difficulty is in making correct inferences about the clinical significance of a patient's experiences, behaviours, and modes of verbal and non-verbal communication which may be unfamiliar to the clinician. A further problem is that the clinician's unfamiliarity with the patient's culture may mean that he or she is not even sure what information should be sought (and from whom) in order to clarify significant clinical uncertainties. Several types of diagnostic error may occur on the basis of misinterpretation of the experience of patients from a different cultural background. Each of these is more likely to occur when patient and clinician do not have a common language in which they can communicate. These diagnostic errors are listed below:

1. Failure to identify the type of psychopathology, leading to mistaken diagnosis, for example, intrusive recollections of a traumatic event, particularly when there are communication difficulties between patient and clinician, may be incorrectly interpreted as obsessional ruminations or hallucinations.

2. Errors in assessment of severity of psychopathology, for example, in a patient who uses a somatic rather than a psychological idiom of distress the severity of depression and suicidal risk may be seriously under-estimated.

3. Diagnosis of psychopathology when it is not present, for example, mistakenly identifying culturally appropriate experience or behaviour as psychopathology.

4. Failure to recognise psychopathology when it is present, for example, mistakenly attributing illness-related experience or behaviour solely to cultural or situational factors.

Cultural issues in the treatment of PTSD

Psychiatric assessment and treatment cannot be adequately carried out if there is a wide divergence between the views of the patient and the clinician concerning the nature of the disorder, its cause, its expected course and outcome, and what needs to be done about it. These differences must be explicitly acknowledged and explored and resolved, if possible, so that patient and clinician can work with a common understanding of the nature of the problem, the goals of treatment, how the goals are to be achieved, and the probable outcome of treatment. In order to achieve such a common under-standing it is frequently necessary (even when patient and clinician come from the same culture) for clinician and patient to negotiate these issues.

The elements of the negotiation process outlined below are adapted from Kleinman (1982):

1. The clinician elicits the patient's understanding of the nature and origins of his illness, its expected course and outcome, and the patient's goals for and expectations of treatment.

2. The clinician clearly and fully presents to the patient, in plain language and, if possible, in a conceptual framework that makes sense to the

patient, their understanding of the patient's problems and their treatment recommendations.

3. Most commonly patients will respond by shifting their understanding of the problem towards that of the clinician, making a treatment alliance possible. The reverse may also occur, where the clinician, having acquired a clearer understanding of the patient's problems and their way of thinking about them, may change the clinical recommendations, shifting towards the patient's expectations of treatment.

4. If significant discrepancies in conceptualisation remain, the two should acknowledge the situation and try to clarify matters. In most cases a mutually acceptable course of action can be agreed.

5. Where the conflict in conceptualisations, particularly about treatment, cannot be resolved, and the patient's requests are thought to be unacceptable on professional or ethical grounds, then the therapeutic alliance is broken. The patient has the right to reject the clinician's perceptions and treatment advice.

This negotiating approach to the clinical encounter makes it possible to achieve an adequate understanding of the patient's illness and their treatment goals, work within a cognitive framework that makes sense to the patient, and avoid imposing a view of the illness which is culturally inappropriate.

A large part of the still very patchy literature on cross-cultural treatment of PTSD is concerned with South-east Asian refugees but the issues raised in this work are probably relevant to the cross-cultural treatment of PTSD.

TREATMENT SETTING

Kinzie and Fleck (1987) draw attention to aspects of the therapeutic setting and process of psychiatric assessment which, for refugees, may exacerbate the disorder by reminding them of the original traumatic incidents: 'The interview setting — a small, closed room where the patient, particularly a female, is surrounded by a male physician and an interpreter — could stimulate past memories' (Kinzie & Fleck, 1987, p. 84). They suggest removing threatening elements of the physical setting in which assessment and treatment are undertaken, so that it should not resemble 'a jail cell' (p. 87). Clinical staff should adopt a polite, low-key, relaxed and non-confronting approach in order to maximise the difference for the patient between the therapeutic atmosphere and one which may connote interrogation. They suggest also that it is helpful to have a female staff member present during the session to enhance this difference. These considerations are particularly relevant to people who have been subjected to torture.

INTERVIEW STYLE AND FOCUS

Kinzie and Fleck (1987) report that adopting an active and directive interview approach with South-east Asian refugees may promote their increased avoidance and withdrawal. They suggest letting the patient lead the process of information gathering by the examiner. Moore and Boehnlein (1991b) make similar suggestions, particularly because of the greater focus of South-east Asian groups on somatic complaints:

> It has been important in treatment to take somatic concerns seriously and treat them symptomatically ... This approach follows the general guideline that it is wise to accept what the patient offers. After discussing their somatic concerns it is often possible to inquire about psychological symptoms and to discuss other family and cultural problems. If the somatic problems are pushed to the side, the patients feel that they have not been taken seriously, the doctor has not fulfilled his or her duty, and is not adequately concerned with their welfare (p. 1032).

Mollica, Wyshak, and Lavelle (1987) suggest that an unhurried, unobtrusive clinical approach to diagnosis and treatment is more congruent with the nature of interpersonal relationships in South-east Asian cultures and is therefore a more appropriate therapeutic approach to take with victims of torture and trauma from these cultures. A probing psychiatric interview, particularly with trauma victims, may lead to underdiagnosis of PTSD and disruption of the therapeutic alliance.

Social, ethnic and cultural differences ought to become subjects for discussion, exploration and explanation in assessment and in treatment. Clinicians would do well to say, 'I don't know much about ...' and invite patients to educate them. A genuine interest in the patient's culture, values, etc. is a good start to a productive therapeutic relationship. Some simple, practical issues are often overlooked, for example, one's name is central to a sense of identity and self. Clinicians who take the trouble and care to learn how to properly pronounce patients' names, their preferred form of address, and so on, provide an opportunity to demonstrate their genuine respect for their patients. It is surprising how rarely clinicians take the trouble to do this.

Keeping in mind the importance of the family in many cultural groups is essential. Patients should be asked whether they want their families to be involved in discussions to do with the illness. Exclusion of the family is one of the more common causes of difficulty in the assessment and treatment of an individual from a different culture. The role and status of certain family members must be acknowledged and respected.

CLINICIAN CREDIBILITY AND AUTHORITY

An understanding of patients' beliefs concerning their illness, as outlined above, is essential in developing a therapeutic alliance between the therapist and a patient from a dissimilar culture. Sue and Zane (1987) provide a useful analysis of how culture may influence the therapeutic relationship, pointing to the significance of the credibility of the therapist and his or her approaches. They suggest that if credibility is not established within the first two or three sessions there is a risk of poor compliance and premature termination of the therapeutic alliance. In order to achieve credibility as healers, clinicians must be alert to their patients' knowledge and expectations of the therapeutic relationship. The discontent reported by Moore and Boenhelein (1991b) in patients whose somatic symptoms were disregarded is a good example of failure by the clinician to achieve credibility — patients expect the 'doctor' to treat medical problems. Therapists can achieve credibility by responding in ways which convey understanding of patients' cultural constructions of illness, through their requests for culturally consistent (and avoidance of culturally dissonant) responses and efforts from patients, and through a congruence of therapeutic goals as understood by both patient and therapist (Sue & Zane, 1987). Therapists must be in a position to give to patients some immediate benefit through the interaction. This will usually be some form or symptomatic relief, normalisation of mystifying 'psychopathological' experiences, hope for relief or recovery, or other 'gifts'. These features are recognisable in Kinzie and Fleck's (1987) approach, particularly in the emphasis on providing adequate support in domains outside the range of traditional psychiatric therapeutic strategies. Furthermore, in view of the often chronic course of the disorder, clinicians are more credible if they make a long-term commitment to their therapeutic relationship with the patient. These factors, and the central role of empathy, have been referred to by several authors writing about the treatment of PTSD in South-east Asian refugees (Mollica et al., 1987; Kinzie & Fleck, 1987).

DISCLOSURE

Cultural values and beliefs may influence the process of disclosure in relation to traumatic incidents. Kroll et al. (1989) found it difficult to assess the frequency of rape experiences in South-east Asian refugee women. They suggested that the tremendous shame attached to rape in this culture may have inhibited disclosure, either to a Western therapist or compatriot interpreter, in addition to the common reluctance of PTSD patients to recount traumatic incidents.

THERAPEUTIC GOALS: CATHARSIS OR SUPPRESSION?

Different therapeutic goals may be relevant to different cultural groups. The goals of the clinician are not necessarily those of patients and their families.

Mollica et al. (1987) suggest empathic review of the traumatic experiences, concurrent with 'reframing' these towards the view that the patient's reactions are understandable and normal in the context of an abnormal situation. Through this they suggest that the patient can move out of the 'crazy patient' (Kinzie et al., 1990, p. 917) role into a 'survivor role'. This helps to minimise the patient's identification with mental illness, which carries tremendous social stigma in Asian cultures (Lien & Rice, 1992). Morris and Silove (1992) report the efficacy of similar reframing techniques with torture survivors from Latin American countries. In such techniques, there is an emphasis in redirecting anger and aggression towards the torturers rather than towards the self (Morris & Silove, 1992, p. 821).

Kinzie & Fleck (1987) place value on supporting the psychological defenses and concurrently avoiding promotion of 'cathartic reminiscences' during treatment of refugees with PTSD. They suggest that cathartic reminiscence may be contraindicated in South-east Asian patients, since recounting traumatic events during the psychiatric evaluation has, in their experience, led in many instances to emergence of the disorder in previously asymptomatic patients. In some the symptoms lasted for several months (Kinzie & Fleck, 1987). In their view, psychological defences, including suppression and avoidance, are an adaptive form of management of PTSD symptoms and not merely a temporary device which interferes with the 'real' therapeutic ingredient of processing or integrating the traumatic experiences (Horowitz, 1986). They suggest also that it is important to deal with emergent situational problems (for example, housing and welfare) and current life stresses as these arise. Patients under this approach of 'covering over' the traumatic conflicts, reportedly gain, 'some sense of relief and begin hoping for a more productive life' (Kinzie & Fleck, 1987, p. 92).

As already mentioned, such an approach runs counter to views that the therapeutic goal should always be the processing of the traumatic events through cathartic reminiscences (e.g. Horowitz, 1986; Grinker & Spiegel, 1945). Morris and Silove (1992) review studies which support the effectiveness of reminiscence approaches adopted by the Copenhagen clinic for treating torture survivors from South American countries and the similarly effective suppression approaches taken with South-east Asians (e.g. Kinzie & Fleck, 1987). They suggest that cultural background may have influenced the choice and efficacy of the two approaches. Recent studies in Western cultures (e.g. Creamer, Burgess, & Pattison, 1992) suggest that intrusive phenomena are negatively correlated with subsequent symptom levels. This would suggest that some form of cognitive processing of the trauma may occur as mediated by intrusive traumatic imagery, perhaps in the manner suggested by Horowitz's (1986) model. However, whether catharsis emotional processing, readjustment of internal schemata, integrating the trauma, and the like, are universally necessary, or even culturally relevant, for recovery from PTSD in patients from varied cultural backgrounds remains unclear (Fairbank & Nicholson, 1987; Solomon, Weisenber, Schwarzwald, & Mikulincer, 1987). What is clear, however, is that the therapeutic approach needs to be culturally appropriate, and therefore will differ for patients from different cultures. The task of the clinician is to sensitively determine which approaches are likely to be of most benefit for which patients. It is likely that patients from different cultural groups use different recovery pathways which are consistent with their particular illness conceptions. If suppression and avoidance are salient features of South-east Asian adaptation to traumatic events, supporting and promoting such processes is enough to achieve the therapeutic goal. If emotional expression and personal disclosure are the predominant means of adapting to trauma in Latin American cultures, then reminiscence and cathartic approaches may be best for these patients. It is essential, however, that clinicians do not rely on cultural stereotypes when framing assessment and treatment approaches, but rather must rely on their knowledge of particular patients in their cultural context. Cross-cultural research which focuses on treatment models and their efficacy in patients from different cultures is necessary to resolve such issues. For patients from some cultures, re-experiencing as part of a therapeutic process may simply result in more traumatisation.

GROUP TECHNIQUES

Group therapeutic approaches, in the view of Kinzie and colleagues (Kinzie & Fleck, 1987; Kinzie et al., 1988), have not proved valuable either with the wider population of South-east Asian patients (Kinzie et al., 1988) or with those suffering from PTSD (Kinzie & Fleck, 1987). Problems with group-oriented approaches included segregation of the group between those who were more acculturated and those who maintained traditional beliefs and values, and difficulties with managing the language barrier between patients and clinical staff (Kinzie et al., 1988). Nevertheless there are some advantages to approaches which use both individual techniques and group sessions (Kinzie et al., 1988; Moore & Boehnlein, 1991b). Group approaches have been found useful as a framework for discussing continu-ing, shared concerns arising from the process of acculturation and adapta-tion to the host society (Moore & Boehnlein, 1991a) and for the development of a social network and a general supportive environment (Kinzie et al., 1988).

Future cross-cultural research on PTSD

Most of the research on PTSD in different cultural groups has focused on its prevalence. Although there have been some recent studies of cultural factors which may influence psychotherapy and pharmacotherapy (Kinzie & Leung, 1989; Kinzie, Leung, Boehnlein, & Fleck, 1987; Moore & Boehnlein, 1991a), these have been largely restricted to South-east Asian groups. Very few investigations have focused on the effects of culture on the ways in which different groups react to severe trauma, and on the course and outcome of PTSD. Nevertheless, the limited available literature contains sufficient indications of the importance of culture in PTSD. Attention to cultural factors will be important in further clarifying the range of responses (including the development of psychopathology) to extreme stress and in developing relevant and effective treatment approaches for people from a wide variety of cultures.

Conclusion

An important first step in recognising the cultural dimensions in patients with PTSD is to become aware of one's own culturally derived beliefs and assumptions. Awareness of one's own information (or lack thereof) about the patient's culture is a critical step. Understanding the socio-cultural milieu in which a person lives and functions is crucial in assessing not only psychopathology but also skills, resources, and coping behaviour (Westermeyer, 1985).

It is necessary to go beyond general sensitivity to people from other cultures to specific knowledge and attitudes (Leong, 1986). Cross-cultural diagnosis and treatment depends on the clinician's basic methods and skills, augmented by special techniques and assistance as described. These may include extra time for the establishment of rapport and eliciting the necessary information, and knowledge about behavioural, attitudinal and cognitive norms in the patient's culture.

References

Angel, R., & Thoits, P. (1987). The impact of culture on the cognitive structure of illness. *Culture, Medicine and Psychiatry, 11*, 465–494.

Baker, R., & Briggs, J. (1975). Working with interpreters in social work. *Australian Social Work, 28*, 31–37.

Berry, J.W. (1990). Psychology of acculturation: Understanding individuals moving between cultures. In R.W. Brislin (Ed.), *Applied Cross-Cultural Psychology* (Vol. 14, pp. 232–253). Beverly Hills, CA: Sage Publications Inc..

Castles, I. (1989). *Overseas born Australians 1988: A statistical profile.* (Australian Bureau of Statistics Catalogue No. 4112.0). Canberra, ACT: AGPS.

Christenson, R.M., Walker, J.I., & Ross, D.R. (1981). Reactivation of traumatic conflicts. *American Journal of Psychiatry, 138*, 984–985.

Creamer, M., Burgess, P., & Pattison, P. (1992). Reaction to trauma: A cognitive processing model. *Journal of Abnormal Psychology, 101*, 452–459.

Demetriou, S. (1991). Interpreters and psychiatry. In I.H. Minas (Ed.), *Cultural diversity and mental health* (pp. 65–69). Melbourne: Royal Australian & New Zealand College of Psychiatrists and Victorian Transcultural Psychiatry Unit.

Fairbank, J.A., & Nicholson, R.A. (1987). Theoretical and empirical issues in the treatment of post-traumatic stress disorder in Vietnam veterans. *Journal of Clinical Psychology, 43*, 44–55.

Friedman, M.J., Schneiderman, C.K., West, A.N., & Corson, J.A. (1986). Measurement of combat exposure, posttraumatic stress disorder, and life stress among Vietnam combat veterans. *American Journal of Psychiatry, 143*, 537–538.

Good, B.J., & Good, M-J. D. (1980). The meaning of symptoms: A cultural hermeneutic model for clinical practice. In L. Eisenberg, & A. Kleinman (Eds.), *The relevance of social science for medicine.* (pp. 197–222). Dordrecht: D. Reidel.

Grinker, R.R., & Spiegel, J.P. (1945). *War neuroses.* Philadelphia: The Blakiston Company.

Hierholzer, R., Munson, J., Peabody, C., & Rosenberg, J. (1992). Clinical presentation of PTSD in World War II combat veterans. *Hospital and Community Psychiatry, 43*, 816–820.

Horowitz, M.J. (1986). Stress-response syndromes: A review of posttraumatic and adjustment disorders. *Hospital and Community Psychiatry, 37*, 241–249.

Jablensky, A. (1988). Epidemiology of schizophrenia. In P. Bebbington & P. McGuffin (Eds.), *Schizophrenia: The major issues*. Oxford: Heinemann.

Jablensky, A., Sartorius, N., Ernberg, G., Anker, M., Korten, A., Cooper, J. E., Day, R., & Bertelsen, A. (1992). Schizophrenia: Manifestations, incidence and course in different cultures. A World Health Organisation 10-country study. *Psychological Medicine*. (Monograph supplement 20).

Jupp, J. (1990). Two hundred years of immigration. In J. Reid & P. Trompf (Eds.), *The health of immigrant Australia: A social perspective* (pp. 1–38). Harcourt Brace Jovanovich: Sydney.

Keesing, R. M. (1981). *Cultural anthropology: A contemporary perspective*. New York: Holt, Rinehart & Winston.

Kinzie, J.D., Boehnlein, J.K., Leung, P.K., Moore, L.J., Riley, C., & Smith, D. (1990). The prevalence of posttraumatic stress disorder and its clinical significance among Southeast Asian refugees. *American Journal of Psychiatry, 147*, 913–918.

Kinzie, J.D., & Fleck, J. (1987). Psychotherapy with severely traumatized refugees. *American Journal of Psychotherapy, 41*, 82–94.

Kinzie, D.J., & Leung, P. (1989). Clonidine in Cambodian patients with posttraumatic stress disorder. *Journal of Nervous and Mental Disease, 177*, 546–550.

Kinzie, D.J., Leung, P., Boehnlein, J.K., & Fleck, J. (1987). Antidepressant blood levels in Southeast Asians: Clinical and cultural implications. *Journal of Nervous and Mental Disease, 175*, 480–485.

Kinzie, D.J., Leung, P., Bui, A., Ben, R., Keopraseuth, K.O., Riley, C., Fleck, J., & Ades, M. (1988). Group therapy with Southeast Asian refugees. *Community Mental Health Journal, 24*, 157–166.

Kirmayer, L.J. (1989). Cultural variations in the response to psychiatric disorders and emotional distress. *Social Science in Medicine, 29*, 327–339.

Kleinman, A. (1982). The teaching of clinically applied medical anthropology on a psychiatric consultation-liaison service. In N.J. Chrisman & T.W. Maretzki (Eds.), *Clinically applied medical anthropology: Anthropologists in health science settings* (pp. 83-115). Dordrecht: D. Reidel.

Kleinman, A. (1980). *Patients and healers in the context of culture: An exploration of the borderland between anthropology, medicine and psychiatry*. Berkeley, CA: University of California Press.

Kroll, J., Habenicht, M., Mackenzie, T., Yang, M., Chan, S., Vang, T., Nguyen, T., Ly, M., Phommasouvanh, B., Nguyen, H., Vang, Y., Souvannasoth, L., & Cabugao, R. (1989). Depression and posttraumatic stress disorder in Southeast Asian refugees. *American Jounal of Psychiatry, 146*, 1592–1597.

Leong, F.T.L. (1986). Counselling and psychotherapy with Asian-Americans: Review of the literature. *Journal of Counselling Psychology, 33*, 196–206.

Lien, O., & Rice, P. (1992). Concepts of mental illness of Vietnamese and the attitude toward psychiatric service. *Tap San Y Si. Hoi Y Si Viet Nam Tai Canada Chu Truong [Medical Journal. Vietnamese Medical Association, Canada.], 115*, 69–77.

Lin, K-M., Tazuma, L., & Masuda, M. (1979). Adaptational problems of Vietnamese refugees: I. Health and mental status. *Archives of General Psychiatry, 36*, 955–961.

Lombard, G. (1993). Refugee issues in the post-cold war world: An overview. In I.H. Minas (Ed.), *Refugee communities and health services* (pp. 5–10). Melbourne: Victorian Transcultural Psychiatry Unit.

Marcos, L.R., Urcuyo, L. Kesselman, M. et al, (1973) The language barrier in evaluating Spanish-American patients. *Archives of General Psychiatry.* 29, 655-659.

Marsella, A.J. (1988). Cross-cultural research on severe mental disorders: Issues and findings. *Acta Psychiatrica Scandinavica, 78* (Supp 344), 7-22.

Masuda, M., Lin, K-M., & Tazuma, L. (1980). Adaptation problems of Vietnamese refugees: II. Life changes and perception of life events. *Archives of General Psychiatry, 37*, 447-450.

McGorry, P. (1988). The sequelae of torture and the implications for health services in Australia. In E. Chiu & I.H. Minas (Eds.), *Mental health of ethnic communities* (pp. 65–78). Melbourne: Department of Psychiatry University of Melbourne, St.Vincent's Hospital and Victorian Transcultural Psychiatry Unit.

Minas, I.H., Klimidis, S. Ata, A., & Stuart, G. (1993). *Psychological distress and of level of exposure to pre-migration traumatic stress in Australian-Vietnamese adolescents.* Unpublished manuscript. Victorian Transcultural Psychiatry Unit.

Minas, I.H., Klimidis, S., & Stuart, G. (1993). *Prevention of psychiatric disorder in Melbourne's Turkish community: Final report to the VHPF.* Melbourne: Victorian Transcultural Psychiatry Unit.

Mollica, R.F., Wyshak, G., & Lavelle, J. (1987). The psychosocial impact of war trauma and torture on Southeast Asian refugees. *American Journal of Psychiatry, 144*, 1567–1572.

Moore, L.J., & Boehnlein, J.K. (1991a). Posttraumatic stress disorder, depression, and somatic symptoms in U.S. Mien patients. *Journal of Nervous and Mental Disease, 179*, 728-733.

Moore, L.J., & Boehnlein, J.K. (1991b). Treating psychiatric disorders among Mien refugees from highland Laos. *Social Science and Medicine, 32*, 1029–1036.

Morris, P., & Silove, D. (1992). Cultural influences in psychotherapy with survivors of torture and trauma. *Hospital and Community Psychiatry, 43*, 820–824.

Murphy, H.B.M. (1977). Migration, culture and mental health. *Psychological Medicine, 7*, 677-684.

Nicassio, P.M., & Pate, J.K. (1984). An analysis of problems of resettlement of the Indochinese refugees in the United States. *Social Psychiatry, 19*, 135–141.

Peck, E.C. (1974). The relationship of disease and other stress to second language. *International Journal of Social Psychiatry 20*, 128–133.

Ramondo, N. (1991). Cultural issues in therapy: On the fringe. *Australian & New Zealand Journal of Family Therapy, 12*, 69–78.

Ramsay, R., Gorst-Unsworth, C., & Turner, S. (1993). Psychiatric morbidity in survivors of organised state violence including torture. *British Journal of Psychiatry, 162*, 55–59.

Ranieri, N. (1992). *Differential acculturation in Vietnamese adolescents and parents: Is it related to intergenerational conflict?* Unpublished manuscript, Graduate Diploma in Child and Adolescent Psychology, University of Melbourne, Melbourne.

Solomon, Z., Weisenber, M., Schwarzwald, J., & Mikulincer, M. (1987). Posttraumatic stress disorder among frontline soldiers with combat stress reaction: The 1982 Israeli experience. *American Journal of Psychiatry, 144,* 448–454.

Stanton, J. (1993). Health of survivors of torture. In I.H. Minas (Ed.), *Refugee communities and health services* (pp. 68–72). Melbourne: Victorian Transcultural Psychiatry Unit.

Sue, S., & Zane, N. (1987). The role of culture and cultural techniques in psychotherapy: A critique and reformulation. *American Psychologist, 42,* 37–45.

Van Dyke, C., Zilberg, N.J., & McKinnon, J.A. (1985). Posttraumatic stress disorder: A thirty-year delay in a World War II veteran. *American Jounal of Psychiatry, 142,* 1070-1073.

Westermeyer, J. (1985). Psychiatric diagnosis across cultural boundaries. *American Jounal of Psychiatry, 142,* 798–805.

Zborowski, M. (1952). Cultural components in responses to pain. *Journal of Social Issues, 8,* 16–30.

Taking Care of the Deceased

Priscilla Nelson-Feaver and Ian Warren

THE death of a loved one can be a stressful time for any family as well as possibly a trying time for any professional carers involved in providing support. Bereaved people can be greatly assisted by professional people at the time of death, and this appendix discusses some of the knowledge required to fulfil this important function.

Cultural needs

Carers involved in counselling the bereaved need to be familiar with cultural differences. It is necessary to recognise the importance of these rituals and special customs, and include these traditions in planning the events following a death. As Parkes (1972) said:

> During a period of mourning social customs determine the roles to be played by members of the dead person's family, impose restrictions on the activities of those most closely related to the dead, and sanction the expression of emotion, usually. (p.5)

Australia is a multi-cultural country, and therefore composed of numerous religions and ethnic groups with differing customs and beliefs. For example, many Greeks view death as personified — that death's physical form is that of a man, his character being cold, objective and impartial; while Sikhs view death as an illusion. Australian Aborigines view death as a natural passing on from one spiritual world into another, while Muslims believe that a person's soul does not die but merely returns to its original home. Roman Catholic Italians believe that the soul is immortal, while

Vietnamese Buddhists believe that birth and death are predestined — everyone is born, dies, decays, and is born again.

When assisting families with such different beliefs, remember that although their customs and beliefs may be different to your own, they still, as human beings, require compassion, empathy, and understanding. To have some knowledge of their beliefs and cultures is obviously helpful, but one must also look beyond that to see if the rituals are meeting the needs of each individual.

Some cultures, such as Judaism and Islam, have strict codes of practice following a death. These rituals provide methods of mourning for the bereaved. It is important to realise, however, that occasionally individuals within a certain cultural group will need additional support to meet their needs. In order to provide personalised additional support, the particular cultural or ethnic traditions must be respected; for example, carers may need to know that the body of a Chinese person should not be enclosed in a sealed coffin until 24 hours after the death to enable the spirit to leave the body.

Below is a general outline of some of the different customs performed at or following the time of death in different cultures. Understanding these will help in dealing with individuals from a variety of ethnic backgrounds as they go through the mourning process.

GREEK ORTHODOX

Death in the Greek Orthodox faith is always considered a tragedy, whether it happens to a young or old person; emotions are expressed very openly. Death is never mentioned by name in the sick room, since death is personified and feared — and using the dead person's name may make him or her come back. The body is considered to be holy and therefore is treated with high respect and gentleness. After death, some families may want to wash the body themselves, while others will leave this to nursing staff. The body is then dressed in a white linen cloth and placed in the best clothes the person possessed. At the time of death a priest is called to the hospital, or home of the deceased, where he performs the first prayers for the expiation and repose of the soul of the deceased.

HINDUISM

The Hindu priest is often called to see dying patients and help them with their acts of *puja* (acts of worship) and to accept their death philosophically (a strong feature of Hindu religious outlook is the acceptance of the inevitable). When death takes place some Hindus may want to place the body on the floor, light lamps, and burn incense; however, this is not a common practice among Australia Hindus. There is usually no restriction on non-Hindus handling the body, provided it is wrapped in a plain sheet. Post-mortems are usually considered extremely objectionable, since the act of opening up the body is considered to be disrespectful to the dead person and his or her family.

JAPANESE

About 80 per cent of Japanese are Zen Buddhist and nearly 20 per cent follow Shintoism. Customs vary depending on the sect, but certain common rites and customs are generally observed.

As death approaches, the dying receive the 'last water' from family members who moisten the lips of the person with a wet brush. After death takes place, the body is washed with hot water and then dressed in white garments. It is laid with the head toward the north, without a pillow, and is covered with a white sheet. A knife, believed to drive evil spirits away, is placed on the chest in Buddhist rites and beside the head in Shinto rites. A small table is placed near the body with a vase, candle holder, and incense burner. Candles and incense sticks burn continuously as the Buddhist priest performs religious rites.

JUDAISM

Jewish practices at the time of death and dying arise from a combination of biblical commandments, Rabbinic law, and tradition. All laws and customs for treating the dead are meant to ensure that the body is treated with respect and dignity. Since members of the Jewish faith belong to one of the three major groups — Reform, Conservative, or Orthodox — their practices at the time of death vary.

After death, the body is laid out with the arms straight beside the body and eyes closed. This is traditionally done by the family. The body is not to be left alone and someone sits with the body, day and night. The burial normally takes place within 24 hours. A post-mortem is not allowed, unless ordered by the civil authorities.

VIETNAMESE BUDDHIST

Generally Vietnamese believe that birth and death are predestined and death is seen as going to the eternal home-place. With this in mind, death is not feared, rather it is waited for, especially by older people. When death is imminent, the dying person is placed with their head facing east. If a sick person appears to have stopped breathing, a burning incense stick is placed in front of their nostrils — if the smoke is not blown by breath, they are considered dead. One of the relatives will then loudly call the name of the dead person, hoping that they will return. After death, the body is placed on the ground for a few minutes. If there is no response, they give up all hope. The exact time is noted, as it is believed there are good and bad times to die. The body is usually washed by one of the children of the dead person.

HELPING THE BEREAVED

When assisting families from whatever cultural background, it is always best to ask them how you can help. Many are pleased to describe their customs and beliefs, for even within cultural groups there can be differences arising from their own community and/or family. For instance, you may assist one

Vietnamese family and become familiar with their customs, the next Vietnamese family you meet may have slightly different traditions. A golden rule is always to ask how you may be of help. Religion and traditions can provide great comfort to the bereaved. A caring helper will acknowledge, respect and provide opportunities for the fulfilment of the customs of the bereaved.

Children's needs

Death can be a very difficult subject to raise with children, particularly at the time of death of a loved one. However, education about death can start at a very young age, with children as young as three years of age being able to understand the concept of death. At this age they often experience death as separation or abandonment and show signs of being upset and angry. Although young children may not comprehend words suggesting the finality of death — such a concept is beyond their own experiences — they can still feel a sense of loss and desertion. Important issues of life and death should be raised at a young age. Nagy's study, for example, (cited in Feifel, 1977) of 378 Hungarian children ranging in age from 3 to 10 years found that there are three primary developmental stages concerning children's comprehension of death. She noted that in the 3–5 age group, death is considered a departure, gradual, or temporary but also reversible. To this age group, sleep and death are often synonymous. To die means the same as to live, but under changed circumstances.

In the 5–9 age group, Nagy found that there is a personification of death as a person or being and death takes on more reality. Children in this age group were able to grasp the finality of death, but also believed that it happens only to other people. This means that by age 9, children usually begin to understand the cessation of bodily activities and the universality and inevitability of death. Between 7 and 8 years, Nagy found that children reach a turning point in their understanding of death and begin to suspect their own mortality.

So how does we talk to children about death in order to prepare them for it? Whether we like it or not, children are learning about death almost every day, but in a random, unplanned, and often counterproductive manner. When children learn about death through their own life experiences, without the help and support of an adult, it can result in many fears and unanswered questions. Education about death can and will remedy this lack of information and support children's experiences, as well as help retain a proper perspective toward the value of life. Focusing on nature, looking at growth and then decay, is an excellent approach to discussing the life cycle with children. They will learn that things are born, grow, and ultimately die. They will see death, not as a thing to be feared, but as part of life.

When a person a child loves has died, the child should be told and given an opportunity to be involved in the events that follow (the grieving, the funeral, and so on). Many adults question whether children should attend funerals. A funeral is meant to be a time of sharing, of saying goodbye to the person, of celebrating their life. Children are part of the family, part of the community, and like other members, are better off if allowed to participate in this significant event. An explanation of the funeral service should be given to the child before attending a funeral. Children should never be forced to go to a funeral, but instead their participation should be encouraged. For example, instead of asking, 'Do you want to go to the funeral home to see grandma?', a more appropriate question might be, 'We are all going to the funeral home tonight to say goodbye to grandma. Would you like to come with us?' Just as adults need to share their sadness and be with others, so do children. Attending a funeral and being given permission to participate in the events surrounding the death, will help children accept the reality of death.

Viewing the body of the deceased

Viewing the body of a deceased family member is a very personal decision. Some people do not need to see the body of those they love in order to work through their grief. However, a significantly high number of people have great difficulty in coming to terms with the death when they have not viewed the body. Many bereaved families report that viewing the body of a loved one assisted them in facing the reality of the death. Research (Raphael, 1984; Wright, 1991) supports these comments by indicating that viewing the body of the deceased helps fulfil the psychological needs of those who are left behind, including children. Commonly, when bereaved family members do not see the deceased person, they can remain in a state of partial denial. This denial may or may not be incapacitating. Viewing the deceased also helps the process of remembering and letting go.

Some family members may not have seen the dead person recently, and will often have a strong desire to view the deceased to say their goodbyes, and perhaps say things they may have wanted to say when the person was alive: this is often part of the tragedy of sudden death. Viewing the body is a chance to psychologically and emotionally complete unfinished business. Viewing should, therefore be encouraged soon after death, since it aids in establishing the finality that death brings to a person's life on earth. It should not be hurried, but dealt with in a sensitive manner, and within an environment which permits the open expression of grief.

A family should see the deceased for the first time in privacy, except perhaps for their clergy and/or other close associates they may want with them. Tensions often build up among many of the immediate family at this moment. Funeral directors may ask the family something like: 'When would you like to spend time with … ', or 'It may be helpful to see … before you leave, others have found it very beneficial'.

If the body has been mutilated, that part may be covered, and only other parts revealed. One family asked only to see the family member's hand, since this was the only recognisable feature. Seeing just the hand brought great relief to this family in accepting that this person had died.

Families need to be prepared for the viewing of their dead family member. Bereaved people who have never seen a dead person before will need to have the situation described to them. The dead person may look different and feel cold to the touch, because circulation has ceased. Let them know how long they can spend with the deceased (hopefully they can spend as much time as they need), and that a funeral director can stay with them for support, or they can be alone. The funeral director may even touch the body on the hand, or stroke the hair. This action helps the family come close to the person, and show them that it is perfectly acceptable to touch, or even kiss the body if they desire. Chairs may be placed at the side of the coffin to allow time for sitting and talking or thinking.

Viewing the dead is an integral part of the parting process. It often initiates the emotional response to grief and may give rise to both positive and negative feelings. It is of course, distressing to most bereaved families, but is also vitally important as an ingredient in the total resolution of grief.

WHEN A BABY DIES
The death of an infant can be one of life's greatest heartaches, leaving behind the sadness of what might have been. The days surrounding the death of an infant will be particularly stressful and sometimes very frightening. Parents are usually inexperienced in making decisions such as what to do at the hospital, planning the funeral, plans for the future, and are therefore often confused and deeply saddened by the whole experience. They may be helped by the people around them, including professional carers, remembering and cherishing the deceased infant, talking about the baby, calling it by its name, taking a photo of the baby, a footprint or a cutting of hair, permitting and encouraging the parents to see, touch and/or hold the dead baby. Making funeral arrangements and storing the infant's belongings, often act as important releases for parents' feelings and can provide a sense of 'giving' to the infant. A funeral may be the only gift a couple can offer their infant.

The needs of the family when an infant dies are the same as when an adult dies. Family members often need to hold, touch, and see the body and take part in the funeral service. Parents that are allowed to participate in such ways with their infant seem to be able to accept and live with the loss more easily.

The funeral

ITS VALUE
When a death occurs, one of the most common feelings the family experiences is denial: 'it really has not happened'. They will often go into a state of shock and feel isolated from what is going on around them. Being involved

in the preparation and services of the funeral helps the family come to terms with these feelings. Preparation for the funeral, the timing of it, needs to take into account the importance of viewing and family involvement.

For the next of kin, the funeral forms a base or starting point for them to work through their grief. It helps them accept the death and allows them to pay their last respects. The funeral is also a time for memories. It often brings to mind the times shared with that family member and reminds them about what endeared that person to them. This process usually begins when they are preparing the format of the funeral service with the officiating person. This is very important in helping the family come to terms with the loss.

A funeral also gives the community a chance to recognise the loss of one of its members, to honour and pay tribute to that person. The funeral demonstrates that a life has been lived and that it has had meaning. It helps to recognise that life will go on for family and friends, though it will never be the same without that person. The funeral service should initiate thinking about the person's life and highlight major events. It should also give the community a chance to pay their own last respects. The funeral provides the community with a formal opportunity to show sympathy and offer support to the bereaved.

Often it is the first time many friends are able to meet the family after the death has taken place. This is usually a difficult experience for people to handle, but one that is important for the family. For many, if it was not for the funeral, they would not get to see the family as they may feel they do not know what to say, and may avoid meeting them so as not to say the wrong thing. Others may not want to see their friends upset, or they may even feel that since everyone else is visiting them, their own visit may simply be an added burden. The family can often miss out on support from their friends, due to people's misunderstandings and uncertainty about their own feelings. Simply being present at a funeral can give great support to the bereaved family through just knowing that you care and are thinking of them at the time of their loss. An issue that sometimes arises for professional people is whether or not to attend the funeral. If they do not attend, how else will they express support for the family, and express their own sense of loss for the deceased?

The main role most people associate with a funeral is the disposal of the remains. While this is an important role, it is certainly not the only one. The funeral is for the living, and not for the dead; even the disposal is for the living. Most people who choose a burial wish to see the coffin or casket lowered into the grave, many return to the site in the immediate months following the death. Cremation follows the same path, by those choosing to go to the crematorium to watch the coffin or casket disappear from sight. This act in itself helps mourners to accept the finality of the death.

One of the last tasks the funeral accomplishes, which varies in its degree of importance from one person to the next, is the expression of religious or philosophical beliefs. To many, the expression of their faith acts as a great source of comfort and strength. It assists them in putting the concepts of 'life and death' into true perspective.

FUNERAL OPTIONS

When someone dies a doctor must be called to certify that the death has occurred. Once the person has been certified dead, a funeral director can be contacted to transfer the body to their premises. There is no set time for how soon the transfer has to be made after the death. It is not uncommon for the deceased to remain in the home for several hours. This time allows relatives to view their family member before the transfer. Though not usual, some families wish to have the body at home for a number of days and to be there prior to the funeral. There is no legislation against this but funeral directors recommend that the deceased be embalmed first.

Earth burial, or interment, is common and may take place in a lawn or monumental cemetery (a lawn cemetery has no tombstones but small plaques marking the place of interment).

Cremation is the alternative to interment. Through cremation, the coffin/casket containing the body is reduced to small skeletal fragments and ash by intense heat and evaporation. These fragments are then crushed through a 'cremulator' into finer ash. The families have the option to do what they want with the ashes — whether to place them in a memorial garden at a cemetery, bury them in an existing grave, scatter them at sea or another meaningful location, or store them in their own home in an urn, etc.

Families should choose the kind of final disposition they feel is meaningful for them, and most appropriate for the deceased. In city areas, the number of cremations is higher than burials, due, in part, to the proximity of the crematoriums. In country areas, burials are more common. Some religions/cultural groups prefer one method of disposition to another; for example, Muslims opt for interment, Hindus for cremation.

Most funerals in Australia take place within two or three days of the death, but some people think it is better to move more slowly than this, since getting the funeral over quickly is no guarantee that grief will be resolved more quickly. Extra time may help the impact of the loss to be absorbed and also allow the arrangement of a more meaningful funeral service.

All burials must take place in a recognised cemetery. Some cemeteries are privately owned and operated, while others are run by a board of trustees. Burial on private property is only allowed by approval from the local government and the State health department. Approval is usually only given in outlying areas where there is no cemetery nearby.

FUNERAL COSTS

The expenses for a funeral can be divided into three main groups. Firstly, there are the funeral directors' professional fees, or service charges. The second is the cost of the casket or coffin. Most funeral directors keep a wide range so families can select something to meet their needs and requirements. The last cost is for disbursements, or cash payments, which the funeral director makes on behalf of the family. Usual disbursement fees include press notices, cemetery or crematorium fees, clergy offering, floral tributes, and doctor's fees for cremation certificates. In some cases, funeral benefits are payable by various agencies for people on a Social Security or Department of Veterans Affairs pension. As the eligibility differs for each individual, the local branch of the relevant government department should be contacted for additional information. Any funeral director should be willing to discuss the specific charges for providing a funeral and final disposition to meet a family's needs.

When a person is dying because of illness, the family should have had the chance to discuss options, and to make preparatory arrangements. Some people design their own funeral, select their casket, and ensure all possible decisions are made. In the case of sudden death, this may not have happened.

LEGAL RESPONSIBILITIES

When the deceased has made a will and appointed an executor, it is technically the executor's responsibility to arrange the funeral. However, in practice, it is usually the next of kin who does this. If the executor were to arrange the funeral, in most cases, they would respect the wishes of the next of kin. When an executor has not been appointed because the deceased had not made a will, the funeral arrangements are made by the next of kin. When the deceased does not have any next of kin, and has made no will, the Public Trustee handles the funeral arrangements.

Coroner's case

The coroner will investigate the death of a person if they died:

- unexpectedly
- from anything other than natural causes
- from an injury or in an accident
- during or as a result of an anaesthetic being administered
- while they were held in an institution, in prison, in a drug or alcohol rehabilitation centre, or by police
- and their identity was not known

If any of these conditions apply, the situation needs to be explained to the family in a sensitive way. These types of deaths are called reportable deaths. All reportable deaths must be investigated by the coroner. Once the death has been reported to the coroner, the coroner puts out a contract for the transfer of the deceased person whose death is being investigated, from the place of death to the coroner's mortuary. Funeral directors tender for this contract, which usually covers a geographical location. The funeral director who is successful in tendering for the contract is only acting as the coroner's agent. The family are free to choose whichever funeral director they desire for the funeral.

The coroner will require the deceased person to be identified, and usually an autopsy will be performed. Sometimes the identification can be done at the hospital before the person is transferred by the coroner's staff. If there are case notes, the coroner's staff will also need these to assist with their investigation.

The autopsy is performed in order to establish the exact cause of death. The family may have strong reactions to the necessity of an autopsy, and require help at this time. Providing extra support, including information as to the autopsy's necessity, and opportunity to express their reactions are all important.

The coroner must hold an inquest if:

- the coroner suspects homicide
- the deceased person was in a prison or institution
- the person's identity is not known.

In other cases the coroner will decide whether or not an inquest is needed.

An inquest is a court hearing conducted by the coroner to decide the circumstances of the death. The coroner can summon people to be witnesses or to bring papers or other items. Evidence is given on oath, and witnesses can be questioned. The coroner will listen to all of the evidence, and then make a finding on the death.

Conclusion

This appendix has aimed to provide some insight into the practical arrangements and bereavement concerns which follow a death.

Professional people, such as health care workers, who are often involved in assisting families make arrangements for their deceased relatives, should be aware of their own and other's needs at this time of loss and stress. In order to offer the most effective help they need to keep up-to-date with the options offered by funeral directors and changes in laws, and to be informed about cultural differences and bereavement issues. Some agencies, including funeral directors, have libraries of books, journals, brochures, and audiovisual material which can be referenced.

References

Feifel, H. (1977). *New meanings of death.* New York: McGraw Hill Inc.

Parkes, C.M. (1972). *Bereavement studies in adult life.* Middlesex: Penguin Books Ltd.

Raphael, B. (1984). *The anatomy of bereavement.* London: Hutchinson & Co.

Wright, B. (1991). *Sudden death.* Edinburgh: Churchill Livingstone.

Index